THE TRAVELS OF PIETRO DELLA VALLE IN INDIA

THE TRAVELS
OF
PIETRO DELLA VALLE
IN
INDIA

FROM THE OLD ENGLISH TRANSLATION OF 1664,

BY G. HAVERS

IN TWO VOLUMES

Edited with a Life of the Author an Introductions and Notes

BY

EDWARD GREY

(LATE BENGAL CIVIL SERVICE)

VOL. II

GYAN

Published by

Gyan Publishing House
5, Ansari Road
Daryaganj, New Delhi-110002
Phone: 011-47034999, 9811692060
E-mail: books@gyanbooks.com

Distribution Network
gyanbooks.com
India, USA, Canada, UK, Australia, France

ISBN : 978-81-212-4163-2 (Set)
ISBN : 978-81-212-4702-3 (PB)
First Published, 1892

2nd Impression 2020

Printed at: Gyan Press, Delhi.

The Travels of Pietro Della Valle in India Vol. II
Author: G. Havers

THE TRAVELS

OF

PIETRO DELLA VALLE

IN

INDIA.

FROM THE OLD ENGLISH TRANSLATION OF 1664,
BY G. HAVERS.

IN TWO VOLUMES.

Edited, with a Life of the Author, an Introduction and Notes,

BY

EDWARD GREY

(LATE BENGAL CIVIL SERVICE).

VOL. II

LONDON:
PRINTED FOR THE HAKLUYT SOCIETY,
4, LINCOLN'S INN FIELDS, W.C.

M,DCCC.XCII.

COUNCIL

OF

THE HAKLUYT SOCIETY.

LETTERS OF PIETRO DELLA VALLE.

VOL. II.

TABLE OF CONTENTS.

LETTER IV.

LETTER V.

LETTER VI.

LETTER VII.

LETTER VIII.

LETTER IV.

From Onor, Octob. 30, 1623.

BEING departed from *Goa* and arriv'd at this Port of *Onor*[1] I shall give you some account of what hath happened in my observation during the few days since the last that I writ to you, on *October* the tenth; and because I understood that it lay still at *Goa*, with the two Ships which were to go thence for *Persia*, I have thought fit to send this to accompany it, and I hope you will receive both of them together, and that not without as much delectation of my News, as I am pleas'd in writing to you from several places, and (when I can get opportunity) from those very places which afford the Novelties and matters whereof I write, which therefore may possibly be more grateful in the reception as being native of the Country.

I took ship with our *Portugal* Ambassador, Sig. *Gio. Fernandez Leiton*, about Evening, *October* the fourteenth, and, departing from *Goa*, we remov'd to a Town call'd *Pangi*[2] in the same Island, but lower, near the place

---

[1] See *ante*, p. 190, *note*.

[2] Now called Panjim, or New Goa, on the left bank of the Mandovi river, three or four miles from the sea. It was made the seat of government in 1759, and was formally raised to the dignity of being the capital by Royal Proclamation in the year 1843. Fonseca (pp. 97 to 103) describes it in detail, and speaks of it as having a "picturesque

where the River enters into the Sea, and whither the Vice-Roys used to retire themselves frequently to a House of Pleasure which they have there, besides many other like Houses of private persons upon the River likewise, and where also at the mouth of the Sea, or Bar, as they call it, which is a little lower, almost all Fleets that depart from *Goa* are wont to set Sail. We might have performed this journey by Land along the Sea-coast, passing along the other lands of *Adil-Sciáh*[1] till we came to those of *Venk-tapà Naieka.*[2] But to avoid expences and occasions of disgust with many Governours of those Territories subject to *Adil-Sciáh*, who sometimes are little courteous and impertinent, the Vice-Roy would have us go by Sea, and for more security sent five of those light Frigats or Galeots, which the *Portugals* call *Sangessis*,[3] to accompany us as far as *Onor*, where we were to land. So that we were in all ten Ships or Galeots, to wit, one which carry'd the *Portugal* ambassador and us, another in which *Venk-tapà Naieka's* Ambassador the Brachman[4] went; three others laden with the baggage of the two Ambassadors (and particularly with Horses and other things which the Vice-Roy sent for a present to *Venk-tapà Naieka*, and other Horses which I know not who carry'd thither to sell)[5]; and the five Ships of war, whereof Sig. *Hettor Fernandez* was Chief Captain or General. Nevertheless we parted from *Goa* the aforesaid Evening onely with our own Ship, the rest

---

appearance"; and C. de Kloguen (p. 142) says: "It is now (1831) a very handsome town, all the houses being well built and the streets being broad and well paved."

[1] See *ante*, p. 143, *note*. [2] See *ante*, p. 168, *note*.

[3] Properly "Sanguiçel". (See Vieyra's *Dictionary*.)

[4] See *ante*, p. 191.

[5] The horse trade was a great business on the west coast of India. (See *Commentaries of A. Dalboquerque*, vol. ii, pp. 76, 77, 107, and 111; vol. iii, p. 21; and Col. Yule's *Marco Polo*, vol. i, pp. 84, 88, 324, 333, etc., and Index.)

being already fallen down lower toward the Sea, and the Ambassador *Vitulá* was above a day at *Pangi* expecting us, where we arriving the abovesaid night did not land, because it was late, but slept in the Vessel.

II.—*October* the fourteenth. We went ashore in the Morning at *Pangi*, and the two Ambassadors saw one another upon the Sea-side, where, I being present with them, Sig. *Gio. Fernandez* told the Brachman Ambassador who I was, and that I went with them out of curiosity to see his King, wherewith he testified great contentment, but was much more pleas'd with the Pendant which I wore at my left ear, as I have us'd to do for many years past for remedy of my weak sight, because wearing Pendants at the ears is a peculiar custom of the *Indians*, especially of the *Gentiles*, who all wear them in both ears[1]: and because this is among the *Portugals* a thing not onely unusual, but ignorantly by some of the ruder sort of them held for unlawful onely because 'tis us'd by *Gentiles*, therefore the Ambassador marvelled that I, being of the *Portugal's* Religion, nevertheless us'd it; but being told that it was not forbidden by our Law, but onely customarily disus'd, and that in *Europe* it was us'd by many,[2] he commended the

[1] See Quintin Craufurd's *Sketches relating to the History, etc., of the Hindoos:* "In the ears all the Hindoos wear large gold rings ornamented with precious stones." The custom of wearing ear-rings has been adopted by males as well as females in India, as is well known, from time immemorial. They are frequently of large size. (See Burton's *Goa and the Blue Mountains*, p. 232.) Instances have been known in which their weight amounted to no less than 2 lbs. In some parts pieces of shell are inserted in the lobes of the ears, and in Burma cheroots are carried in this way. Nose-rings are commonly worn by women. (See Sir M. Williams' *Modern India*, p. 61.) Ear-rings are mentioned as being generally worn by Indians in Arrian's *Indica*, chap. xvi. Mr. Forbes (*Oriental Memoirs*, p. 390) says: "The Malabar women's ears, loaded with rings and heavy jewels, reach almost to their shoulders."

[2] It is said that Charles I. of England wore pearl ear-rings, and that

custom, and bid the *Portugals* see how well I shew'd with that Pendant, and better than they who wore none; so powerful is use to endear things to the eye, and make that fancy'd and esteem'd by some, which others, through want of custom, dislike, or value not.[1]

This day we departed not, because one of the Frigats of the Armado which was to accompany us was unprovided with Sea-men, for which we were fain to stay till the day following, and then were not very well provided. The cause whereof was that there was at this time a great Scarcity of Mariners in *Goa*, because the Governours of the maritime parts of the Continent subject to *Idal-Sciàh*[2] would not permit their Ships to come, as they were wont, to supply Mariners for the *Portugal* Armado; which seem'd an argument of some ill will of that King against the *Portugals*, of which, were there nothing else, their being weaker and more confus'd in their Government than ever, and all things in bad order, was a sufficient ground; for remedy of which they took no other course, but daily loaded themselves with new, unusual and most heavy Impositions, to the manifest ruine of the State, taking no care to prevent the hourly exorbitant defraudations of the publick Incomes, which otherwise would be sufficient to maintain the charge without new Gabels[3]: but if such thefts continue both the publick Incomes and the new Gabels, and as many as they can

---

he gave one of them to Bishop Juxon, the day before his execution, for his daughter, the Princess Royal. They were at one time much worn in Europe, as being good for the eyes.

[1] See Shakespeare (*Two Gentlemen of Verona*, act v, sc. 4): "How use doth breed a habit in a man!"

[2] Should be Adil Shah. See *ante*, p. 143, *note*.

[3] This word (said to be derived from the Arabic *Kabāla*, "a tax") was in France specially applied to a tax on salt, and is said to have led King Edward III. to the perpetration of a pun in remarking that King Philip, who imposed the tax, was the author of the "Salique law".

invent, will be all swallow'd up. Nevertheless the *Portugals* are heedless according to their custom, and out of fatal blindness, making no reckoning of these signs which shew the evil mind of their neighbour *Adil-Scidh*, think he knows nothing of these disorders, and that this with-holding of his Subjects is onely an impertinence of his Officers. What the event will be Time will shew.

III.—But to return to my purpose. Not being to depart this day we went to dine and pass the time, with intention also to lodge the following night, in the house of Sig. *Baldassar d'Azevedo*, who liv'd constantly in a fair House there by the Sea-side, a little distant from the *Villa*, or Fort,[1] where the Vice-Roys lodge in *Pangi*.[2] Whilst we were recreating our selves, Sig. *Fernandez*, bethinking himself of what, perhaps, he had not thought of before, ask'd me whether I had the Vice-Roy's Licence to go with him this Voyage, and I telling him that I had not because I did not think it needful, he reply'd that it was needful to be had by any means if I intended to go, otherwise he could not venture to carry me, for fear of giving malevolous[3] persons occasion to criminate him, by saying that he had carry'd me, a stranger and without the Vice-Roy's licence, into suspected places, where matters of State were to be handled; in brief, knowing the matter to be blameable, and the wonted cavils of many of his own Nation, and being admonished by many and great troubles befallen others, and particularly a Kinsman of his, very innocently for very slight causes and much inferior to this, he told me resolutely that without the Vice-Roy's Licence it was no-wise good, either for him or me, that I should go. Wherefore, being[4] we were not to depart that day, he advis'd me to return to the City, and procure the said Licence, if I

---

[1] Built by Yusuf Adil Shah. [2] See p. 193, *note*.

[3] An obsolete word for "malevolent".

[4] For "since" see *ante*, p. 27, *note*.

intended to go, and he would stay for me till the next Morning; but without the Licence I must not return to take Ship, nor would he by any means venture to carry me. I who well understood the procedures of the *Portugals*, and what rigor they use in their Government,[1] and to what suspicions and malevolences they are prone, which cause a thousand ill usages and injustices, was sensible that Sig. *Fernandez* had reason, and that the not having gotten this Licence was an inadvertency, because I accounted it not necessary; but to obtain it of the Vice-Roy, who knew me well and had shewn himself courteous to me, I look'd upon as not difficult. Wherefore, being loathe to lose my intended voyage, as soon as I had din'd with these Gentlemen, I went by boat to the City, and having first given account of my business to Sig. *Antonio*, and Sig. *Ruy Gomez* his Brother, (to whose House I repair'd, having left that which I had hir'd, and remov'd my Goods to that of the said Sig[ri] *Barocci*), I went with the same Sig. *Ruy Gomez* to speak to F. *Moryad*, a Jesuit and the Vice-Roy's Confessor and my Friend, whom I desir'd (as the fittest person to do it in the short time left me) to get me a Licence from the Vice-Roy. He went immediately to speak to the Vice-Roy about it, and had the fortune to find him before he enter'd into a Congregation, or Council, which was to sit till to-night; and the Vice-Roy presently writ a Licence for him with his own hand, directed to the Ambassador *Gio. Fernandez*, wherein he told him that, whereas I desir'd to go along with him, he might carry me and shew me all kind of Civility and

---

[1] The policy of Admiral Dalboquerque, first Viceroy of Goa, which, it may be presumed, was adopted in a general way by his successors, is thus described by Fonseca (*Historical Sketch of Goa*, p. 144): "While on the one hand he treated the Muhammadans with undue severity and harshness, he showed marked favour to the Hindoos, but punished with merciless rigour every species of oppression practised on the merchants and traders."

Honour as a deserving person, with other like courteous and high expressions.

Having gotten my Licence, I went with F. *Ruy Gomez Baroccio* to visit the Bishop of *Cocin*,[1] who in the vacancy of the See administred the Arch-bishoprick of *Goa*,[2] and whom I had not yet visited; and understanding that he was desirous to know me, and was a Prelate of great merit, not only as to Ecclesiastick matters but also in point of Government and War (for he took divers strong places, and perform'd other exploits in *India* for the service of his King with great valour) I would not depart without first visiting him and making myself known to him. This Prelate is called *Frà Don Sebastiano di San Pietro*[3] and is an *Augustine* Fryer. We discours'd above an hour together concerning things of *India* and *Persia*, and other matters, and I recommended to him, with the F. Confessor, the *Augustine* Fathers of his

---

[1] In original Cocin—generally written Cochin—on west coast of India, in lat. 9° 58′ N. Properly Kachhi or Kuçhi, called also Gutschin, Couhi, and Cocym. According to Sir H. Yule (*Cathay*, vol. ii, p. 455), it is first mentioned by Conti, under the name of "Cocym". Now the chief port of Malabar. The town gives its name to the adjacent territory, which is governed by a native ruler, who pays a tribute of 200,000 Rs. annually to the British Government. A Portuguese fort was erected here in 1503 by Admiral Dalboquerque. In 1663 it became the capital of the Dutch possessions in India, and in 1796 was taken by the British. It is at present remarkable as the residence of the black and white Jews, and of the sect of Christians called Nazaranis or Nestorians, who ascribe their conversion to St. Thomas. (Eastwick's *Handbook of Madras*, pp. 316, 317.)

[2] Goa was made a metropolitan, or archiepiscopal, see by Pope Paul IV in 1557, and two suffragan bishoprics were created at the same time, viz., those of Cochin and Goa, of which the former extended from Cranganur to the Ganges, and the latter from Cranganur to Cape of Good Hope. (See C. de Kloguen, p. 58.) There were afterwards seven suffragan bishoprics altogether, viz., Cochin, Malacca, Macao, Tunay (Japan), Meliapur, Nankin, and Pekin.

[3] He was the first Bishop of Meliapur, and was confirmed as Archbishop of Goa in 1629. He completed the cathedral begun in 1616.

Religion in *Persia*, giving him an account of their necessities, and how he might help them.

Night being come, I went to make a Collation in the House of Sig^ri *Barocci*, and when it was grown dark I return'd to imbark in the Ship which expected me, and went to the Town of *Pangi*[1] to find Sig. *Gio. Fernandez* and my other Companions, who were very glad at my return with the Vice-Roy's Licence so favourable and courteous to me, because they were loath to have gone without me; and so I slept with them that night in the same House. My charge, *Mariàm Tinatìn*,[2] went not with me this journey because it was not expedient, being[3] I was to return to *Goa*, but stay'd still in the House of Sig^ra *Lena da Cugna:* onely *Cacciatùr*[4] went with me to serve me.

October the fifteenth. A little before night we were ready to set sail, had we not been necessitated to stay for certain Mariners till the next Morning, when we went to hear Mass in a Church of Saint *Agnes*[5] belonging to the *Augustine* Fryers[6] and standing in the Island of *Goa*; after which, being imbark'd, we stay'd a while longer waiting for the Brachman Ambassador, for what reason I know not, unless, perhaps, he was minded to make us stay for him, as we had made him stay for us. At length being got out of the mouth of the River we continu'd sailing all night, but with

---

[1] See *ante*, p. 193, *note*.

[2] See *ante*, p. 24, *note*.

[3] For "since", see *note*, p. 27.

[4] See p. 126.

[5] A small church in the village of St. Agnes, to the west of Panjim. In this parish is one of the three palaces of the Archbishop. Of the other two palaces, one adjoins the cathedral and the other is in the parish of St. Peter.

[6] The Augustine Friars were the fourth religious order established in Goa, where they came in 1572 under Fra Antonio de Paixão. Their convent is described by Cottineau de Kloguen as "the most beautiful and stately convent or building in Goa", and he adds that "few cities in Europe can boast of a finer edifice of the kind". For a description of it, see De Kloguen's *Goa*, p. 122; and for some general observations on the religious orders at Goa, see the same, p. 133.

a small wind. Our course was always Southward almost directly, and we coasted along the land at a little distance.

October the sixteenth. In the Morning we discern'd four Ships of *Malabar* Rovers[1] near the shore (they call them *Paroes*[2] and they go with Oars, like Galeots or Foists[3]). We gave them chase for above an hour, intending to fight them, but we could not overtake them; onely we lost much time and much of our way. Night came upon us near certain Rocks, or uninhabited little Islands, which they call *Angediva*,[4] which signifies in the Language of the Country *Five Islands*, they being so many in number. We found fresh water in one of them; they are all green and have some Trees. We set sail from thence the same night, but had little or no wind and violent rain.

October the seventeenth. Continuing our course the next day with a very small gale we saw the bound of the States

---

[1] The whole line of coast here (called Ariake by the Greeks, Kemkem by the Arabs, and Kukan, or Konkan, by the Hindús) has always been infamous for the piratical propensities of its inhabitants, whose ancient occupation is well favoured by the multitude of small ports, an uninterrupted view along the coast, high ground favourable to distant vision, and the alternate land and sea-breezes that oblige vessels to hug the shore, and by the fact that the ports, besides being shallow, are protected against large ships by bars. Pliny notices the depredations committed by these pirates, and our early travellers are full of horrible tales about them. (See Sir R. Burton's *Goa and the Blue Mountains*, pp. 12 and 13.)

[2] For *Prau*, or *Prahu*, a Malay word for a kind of swift sailing-vessel, used in the Malayan archipelago and on the Malabar coast. See *Commentaries of Dalboquerque*, vol. ii, pp. 87 and 91.

[3] An obsolete word for a small sailing-vessel, called *Fustas* by the Portuguese. (See *Commentaries of A. Dalboquerque*, vol. ii, pp. 86, 87, 99, and 100.)

[4] Probably for Panjdwipa, or "five islands" (Sanskrit), a favourite anchorage of the early Portuguese, in lat. 14° 30′ N. Called also "Anchediva", and, in Dourado's map of 1546, "Amgedina". They were fortified by the Viceroy of Goa, Don Francis de Taura, in 1683, when the Portuguese were at war with Sambaji, the Mahratta chief.

of *Adil-Sciàh*[1] and *Venk-tapà Naieka*,[2] which is onely a brackish River,[3] such as are frequent upon the Coast of *India*. The wind was but small still, so that all this day we could not arrive at *Onor*[4]; but when it was night, because 'tis no good ent'ring into the Port of *Onor* in the dark and with ebbing water, as it was now, we cast Anchor, and remain'd all night under an uninhabited small Rock, which they call the Rock of *Onor*. After mid-night the Tide began to flow, but yet we stirred not.

October the eighteenth. About break of day we mov'd along, and by the help of Oars finished the remainder of the way, arriving at *Onor* in good time. This whole voyage from *Goa* to *Onor* is not above eighteen Leagues, but it took up so much time because we had onely a very small wind.

V.—*Onor* is a small place by the Sea-side, but a good Port of indifferent capacity, which is formed by two arms of Rivers,[5] which (I know not whether both from one or several heads) running one Southward and the other Northward meet at the Fortress, and are discharg'd with one mouth into the Sea. The habitations are rather Cottages than Houses, built under a thick Grove of Palms, to wit those which produce the Indian Nuts, called by the *Portugals Coco*[6]; and by the *Arabians Narghil*. But the Fortress[7] is of a competent circuit, though the walls are not very

---

[1] See *ante*, p. 143, *note*. [2] See *ante*, p. 168, *note*.

[3] Marked in Wyld's map as the Gungawully river.

[4] Or Honawar. See *ante*, p. 190.

[5] Branches of the river Shiravati, on which are the celebrated Gairsappa, or Gerusappè, Falls. [6] See *ante*, pp. 40 and 181.

[7] This fort previously to 1569, when it was captured by the Portuguese, belonged to the Queen of Gerusappè. It subsequently fell into the hands of the Rajas of Bednur, and afterwards passed into the possession of Haidar Ali, from whom it was taken by the British in 1783, and restored in the following year to Tipu Sahib by the treaty of Mangalùr.

well designed, being just as the *Portugals* found them made by the people of the Country. It stands upon a high Hill of freestone, and, it being very capacious, not onely the Captain lives there, but most of the married and principal *Portugals* have Houses in it, very well accommodated with Wells, Gardens, and other conveniences. The streets within the Fortress are large and fair, besides a great Piazza sufficient to contain all the people of the place in time of a siege. There are likewise two Churches, one dedicated to Saint *Catherine*,[1] and the other to Saint *Anthony*[2]; but ordinarily there is but one Priest in *Onor*, who is the Vicar of the Arch-Bishop of *Goa*; and therefore in Lent other religious persons always go thither. Out of the Fort, in the country, is the *Bazar* or Market, but a small one, and of little consideration; nothing being found therein but what is barely necessary for sustenance of the inhabitants.

Our Ambassador Sig. *Gio. Fernandez* lodg'd with us, not in the Fort but without in the House of a private man; and, I believe, it was because he had rigorous Orders from the Vice-Roy against the Captain, and commission to redress many Disorders which he had committed in his Government, especially to compose matters between him and the people of the Country, as also between him and

---

1 St. Catherine was held in special honour by the Portuguese, as it was on the festival day of that saint (Nov. 25th, 1510) that Goa was finally captured by Admiral Dalboquerque. (See *Commentaries of A. Dalboquerque*, vol. iii, p. 9.) That event is commemorated in Camões' *Lusiada* (x, 42, 43), in certain stanzas, of which the last two lines are thus translated by Fanshaw:—

> "Upon the Feast (as put in by designe)
> Of Egypt's Virgin Martyr, Katherine."
> (*Commentaries of A. Dalboquerque*, vol. i, p. 1.)

2 There were, as is well known, two St. Antonies, one of Egypt, the other of Padua. This church was dedicated to the former saint. (See *post*, p. 209.)

the Vicar, betwixt whom there were great Disorders, the fault of which was charg'd upon the Captain.

When we were settled in our House, first the Vicar, call'd F. *Henrico Rabelo*, and afterwards the Captain, call'd Sigr. Don *Christoforo Fernandez Francisco*, with almost all the principal persons of the place, visited Sig. *Gio. Fernandez*, who presently beginning to treat of business, and presenting to the Captain the Vice-Roy's Letters and Orders, the Captain being terrifi'd therewith on the one side, and on the other oblig'd by the civil terms of Sig. *Fernandez*, forthwith offer'd himself ready to give the Vice-Roy satisfaction in whatever he commanded, and began immediately to put the same offer in effect ; releasing one whom he held Prisoner, and performing other things which Sig. *Fernandez* appointed him.

October the nineteenth. The Captain inviting the Ambassador and all the company to dine in the Fort, we went first to visit him, and afterwards to hear Mass in Saint *Catherine's* Church which is the Vicar's See ; which being over, the Ambassador visited a Gentlewoman who was a Kinswoman of the Vicar's, and then retir'd in private with the Captain, not without manifest signes that his re-pacification was rather upon necessity than out of good will. *Causa mali tanti fœmina sola fuit.* The original of most of the Disorders between the Captain and the Vicar, they say, was occasion'd by the Captain's Wife,[1] who had banished out of *Onor* a servant of his whom he had employ'd as his instrument to other Women, and who had been formerly punished for the same fault. In the mean time we walk'd up and down, but saw nothing worth mentioning ; and at dinner-time we went to the Captain's House where we all din'd, namely Sig. *Gio. Fernandez* the

---

[1] "Hell has no Fury like a woman scorned." (Congreve's *Mourning Bride*, act iii, sc. 8.)

Ambassador, the Chief Commander of the Fleet, call'd *Hettor Fernandez*, F. *Bartolomeo Barroso* the Ambassador's Chaplain, Sig. *Gonsalvo Carvaglio* and I, who came in the Ambassador's Company. The entertainment was very well served ; dinner ended, we returned to our House.

VI.—*October* the twentieth. In the Evening the Chaplain and I went in a *Palanchino* a mile out of *Onòr* to see a fine running water, which issuing out of the earth in a low, or rather hollow place, as it were the bottom of a Gulph, falls into a *Tanke* or Cistern built round with stone ; and, this being fill'd, it runs out with a stream, watering the neighbouring fields. The water is hot,[1] to wit not cold ; and therefore the Country people come frequently to bathe themselves in it for pleasure. The Cistern is square, every side being five or six yards, and the water would reach to a man's neck ; but by reason of the ruinousness of the walls in some places it is not very clean. Within it are small fishes,[2] which use to bite such as come to swim there, yet without doing hurt, because they are small ; and the place being low is consequently shady and so affords a pleasant station at all times. The Gentiles have this Cistern in Devotion, and call it *Ram-tirt*,[3] that is, Holy Water, Water of Expiation, etc. The

---

[1] Hot springs are found in many places in India, and are generally regarded by the natives as objects of veneration. Some are constant in their flow, others intermittent. One such spring is near Rájápur (near Goa), and others are at Máhár, Dábul, and elsewhere. At one place not far from Rájápur there are fourteen singular intermittent springs, which flow for some months in the year only. (See Eastwick's *Handbook of Bombay Presidency*, 2nd ed., p. 219.) There are hot springs also near Gáyá, in the Bengal Presidency.

[2] Fish are not generally found alive in hot water, but one species (mentioned by Humboldt), the *Pimelodus Cyclopum*, is said to be found sometimes in volcanoes.

[3] The correct meaning is the Place of Pilgrimage (*Tirth*) of Ram, or Rama, an incarnation of Vishnu.

Portugals call it *O Tanque da Padre*,[1] that is, the Cistern of the Father, or Religious person, from the Gentile-Monastick who uses to remain there. We stript our selves and spent a good while swimming here. The fields about *Onor* through which we passed were very pleasant Hills and Valleyes, all green, partly with very high herbage, partly with wood, and partly with corn.

October the one and twentieth. I took the Altitude of the Sun, and found it distant from the Zenith 24 degrees 20 minutes, upon which day the Sun, according to my manuscripts, was in the 27th degree of *Libra*, and declin'd from the Æquinoctial to the South 10 degrees 24′ 56″, which deducted from 24 degrees 20′, in which I found the Sun, there remain 13 degrees 55′ 4″; and precisely so much is *Onor* distant from the Æquinoctial towards the North. In the Evening the Ambassador *Vitulá Sinay*,[2] who was lodg'd beyond the River more South of *Onor*, came to the City to visit the Captain in the Fort. The Captain with all the Citizens, and Sig. *Gio. Fernandez*, with us of his Company, went to meet and receive him at the place where he landed: three pieces of Ordnance being discharg'd when he entred into the Fort.

October the four and twentieth was the Davàli,[3] or Feast of the Indian Gentiles, and, I believe, was the same that

---

[1] The word "tank", commonly used in India for an artificial reservoir, seems to be the Portuguese word *tanque*, which may be derived from the Sanskrit *Tanghi*. See *ante*, p. 32.

[2] See *ante*, p. 191.

[3] From *Diwali*, meaning "a row of lamps". This festival takes place in honour of Káli (otherwise called Bhawáni), wife of Siva, and of Lakshmi, wife of Vishnu, goddess of prosperity and abundance, on the last two days of the dark half of the month Asan, and at the new moon, and four following days, of the following month Kartik (October), when all the houses of Hindús are illuminated with rows of lamps. As is well known, the Chinese have a somewhat similar

I had seen the last year celebrated in *Bender di Combrù*[1] in *Persia*. The same day, if I mistake not in my reckoning, the *Moors* began their new year 1033. In the Evening I went to see another great town of *Gentiles*, separate from that which stands upon the Sea near *Onor*, and they call it the *Villa di Bahmani*, because most of the inhabitants are *Brachmans*[2] whereas they that live by the Sea-side are Fishermen, and of other like professions. This Town of the *Brachmans* stands about a Canon's shot within land, remote from the Fortress of *Onor* towards the North-East. The inhabitants keep Cows, or Buffalls,[3] and live by other Trades. In the entrance of the City is built for publick use a handsome square Cistern, or Receptacle for Water, each side of which measured about a hundred of my paces in length; 'tis fill'd with rain-water, which lasts for the whole year.

VII.—*October* the five and twentieth. News came to *Onor* how on *Thursday* night last, *October* the nine and twentieth, *Venk-tapà Naieka*[4] lost his chief Wife, an aged Woman and well belov'd by him; her name was *Badra-Amà*,[5] Daughter of a noble-man of the same Race of

---

festival, called the "Feast of Lanterns". The use of lighted lamps at this festival is to commemorate the slaying of a giant by Vishnu, on which occasion women went to meet him with lamps lighted in his honour.

[1] See *ante*, p. 3, *note*, and p. 107, *note*.

[2] It is a common custom in Indian towns and villages to assign certain specific quarters (called *páras*) as the residence of particular castes, or trades.

[3] Or buffaloes (*Bubalus buffelus*), a Spanish, or Portuguese, word, from the Greek *Boubalos*, hence our word "buff", originally applied to the leather made of buffalo hide, but now to the colour resembling that of such leather.

[4] See *ante*, p. 168, *note*.

[5] More correctly *Bhadr Amma* (Kanarese), "good mother". As an instance of singular perversion of terms it may be noticed that in the Tuluva dialect *Amma* means "father", and *Appa* (Karanese for "father") means "mother". (See *Handbook for Madras*, by E. B. Eastwick, C.B., p. 302.)

Lingavant,[1] which *Venk-tapà* himself is of. Badrà was her proper name, Amà her Title, denoting Princess or Queen. We stayed all this while at *Onor*, because as soon as we arriv'd there *Vitulà Sinay* writ to *Venk-tapà Naieka,* his Master, giving him an account of our arrival; and so it was necessary to stay for his Answer and Orders from the Court: we also waited for men to carry us upon the way (the whole journey having to be made in Litters, or Palanchinos), together with our Goods and Baggage, which were likewise to be carry'd by men upon their shoulders; and the *Davàli*, or Feast of the *Gentiles*, falling out in the meantime, we were fain to stay till it was passed; and I know not whether the Queen's Death and Funeral may not cause us to stay some time longer.

I will not suppress one story which is reported of this Lady. They say that twelve or thirteen years since, when she was about five and thirty years old, it came to her ears that *Venk-tapà Naieka*, her Husband, having become fond of a Moorish Woman, kept her secretly in a Fort not far from the Court, where he frequently solac'd himself with her for two or three dayes together; whereupon *Badrà-Amà*, first complaining to him not onely of the wrong which he did thereby to her, but also more of that which he did to himself, defiling himself with a strange Woman of impure Race (according to their superstition), and of a Nation which drank Wine and ate Flesh and all sort of

---

[1] Lingavats (vulgarly Lingaits), worshippers of Siva, whose symbol is the "Lingam", or emblem of generative power. They were originally followers of a leader named Basava (Sanskrit *Vrishabha*), who became prime minister of the State of which Kalyanpùr was the capital, and wear a "Lingam" as a neck ornament, which must be always carried about, and hence is called *Jangam*, or "movable". They abjure all respect for caste distinctions and observance of Brahmanical rites and usages. A great part of the Kanarese population below Kolapur and in Maisur is Lingait. (See Sir Monier Williams, *Modern India*, p. 194; and Eastwick's *Handbook for Madras*, p. 70.)

uncleannesses (in their account), told him that, if he had a mind for other Women, he need not have wanted Gentile-Women of their own clean Race, without contaminating himself with this Moor, and she would have suffered it with patience; but, since he had thus defil'd himself with her, she for the future would have no more to do with him; and thereupon she took an Oath that she would be to him as his Daughter and he should be to her as her Father: after which she shew'd no further resentment, but liv'd with him as formerly, keeping him company in the Palace, tending upon him in his sickness and doing other things with the same love as at first, helping and advising him in matters of Government, wherein she had alwayes great authority with him; and, in short, excepting the Matrimonial Act, perfectly fulfilling all other Offices of a good Wife. *Venk-tapà Naieka*, who had much affection for her, notwithstanding the wrong he did her with his Moor, endeavour'd by all means possible to divert her from this her purpose and to perswade her to live a Matrimonial Life still with him, offering many times to compound for that Oath by the alms of above 20,000 Pagods[1] (Pagod is a gold coin, near equivalent to a Venetian Zecchino[2] or English Angel), but all in vain, and she persever'd constant in this Resolution till death; which being undoubtedly an act of much Constancy and Virtue was the cause that *Venk-tapà Naieka* lov'd her always so much the more.

VIII.—*October* the eight and twentieth. *Vitulà Sinay*

---

[1] A gold coin equivalent to about 3 Rs., or about 4*s*. 6*d*. of our money. The origin of the name is obscure, but Sir H. Yule thinks it is most probably a corruption of *Bhagavati*, the name of an idol, of which the coin bears a representation. (See *Hobson-Jobson*.)

[2] The words "or English Angel" are not in the original. The zecchino (familiarly *sequin*) was worth about 9*s*. 5*d*. of our money. It is so called from *Zecca*, "mint". An *angel* was worth about 10*s*. It was so called from having the figure of an angel on it.

sent to tell our Ambassador that, having sent word of our arrival to the Court, the great Ministers had acquainted *Venk-tapà Naieka* therewith, who was still so afflicted for the death of his Wife that he went not forth in Publick, nor suffer'd himself to be seen; when they told him of this matter he stood a while without answering, and at length said onely that they might come when they please. Whereupon his Courtiers, seeing him in this mood, would not reply further to him concerning provisions of the journey to be sent to the Ambassador, persons to convey his Goods and other such things; wherefore *Vitulà Sinay* said that Sig. *Gio. Fernandez* might consider what to do, whether to put himself on the way towards the Court without further waiting, or to have him write again and stay for an Answer, for he would do which he pleas'd. Sig. *Gio. Fernandez*, as well for the credit of his Embassy as to avoid charges, was desirous to have provisions for the journey, Men to carry his Goods, and other greater conveniences, although in publick, and with us of his company, he did not testifie so much, being willing to have it thought that *Vitulà Sinay* did this Office for him at the Court upon his own motion and not at his request; yet I know that in secret he us'd great instance with *Vitulà Sinay*, both by Writing and by Speech, by the mediation of an Interpreter, that he would write again to the Court and set forth to *Venk-tapà* how that he was the Ambassador of so great a King, the first Monarch of Christians (for so I heard him tell the Interpreter, though he spoke with a low voice), and that it was not seemly for him to go in that manner, but that people should be sent to him for his journey, and persons to receive him, and commands given to *Venk-tapà's* Ministers that he might pass through his Territories with that conveniency and decency which was requisite; that since he was now within two or three days' journey of the Court he would stay another week at *Onor*, and longer, if need were, till a better Answer came; and that, if he thought it expedient, *Vitulà Sinay* himself might go before to do this Office, as he that might do it best, and who ought to arrive at the Court before him, the Ambassador, who afterwards might come thither alone by easie journeys after he had sent him an Answer. The same night the Interpreter returned with this message to *Vitulà Sinay*, who was lodged on the other side of the River in his own King's jurisdiction.

October the nine and twentieth. After we had heard Mass in Saint *Antonie's Ægypt*[1] Sig. *Gio. Fernandez* was minded to go in person to visit *Vitulà Sinay* and speak to him about the above mention'd matter; wherefore, entring with us into one of those boats which they call *Maneive*,[2] going with twenty, or four and twenty, Oars, onely differing from the Almadies[3] in that the *Maneive* have a large cover'd room in the poop, sever'd from the banks of rowers, and are greater than the Almadies, which have no such room, we pass'd out of the Port, and thence from the mouth of the River Southward went to land upon the continent, where *Vitulà Sinay*, having been advertis'd of our coming, expected us under the shade of certain little Hills and Trees, of which all this Country is full. This was the first time that I set foot in any place of the *Gentiles* where they bear sway themselves.

Sig. *Gio. Fernandez* spoke a long while and alone with *Vitulà Sinay*, both of them sitting upon a Carpet spread upon the grass; and at length, the discourse being ended, the Ambassador took boat again, and returned to *Onor*. Upon the way he told us that *Vitulà Sinay* said that in either case of his writing again, or going in person to the

---

[1] Meaning "church of St. Antony of Egypt". See *ante*, p. 203.

[2] Sometimes called Manchua.

[3] See *ante*, p. 122, *note*.

Court, and waiting for a new Answer, many dayes would be lost, therefore it seem'd best to him that we should all put ourselves upon the way without further waiting; and that to carry his (the Ambassador's) Goods they had appointed ten Men according to his King's order; wherefore Sig. *Fernandez* told us he was resolv'd to go by all means, and seeing the ten men allow'd him to carry his Goods were not sufficient, they alone requiring twenty-five, besides those of the rest of his Company, he would hire the rest at his own charge and rid himself of this perplexity.

By this change of opinion after this interview I understood that *Vitulà Sinay* had spoken in such sort that Sig. *Fernandez* perceiv'd that this coldness of sending him greater accommodations for his journey was not so much through the King's melancholy for his Wife's death and the present confusion of the Court, as for some other cause; and the alledging loss of time in waiting for a new Answer was but an excuse of *Vitulà;* but, in fine, the truth could be no other than that they would not give him any greater Provisions, because *Venk-tapà* was not well pleased with this Embassie. And, to confirm this, I know that before Sig. *Fernandez* departed from *Goa Venk-tapà Naieka* writ thither to his Ambassador, *Vitulà Sinay*, that if they sent this Embassie to urge the restitution of the State and Fortress of *Banghel*,[1] which he had lately taken from a small Indian-Prince, neighbour to *Mangalòr*,[2] who lived under the *Portugals*' protection (for whose defence two or three years before the *Portugals* had made warr with *Venk-tapà Naieka*, and receiv'd a notable defeat by him), it was in vain, and that Sig. *Gio. Fernandez* (now first known to him) might forbear

---

[1] Banghel is for Bangher, or Banghervan, a place of no importance.

[2] A port on the west coast, in lat. 12° 54′ N., probably identical with the Mangaruth of Cosmas. (See Yule's *Cathay*, vol. i, p. clxxviii.)

to undertake this journey, for that he was fully resolv'd not to restore it, nor yet to give seven thousand Pagods[1] yearly to that Prince, as he had promised upon agreement, unless he went to live out of those Territories taken from him, either in *Goa*, or in *Mangalòr*, or elsewhere, he pretending at least a purpose to return to live with that annuity in the lands once his own, privately in hopes, perhaps, to raise some new commotion one day. So that, *Venk-tapà Naieka* knowing that one of the principal businesses of this Embassie was that of the Prince of *Banghel*, which little pleas'd him; and feeling also that this year the Ships from *Portugal* were not yet arriv'd (which every year fetch Pepper out of his Dominions, and bring him in a great sum of money, by agreement made with the *Portugals*, who every year were either to take it, or pay for it), so that, neither the Ships nor the money coming this year, they could not easily pay him for the Pepper this year, nor yet for a great part of that of the last, for which, by reason of the loss of their Ships, they still owed him; and lastly, observing the *Portugals* weakened and low, so that they not onely stood in need of him, but now, in some sort, began to submit themselves to him with this Embassie which they sent to him; and remembering the disgrace of their pass'd defeat; 'twas no strange thing that, being become insolent thereupon, as 'tis the manner of the *Barbarians*, and designing to carry it high over them, he not onely shew'd no great liking of the Embassie, but made little account of it; and in a manner despis'd it, that so he might keep himself and his affairs in greater reputation.

IX.—*October* the thirtieth. Sig. *Gio. Fernandez*, being resolv'd to depart the next day, sent some Horses before upon this day, with some of his Family. The same Evening

---

[1] See *ante*, p. 200, *note*.

one from *Goa* brought News of the arrival there of some *Portugals* of the fleet[1] which came this year from *Portugal*, consisting of four great trading Ships, two Shallops and four Galeons of Warr; which last come in order to be consign'd to *Ruy Freira* for the War of *Ormuz*, the loss of which place, and the deliverance of *Ruy Freira* out of prison, being already known at the Court of *Spain*, but not the loss of the ships of the Fleet last year. The *Portugals* arriv'd in *Goa*, according to the abovesaid intelligence, came in one of the Galeons of the Fleet which is coming, which, being separated from the rest, toucht at *Mozambique*, and there, being old and shatter'd, was lost, onely all the People and Goods were sav'd and came in other ships to *Goa*; and, being[2] the rest of the fleet delays so long, 'tis conceiv'd to have held a course without the Island of Saint *Lorenzo*,[3] which uses to take up more time. They relate also that the Marriage[4] between *Spain* and *England* is concluded, and that the Prince of *England* is now in *Spain*, being come thither *incognito* before the conclusion of the Marriage which was shortly expected.

---

[1] The commercial intercourse between the Portuguese and the native States on the coast was at this time already affected by the rivalry of the Dutch merchants. The system adopted by the Portuguese of depending on fleets despatched at fixed intervals by the Government was unable to cope with the superior vigour of the Dutch traders, who brought their individual energies into play.

[2] For "since", see *ante*, p. 27, *note*.

[3] That is, Island of Madagascar, which was originally named St. Lorenzo, after Lorenzo Dalmeida, who discovered it in 1506. It was afterwards called "Isle Dauphin". For an account of the sack and capture of this island by A. Dalboquerque, see *Commentaries of A. Dalboquerque*, vol. i, pp. 29 and 30, and for another reference to it see *idem*, vol. iv, p. 107, and Barbosa's *East Africa*, p. 13 (Hakluyt edit.). The word "without" means, of course, "westward of".

[4] Or rather "matrimonial agreement", regarding the marriage of Prince Charles with the Infanta, which, as is well known, did not, after all, take place.

It being already very late I shall not longer deferr concluding this Letter, because it is requisite for me to go and take a little rest, that I may be fit for my journey to-morrow Morning, if it please God; to whom I heartily commend you, and with my accustomed affection kiss your Hands. From *Onor*, *October* 30, 1623.

LETTER V.

From Ikkerì,[1] *Novemb*. 22, 1623.

I WRITE to you from *Ikkerì*, the Royal City and Seat of *Venk-tapà Naieka*,[2] whither I am come and where I am present. I shall give you an account of the Audience which our Ambassador hath had of this King, who, in my judgment, should rather be call'd a *Regulus*, or *Royolet*,[3] although the *Portugals* and *Indians* give him the honor of a Royal Title; being[4] he hath in effect neither State, Court, nor appearance, befitting a true King. I shall describe to you every particular that is not unworthy your Curiosity,

---

[1] Called "Eckairee" in modern maps, in lat. 14° 7′ N., and long. 7° 3′ E., to the south-east of Honawar, in the Shivamoga district of Maisúr. Here, according to Sir H. Yule, the coins called Pagodas were first struck. (See *Hobson-Jobson*, article "Pagod".) It is not a place of any importance in the present day, though it was formerly the capital of the Kelâdi chiefs until they removed to Bednur, on the coast, in 1645. (See *ante*, p. 168.) The walls of the town were formerly of great extent and enclosed a palace and citadel. All that now remains is a large stone temple of Aghoreswara. It contains effigies of three chiefs. (See Hunter's *Gazetteer*, sub v.)

[2] See *ante*, p. 168, *note*.

[3] In Italian *Regolo*, a little king; *Royolet*, from *Roitelet*, an old French word meaning the same.

[4] For "since", see *ante*, p. 27, *note*.

and adjoyn some other of my Relations and Descriptions of the Idolatrous *Gentiles*, their vain Superstitions and Ceremonies about their Idols, Temples and Pagods.[1] What I shall now set down mine own Eyes have witness'd to; and I shall not fear being too tedious in describing things, perhaps over minutely, in these Letters, since I know you are delighted therewith and out of your great erudition can make reflections upon the Rites used in these parts of the World, which in many things are not unlike the ancient Ægyptian Idolatry. For I am perswaded to believe, not without the authority of ancient Authors, that the worship of *Isis* and *Osiris*[2] was common to *Ægypt* and this Region, as in *Philostratus* I find *Apollonius* affirming[3] that in *India* he saw the Statues not onely of the Ægyptian, but also of the Grecian, gods, as of *Apollo*, *Bacchus* and *Minerva*.

But to return to the particulars of my journey; on *October* the one and thirtieth, after one a clock in the Afternoon, we departed from *Onor* with Sig. *Gio. Fernandez* in a *Mancina*,[4] or Barge, and the rest of the Family in a less Boat. *Vitulà Sinay*, who was to go with us, we left in readiness to set forth after us, I know not whether by water, or by Land. We row'd up the River, which runs

---

[1] Or Pagodas, a word, as commonly used, synonymous with "temples". See *ante*, p. 209, *note*.

[2] This statement raises a question which cannot be fully discussed in a foot-note. But assuming—as is probably the case, and as is positively stated by Diodorus—that Isis and Osiris really represent the moon and sun respectively, the statement here made may be accepted as probably correct. Sir W. Jones came to the conclusion that the gods of Greece and of India had one common origin, and that "the whole crowd of gods and goddesses of ancient Rome and Hindostan mean only the powers of nature".

[3] This statement of Apollonius cannot be literally true, though he may of course have found no difficulty in connecting the statues of Hindu deities with those of Greek mythology by some outward marks of resemblance.

[4] For Manchua. See *ante*, p. 211.

Southward to *Onor*, against the Stream, making use both of Sail and Oars; and a little before night, having gone about three Leagues, we came to *Garsopà*[1] and there lodg'd. This place was sometimes a famous City, Metropolis of the Province and Seat of a Queen: in which State, as likewise in many others upon the Coast of *India*, to this day a Woman frequently hath the sovereignty; Daughters, or other nearest kinswomen, begotten by whatever Father, succeeding the Mothers; these *Gentiles* having an opinion (as 'tis indeed) that the Issue by the woman-side is much more sure of the blood and lineage of the Ancestors than that by the Man-side.[2]

The last Queen of *Garsopà* fell in Love with a mean Man and a stranger, into whose power she resign'd herself, together with her whole kingdom. In which act, setting aside her choosing a Lover of base blood, upon which account she was blam'd and hated by the *Indians* (who

---

[1] Or Gairsappa (more correctly Gerusappè), well known on account of the magnificent waterfall (on the river Sheravati) in its vicinity, often spoken of as the "Grasshopper falls", a good instance of the transformation of Oriental names. It is curious that P. della Valle makes no reference to this waterfall.

[2] This refers to the custom (called by Sir R. Burton "Murroo-mukata-yum"; see *Goa and the Blue Mountains*, p. 208) prevalent among the Nairs, or Nayars, the ruling race in these parts, of restricting inheritance to the female line, an inevitable result of their system of polyandry. The custom is well known to have prevailed in other parts of the world (see Heriot's *Canada*, vol. i, p. 509, Sir J. Lubbock's *Origin of Civilization*, pp. 87 and 154, and other authorities). A great deal of information on the subject of succession through females may be found in a book, called *The Development of Marriage and Kinship*, by C. Staniland Wake (G. Redway). As to the Nairs and their customs, an interesting account will be found in the *Description of Malabar*, by D. Barbosa (? Magellan), published by the Hakluyt Society in 1866, at p. 124, etc., and also in the Report of the Commission, which, under the orders of the Government of India, made a special inquiry, in 1891, into Malabar customs of marriage and inheritance, and in Sir R. Burton's book already quoted, p. 215 *et seq.*, and in Westermarck's *History of Human Marriage*.

are most rigorous observers of Nobility and maintainers of the dignity of their ancestors in all points) as to giving herself up as a prey to her lover, she committed no fault against her honor; for in these Countries 'tis lawful for such Queens to choose to themselves Lovers or Husbands, one or more, according as they please. But this Man who was so favor'd by the Queen of *Garsopà*, having thoughts as ignoble as his blood, in stead of corresponding with gratitude to the Queen's courtesie, design'd to rebell against her and take the kingdom from her; which design for a while he executed, having in process of time gain'd the affection of most of her most eminent vassals. The Queen, seeing her self oppress'd by the Traytor, had recourse to the *Portugals*, offering them her whole State on condition they would free her from imminent ruine. But the *Portugals*, according as they had alwayes in *India* done by their friends (whereby they have been many times the ruine of others and themselves too) did not succour her till it was too late and then very coldly. On the other side the Traytor (as his ill fate, or rather God's just anger, would have it) call'd to his assistance against the Queene and the *Portugals* his Neighbour *Venk-tapà Naieka*,[1] now Master of those Countries. *Venk-tapà Naieka*, taking advantage of the occasion, enter'd suddenly into the kingdom of *Garsopà* with great diligence and force, so that, shortly becoming Master of the whole Country and the City Royal, and having driven out the *Portugals* who came to defend it, he took the Queen Prisoner and carry'd her to his own Court; where being kept, although honourably, she ended her days in an honourable prison. But the Traytor under-went the punishment of his crime, for *Venk-tapà Naieka* caus'd him to be slain; and, for more secure keeping that State in his power, caus'd the City and Royal Palace of *Garsopà* to be

[1] See *ante*, p. 168, *note*.

destroy'd, so that at this day that lately flourishing City is become nothing but a Wood, Trees being already grown above the ruines of the Houses, and the place scarcely inhabited by four Cottages of Peasants.

II.—But, returning to my travel, I must not omit that the three Leagues of this journey was one of the most delightful passages that ever I made in my life; for the country on either side is very beautiful, not consisting of Plains that afford onely an ordinary prospect, nor of towring mountains, but of an unequal surface, Hills and Valleys, all green and delightful to the eyes, cloth'd with thick and high Groves, and many times with fruit Trees as Indian Nuts, *Foufel*, Ambe, and such like,[1] all water'd with innumerable Rivulets and Springs of fresh water; the sides of the River all shady, beset with Flowers, Herbs and sundry Plants, which, like Ivy,[2] creeping about the Trees and Indian reeds of excessive height, (call'd by the Country-people *Bambù*,[3] and very thick along the banks) make the wood more verdant; through the middle whereof the River strayes with sundry windings. In short, the River of *Garsopà*, for a natural thing without any artificial ornament of buildings, or the like, is the goodliest River that ever I beheld.[4]

Our boats, being large, could not go to the ordinary landing-place at *Garsopà*, because the River, which is discharg'd into the Sea with one stream, is there divided into many, which fall from several Springs upon some neigh-

---

[1] *I.e.*, areca nut and mangoes. See *ante*, pp. 36 and 40.

[2] Probably the plant *Aralia digitata*, common in this part of India, having a resemblance to ivy.

[3] A Malay word. The well-known *Bambusa arundinacea*, or bamboo. The Indian name is *Bāns*.

[4] Mr. Eastwick, in his *Handbook of the Madras Presidency*, speaking of this locality, says: "Even the most phlegmatic person cannot but have his enthusiasm somewhat kindled by the scenery." (P. 308.)

bouring Hills, so that the water is but little. Wherefore we landed at some distance from *Garsopà*, which stands on the South-bank of the River, and walkt the rest of the way on foot, and our goods were carry'd upon the Men's shoulders whom we had hir'd for that purpose. Before we got to our lodging it was night, and we were fain to wade over one of the arms of the River which took me up to the middle of the thigh; the bottom was stony, and not so dangerous to us (who were free) in reference to falling as to the poor men who carry'd burthens upon their heads; so that I wonder'd not that he who carry'd the hamper of my clothes fell down with it and wetted it in the water.

At length we lodg'd, not within the compass of *Garsopà*, which was somewhat within land, but near it upon the River, in a place cover'd with a roof amongst certain Trees, where many are wont to lodge, and where the Pepper is weigh'd and contracted for when the *Portugals* come to fetch it: for this is the Country wherein greatest plenty of Pepper grows; for which reason the Queen of *Garsopà* was wont to be call'd by the *Portugals*, *Reyna da Pimenta*,[1] that is, *Queen of Pepper*. The River is call'd by the *Portugals* the River of *Garsopà*, but by the *Indians* in their own Language one branch is term'd *Ambù nidi*,[2] and the other *Sarà nidi*. From the River's mouth, where it falls into the Sea, to *Garsopà*, the way, if I mistake not, is directly East.

III.—*November* the first. After dinner we departed from our station, and, passing by the Cottages and the places where the City of *Garsopà* sometime stood, we walk'd a

---

[1] Strictly speaking, the "Pimenta", or "Pimento", is the allspice (not pepper) of commerce, being the berry of the shrub *Eugenia pimenta*, which grows only in the W. Indies. Pepper is the product of the plant *Piper nigrum*.

[2] *Nidi* for *nadi*, Sanskrit for "river".

good way Southwards, or rather South South-west, always through an uneven, woody, Country, irrigated with water and delightful, like the banks of the River which I describ'd. Then we began to climb up a Mountain, which the Country people call *Gat*,[1] and which divides the whole length of this part of *India*, being wash'd on the East with the Gulph of *Bengala*, and on the West with the Ocean, or Sea of *Goa*.[2] The ascent of this Mountain is not very rough, but rather easie and pleasant like the other parts, being thick set with Groves of Trees of excessive greatness ; some of them so strait that one alone might serve for the Mast of a Ship. Withall the Mountain is so water'd with Rivulets and Fountains, that, me-thought, I saw the most delightful place of the *Appennine* in *Italy*. If there be any difference, the *Gat* of *India* hath the advantage in this place, because the height is much less than that of our *Appennine*, the ascent more easy, the wood more beautiful and thick, the waters not less plentiful and clear. If the *Gat* yields to it in any thing, 'tis in the frequency of inhabited places, the sumptuousness of buildings, and, lastly, in the beauty which the industrious art of the inhabitants adds to the *Appennine ;* the Indian *Gat* having no other, besides what liberal, yet unpolished, Nature gives it.

About three hours after noon we came to the top of the *Gat*, where, a little beneath the highest cliff, is found a kind of barr'd Gate, with a wall in a narrow pass, which renders the place sufficiently strong ; a little further than which, in the top of all, are found earthen Bulwarks and lines, which guard the passage ; and in this place is a

---

[1] Properly *Ghát*, or *Ghátta*, Sanskrit for "step". See p. 185, *note.*

[2] There are, in fact, two ranges of mountains, called the Eastern and Western Gháts, not one single range, as our traveller supposed, with an elevated table-land between them.

sufficient Fortress, it being a mile and half in circuit. It was sometimes call'd *Garicota*,[1] but now *Govarada-Naghar*. We lodg'd about a Musket-shot without the Fort, in a plane and somewhat low place, where are some Houses like a Village, and amongst them a Temple of *Hamant*,[2] who is one of those two *Scimiones*[3] who were employ'd by *Ramo*[4] for recovering his Wife *Sità*, as their Fables relate; for which good work and their other miracles the *Indians* adore them. Here I saw his Statue in the Temple with burning lights before it, and a consecrated Silver Hand hung up by some devout person, perhaps cur'd of some evil of his Hands.

Below this place where we lodg'd, amongst the little Valleys of the Hill, is a fair and large Cistern, or Receptacle of water, which falls thereinto from a River descending from the Mountain, the over-plus running into the lower Valleys. At night we heard Musick at the Gate of the above-mention'd Temple, divers barbarous Instruments sounding, and amongst the rest certain great Horns of Metal, fashion'd almost into a semicircle. I ask'd the reason of this Festival, and they told me the Idol was to go presently, accompany'd with a great number of Men and Women, in pilgrimage to a place

---

[1] Probably *Girikot*, or "Hill-fort".

[2] Misprint for "Hanimant" in the original. Properly "Hanumán", the monkey-god, son of Pāvana (the wind).

[3] Italian for apes.

[4] A reference to the legend, according to which Rama (darkness), son of Dasanatha (he of the ten chariots), King of Ayodhya (Oude), an incarnation of Vishnu, led an army of apes (generally supposed to have been aboriginal tribes) against Rāvana, the ten-headed demon of Lanka (Ceylon), who had carried off Sita (moon), wife of Rama, daughter of Janaka, King of Viddha. For an interesting explanation of the hidden meaning of this legend, see *Notes on the Early History of Northern India*, by J. F. Hewitt, Part VI, in the *Journal of the Royal Asiatic Society*, Art. XIV, vol. xxii, p. 742.

of their devotion near *San Tome*,[1] a moneth's journey and more; and that it was to be carry'd in a *Palanchino*, as the custom is, and in procession with sundry sounds and songs, almost in the same manner as amongst us Christians the Bodies, or Images, of Saints are carry'd in procession when any Community, or Fraternity, go in pilgrimage to *Loreto*, or *Rome*, in the Holy year. At this time assisted at the service of the Idol, amongst others, a Woman, who, they said, was so abstinent that she did not so much as eat Rice; they held her for a kind of Saint, upon a fame that the Idol delighted to sleep with her, which these silly souls accounted a great spiritual favour; and, haply, it may be true that some incubus-Devil has to do with her and deceives her with false illusions, telling her that he is her God; of which kind of Women there are many among the *Moors*.[2] Divers come to ask her about future things, and she, consulting the Idol, gives them their answer; one of these interrogations was made to her whilst we were present. Others came to offer Fruits and other edibles to the Idol, which one of the Priests presented to it, murmuring his Orisons, and taking half of the things offer'd, (which, after presentation to the Idol, remains to the servants of the Temple), he restores the other half to him that offer'd them; and, were it but an

---

[1] Or St. Thomas. A place on the east coast, reputed to have been the scene of martyrdom of St. Thomas the Apostle, formerly known as Mihiláropye or Mihilapúr, and identified by Prof. H. Wilson with Mailapúr (*Trans. of R. A. S.*, vol. i, p. 161). For further references to this place see Bishop Heber's *Journal* (vol. iii, p. 212, 4th edit.) and Sir H. Yule's *Marco Polo* (vol. ii, p. 290 *et seq.*). Some authorities mention Kalamina as the place of the Saint's martyrdom (A.D. 68). (See Eastwick's *Handbook of Madras*, p. 152.)

[2] The word "Moors" seems to be inserted by mistake for "Gentiles", for the superstition referred to is held rather by Hindus than by Muhammadans. (See *Mœurs des peuples de l'Inde*, by Dubois, vol. ii, p. 59.)

Indian Nut, he splits it in two before the Idol and gives half to him that brought it, who takes the same with reverence, and is afterwards to eat it with devotion as sacred food and tasted of by the Idol.

In the Evening, by the Captain of the Fort (who was a Moor of *Dacàn*,[1] and sometime an Officer under one *Melik*,[2] a Captain of *Adil-Sciàh*,[3] on the Frontiers of *Goa*, but being taken Prisoner in a War between *Adil-Sciàh* and *Venk-tapà Naieka*, and afterwards set at liberty, remained in the service of *Venk-tapà*, and hath been about five-and-twenty years Governour of this Fortress and is called *Mir Baì*)[4] was sent a Present of Sugar Canes, and other refreshments to eat, to Sig: *Gio: Fernandez;* whom also the same night *Vituldà Sinay*, who travell'd with us but apart by himself, came to visit, and entertain'd with the sight of two young men, who fenc'd very well a good while together, onely with Swords made of Indian Canes. On which occasion, I shall not omit to state that amongst the *Indians* 'tis the custom for every one to manage and make use of one sort of Arms, whereunto he accustoms himself, and never uses any other, even in time of War. So that some Souldiers fight onely with Swords, others with Sword and Buckler, others with Lances, others with Bows and Arrows, and others with Muskets; and so every one with his own arms, never changing the same, but thereby becoming very expert and well practis'd in that which he takes to. The way from *Garsopà* to *Govarada Naghar* was about five or six miles and no more.

November the second. Early in the Morning *Vituldà Sinay* first visited Sig: *Gio: Fernandez*, and afterwards

---

[1] See *ante*, p. 141, *note*. [2] See *ante*, p. 34, note 3.

[3] See *ante*, p. 143, note 5.

[4] Literally "noble governor". The last of these two titles is more familiarly known as "Bey", a corruption of the Turkish "Beg".

the Captain of the Fort, accompanied by a great number of his Souldiers with several Arms, but most had Pikes, Lances in the form of half Pikes, and Swords ; onely two had Swords and Bucklers : one of them had a short and very broad Sword like a Cortelax,[1] but the edge-part bowed inwards after a strange fashion. Those two with Swords and Bucklers came before the Captain, dancing and skirmishing after their manner, as if they fought together. The visit was receiv'd in the Porch of the little Temple above mention'd and lasted a good while. *Vitulà Sinay*, who spoke the *Portugal*-Tongue well, serv'd for interpreter between our Ambassador and the Captain, and handsomely[2] intimated to the Ambassador that when he return'd back it was fit to give a present to this Captain and visit him in the Fort ; that the Custom was so, and he had already done the like to the Ambassador ; that since he did it not now he had already made an excuse for it, by telling him that the baggage was gone before, and that he did not go to visit him because he had no present to carry him, but he would do it at his return. At the end of this visit *Vitulà Sinay* caus'd a little Silver basket to be brought full of the leaves of *Betle*,[3] (an herb which the *Indians* are always eating, and to the sight not unlike the leaves of Cedars[4]) and, giving it to the Ambassador, he told him that he should present it to the Captain, the Custom being so in *India* for the person visited to give *Betle*-leaves to the visitant, where-with the visit ends. The Ambassador did so, and the Captain, without taking any of these leaves, whether it were the custom, or that, being a *Moor*, he did not use it, (which yet I believe not) gave it to certain persons

---

[1] From Spanish *cortar*, "to cut", hence our word cutlass (Webster's *Dictionary*).

[2] In the original "con bel modo". [3] See *ante*, p. 36, note 1.

[4] It is difficult to understand how the leaves of *Piper betelium* could be held to resemble those of the cedar. They are more like vine-leaves.

of qualitie, who stood beside him and had accompany'd him; neither did any of them touch the leaves, but the basket went from hand to hand till it was carry'd away as full as it was presented; which being done, the Captain first, and then *Vitulà Sinay*, took leave and departed.

V.—After we had din'd about noon, or soon after, our Ambassador went away alone with his Chaplain, out of impatience to stay longer in that place; the rest of us remain'd, expecting the removing of all our baggage, which was very slow in departing, because the Men who carry'd the same upon their heads were not sufficient and the burthens were too heavy; so that it was needful to hire more and increase the number of Porters to thirty-six besides mine, which I hir'd for myself apart, and, because neither were these enough, it was needful to lade two Oxen, who carry'd Goods for four other Men; and this took up much time, because neither the Men nor the beasts which were hir'd were ready, but were to be sought for here and there.

In the mean time, while the burthens were getting in order, I entertain'd myself in the Porch of the Temple, beholding little boys learning Arithmetick after a strange manner,[1] which I will here relate. They were four, and having all taken the same lesson from the Master, in order to get that same by heart and repeat likewise their former lessons and not forget them, one of them singing musically with a certain continu'd tone, (which hath the force of making deep impression in the memory) recited part of the lesson; as, for example, "One by its self makes one"; and whilst he was thus speaking he writ down the same number, not with any kind of Pen, nor on Paper, but (not to spend Paper in vain) with his finger on the ground, the pavement

---

[1] A similar scene may be witnessed in the village schools of India at the present day. (See Sir Monier Williams' *Modern India*, p. 220.)

being for that purpose strew'd all over with very fine sand; after the first had writ what he sung, all the rest sung and writ down the same thing together. Then the first boy sung and writ down another part of the lesson; as, for example, "Two by its self make two", which all the rest repeated in the same manner, and so forward in order. When the pavement was full of figures they put them out with the hand, and, if need were, strew'd it with new sand from a little heap which they had before them wherewith to write further. And thus they did as long as the exercise continu'd; in which manner likewise, they told me, they learnt to read and write without spoiling Paper, Pens, or Ink, which certainly is a prety way. I ask'd them, if they happen'd to forget, or be mistaken in any part of the lesson, who corrected and taught them? they being all Scholars without the assistance of any Master; they answer'd me and said true, that it was not possible for all four of them to forget, or mistake in the same part, and that thus they exercis'd together, to the end that if one happen'd to be out the others might correct him. Indeed a prety, easie and secure way of learning.

VI.—Having seen this Curiosity, and our baggage being laden, we all set forth after the Ambassador, and *Vitulà Sinay* set out together with us. We travell'd first Eastward, then South-ward, but many times I could not observe which way our course tended; we went upon the ridge of a Hill, and through uneven wayes, sometimes ascending and sometimes descending, but always in the middle of great thick Groves full of Grass and running water, no less delightful then the former Fields. A little more than half a League from the Fort we found a *Meschita*[1] of the *Moors*, built upon the way, with a Lake, or

[1] A Spanish corruption of the Arabic word *masjid*, derived from the verb *sajada*, "to bend", or "bow down", generally rendered in English as "mosque", a Muhammadan temple.

Receptacle of water, but not very well contriv'd by the Captain of the said Fort, which his King had allow'd him to make as a great favour; for the *Gentiles* are not wont to suffer in their Countries Temples of other Religions. Here we found our Ambassador, who stay'd for us; and we tarry'd likewise here above an hour in expectation of our baggage, much of which was still behind.

At length continuing our journey, and having rested a good while in another place, night came upon us in the midst of a Wood, so shady that although we had very clear Moon-light yet we were fain to light Torches, otherwise we could not see our way. The Torches used in *India* are not like ours, but made of metal in form of those wherewith the Infernal Furies are painted, the fire of which is fed with Bitumen and other dry materials, which are put into the mouth, or hollow at the top, into which also they frequently powre a combustible liquor,[1] which the Man that holds the Torch carries in his other hand in a metalline bottle, with a long slender neck, very fit for that purpose; for when he is minded to recruit the flame he distills a little liquor into it, the length of the neck securing his hand from hurt. By the light of these Torches we travell'd a great part of the night.

At length, being unable to overtake the Horses which were led before, and the baggage being behind, for fear of losing our way we stay'd under a great Tree, where some in *Palanchinoes*[2] and others upon the ground spent this night inconveniently and supper-less, having nothing else to eat but a little Bread, which we toasted at the fire that we might eat it hot; and with the same fire which we kindled we allay'd the coldness of the night, which in the

---

[1] The liquor generally used is mustard-oil, made from the seed of *Sinapis Chinensis*.

[2] See *ante*, p. 31, *note*.

top of these Indian Mountains is very cold in regard of their height; yet it was not sharper to us this night than it uses to be at *Rome* in the beginning of *September*, even in temperate years.

November the third. As soon as it was day we follow'd our way, and in a short time came to a Village of four Cottages, call'd *Tumbrè*, where the Horses were lodg'd, and we also stay'd till the baggage came up, which was much later then we; and we stay'd the longer to rest the people that travell'd on foot: for all the Servants, and I know not how many Musketiers, which our Ambassador carry'd with him, were on foot. *Vitulà Sinay* lay there likewise this night, but was gone before we came thither. From *Garicota* to *Tumbrè* is about a League and a half; for in this Country they measure the way by *Gaùs*, and every *Gaù*[1] is about two Leagues, and they said that from *Garicota* to *Tumbrè* was not one *Gaù*.

VII.—When we arriv'd at this Town we found the pavements of the Cottages were varnish'd over with Cow-dung mix'd with water; a custom of the Gentiles in the places where they are wont to eat, as I have formerly observ'd. I took it for a superstitious Rite of Religion; but I since better understand that it is us'd only for elegancy and ornament, because not using, or not knowing how to make, such strong and lasting pavements as ours, theirs being made sleightly of Earth and so easily spoyl'd, therefore when they are minded to have them plain,

---

[1] One meaning of the word is said to be the distance at which the lowing of a cow may be heard, which could hardly be so much as two leagues. There is a native measure of distance called *Gaudia*, the same as the Tamil *Naliguai*, which has probably the same origin. (See Smith's *Dictionary of Greek and Roman Geography*, vol. ii, p. 1092.) Sir Emerson Tennent says that the word in Ceylon "means the distance which a man can walk in an hour" (vol. i, p. 543).

smooth and firm, they smear the same over with Cow-dung temper'd with water, in case it be not liquid (for if it be there needs no water), and plaining it either with their hands, or some other instrument, and so make it smooth, bright, strong and of a fine green colour, the Cows whose dung they use never eating anything but Grass; and it hath one convenience, that this polishing is presently made, is soon dry and endures walking, or any thing else, to be done upon it; and the Houses wherein we lodg'd we found were preparing thus at our coming, and were presently dry enough for our use. Indeed this is a prety Curiosity, and I intend to cause tryal to be made of it in *Italy*, and the rather because they say for certain that the Houses whose pavements are thus stercorated,[1] are good against the Plague,[2] which is no despicable advantage. Onely it hath this evil, that its handsomeness and politeness lasteth not, but requires frequent renovation, and he that would have it handsome must renew it every eight, or ten, days; yet, being a thing easie to be done and of so little charge, it matters not for a little trouble which every poor person knows how to dispatch. The *Portugals* use it in their Houses at *Goa* and other places of *India;* and, in brief, 'tis certain that it is no superstitious custom, but onely for neatness and ornament; and therefore 'tis no wonder that the *Gentiles* use it often and perhaps every day, in places where they eat, which above all the rest are to be very neat.

'Tis true they make a Religious Rite of not eating in any place where people of another Sect, or Race, (in their own opinion unclean) hath eaten, unless they first re-

---

[1] A somewhat pedantic word, for which, however, the authority of Bacon may be cited.

[2] This is an exaggeration, but the practice has, no doubt, some sanitary advantages. (See Moor's *Hindoo Pantheon*, p. 141.)

polish the same with Cow-dung, which is a kind of purification: as we do by washing it with water, and whitening the wall (not as a Religious Rite, but through Custom), in Chambers where any one has dy'd. I said, where people not oncly of different Religion, but also of impure Race, have eaten, because the *Gentiles* are very rigorous and superstitious among themselves for a noble Race not to hold Commerce of eating with others more base; yea, in one and the same Race (as in that of the *Brachmans*, which is the noblest), some *Brachmans* (as the *Panditi*[1] or *Boti*,[2] who are held in great esteem amongst them), will not eat in the Company, or so much as in the House, of a *Brachman*, *Sinay*[3] or *Naieke*,[4] and other Nobles who eat Fish, and are call'd by the general name *Mazari*,[5] and much less esteem'd then those who eat none; yet the *Brachmans*, *Sinay* and *Naieke*, or other species of *Mazari*, who are inferior, eat in the House of a *Pandito*, or *Boto*, without being contaminated, but rather account it an honor.[6]

VIII.—After dinner we departed from *Tumbrè*, travelling through unequal wayes and lands like the former, but rather descending than otherwise; we rested once a while under a Tree, to stay for the baggage, and then proceeding

---

[1] Sanskrit for "learned men".

[2] See *ante*, p. 80, *note*.

[3] Properly *Sinaia*, the name of a Brahman caste.

[4] These are the military caste (from Sanskrit *Nayaka*, "a chief"), who rank next below the Brahmans. The title of "Nair" is supposed by Sir R. Burton (*Goa and the Blue Mountains*, p. 215) to be derived from *Nayaka*.

[5] This term is usually applied to a tribe employed solely in the cultivation of the soil, but is here used in a more general sense to denote a lower caste than that of Brahmans.

[6] More striking instances than this of the veneration with which Brahmans are regarded by inferior castes might be mentioned. For one special instance see Sir R. Burton's *Goa and the Blue Mountains*, p. 213.

again, at almost six a clock after noon we came to the side of a River call'd *Barenghì*, which in that place runs from West to East and is not fordable, although narrow, but requires a boat to pass it. On the Southern bank on which we came were four Cottages, where we took up our station that Night, enjoying the cool, the shadow and the sight of a very goodly Wood which cloaths the River sides with green; but above all where we lodg'd, on either side the way, were such large and goodly Trees, such spacious places underneath for shade and the place so opacous by the thickness of the boughs on high, that indeed I never saw in my dayes a fairer natural Grove; amongst other Trees there was abundance of *Bambù*,[1] or very large Indian canes, twin'd about to the top with prety Herbs. The journey of this day was three *Cos*, or a League and half. This River, they say, is one of those which goes to *Garsopà*.[2] *Vitulà Sinay* we found not here, because he was gone before.[3]

November the fourth. We began in the Morning to pass our Goods over the River; but, because there was but one, and that a small, boat, it was ten hours after noon before we had got all of them over; then, following our journey through somewhat oblique and uneven wayes like the former, we found many trees of *Myrobalanes*,[4]

---

[1] See *ante*, p. 220. It is not usual to find creeping plants twining themselves round the bamboo, as here stated, though they abound on trees of all kinds.

[2] Properly *Gérusappé*. See p. 218.

[3] This statement seems to be an anticipation of Sheridan's celebrated remark in *The Critic*: "The Spanish fleet thou canst not see, because it is not yet in sight."

[4] The *Terminalia Belerica*, of which the fruit formed a considerable article of commerce in former days. See Barbosa's (? Magellan's) *Coast of Malabar*, pp. 80, 222, 223. The Mahratta name is *Hirda*. It is also called *Arjuna*. It is used for calico-printing, but in the present day chiefly for tanning purposes. The name *Myrobolan*,

such as are brought into *Italy*, preserved in Sugar. It hath leaves much like that plant which produces Gum Arabick,[1] by me formerly describ'd[2]; different onely in this, that in that of Gum Arabick the branch, consisting of many leaves, is much less, round or oval, and seems one leaf made up of many long and narrow ones: but in this *Myrobalane* Tree the branch is sufficiently long, and the small leaves composing it in two rows on either side are somewhat larger; nor is the *Myrobalane* Tree prickly, like that of Gum Arabick. The fruit is round, hard, of a yellowish green, smooth, shining, of little pulp, with a great stone, almost round and furrow'd with six circular lines. Being raw it hath an acid and astringent, but, in my judgment, no pleasant taste; but when preserv'd becomes good. They say it is refrigerative and purges Choler.

IX.—Having rested many times upon the way and in all travell'd two Leagues, we ended this day's journey in the onely considerable and populous Town we had hitherto met, which is call'd *Ahinelì*.[3] We lodg'd in the Porches of a Temple of Idols, low after their manner, with very large eaves supported by great Posts; the Pavement rais'd high and dung'd,[4] but not lately; the walls white, sprinkled in the corners and ends with a sort of rosy pigment, ill colour'd; for so is their custom

---

derived from two Greek words signifying "unguent" and "fruit" or "nut", comprehends several species of *Terminalia*, and one of *Phyllanthus*. As to the medicinal and other properties of the fruit, see Sir H. Yule's *Hobson-Jobson*. An allusion to the fruit occurs in Beckford's *Vathek*, "She is sweeter to me than the myrabolan comfit."

[1] Gum-arabic is the product of *Acacia Nilotica* and *Acacia Seyal* the Myrobolan being a *Combretum*.

[2] In one of the letters not included in this translation.

[3] This town seems to be the modern *Honelli*. It is not at present a town of any importance.

[4] See *ante*, pp. 87 and 230.

always in their Religious Structures.[1] The Idol was call'd *Virenà Deurù*,[2] the latter of which words signifies *God*, or rather *Lord*, being attributed also to Men of quality; he stood at the upper end in a dark place with Candles before him ; of what figure he was I could not see well, by reason of the darkness, but they told me 'twas a Man. In the body of the Temple were many other wooden Statues of less Idols, plac'd about in several places, as 'twere for ornament; some of which were figures of their Gods, others not of Gods, but for ornament, of several shapes.

Many of these figures represented dishonest actions. One was of a Woman. Another was of a Man and a Woman kissing, the Man holding his Hands on the Woman's Breasts, and sundry such representations fit indeed for such a Temple.[3] But these were not figures of Gods. Of Gods there was a *Brahmà* with five Heads[4] and three Arms on a side, sitting astride a Peacock, which in their Language they call *Nau Brahmà*,[5] that is *the Peacock*

---

[1] Sir J. Lubbock (*Origin of Civilization*, p. 366) thinks that this red pigment is intended to represent the blood of sacrifices offered to the deities. The use of such red paint is common among idolatrous nations, and in some parts of India no flowers can be presented to idols except those of a red colour. (See Dubois, *Mœurs des peuples de l'Inde*, vol. ii, p. 441.)

[2] A name applied to the Lingam, or emblem of Siva. For the legend regarding the origin of this emblem, see Dubois, *Mœurs des peuples de l'Inde*, vol. ii, p. 417 *et seq*.

[3] Two passages in the original are omitted.

[4] It is unusual for this deity to be represented with *five* heads. It is true that he is said to have been born with five heads, but he lost one of them in a combat with Siva. (See Dubois, *Mœurs des peuples de l'Inde*, vol. ii, p. 396.)

[5] Literally, "the Boat of Brahma," signifying the vehicle by which Brahma was supposed to be conveyed in the ocean of space. A swan, or goose, sometimes takes the place of the peacock. (See Dubois, vol. ii, p. 396.)

of Brahmà; another God was call'd *Naraina,*[1] with four Arms on a side: another with an Elephant's Head and two Hands to an Arm, whom they call *Ganesù,*[2] and others *Bacra-tundo,*[3] that is *Round-mouth;* for one and the same God hath divers names. Another, call'd *Fuenà,*[4] had the shape of a Man, holding a naked Sword in his right Hand and a Buckler in his left. Another had a Man under his Feet,[5] upon whose Head he trampled; and so many others of various sorts.

I observ'd that all these Idols had the same cover of the Head, high, with many peaks, all ending in one long peak, a strange and majestical Diadem not used now in *India;* it might have been of wreath'd Linnen, or Gold, or other solid matter; wherefore I imagine that it is a very ancient covering, at this day dis-us'd; unless haply it be some ensign of Divinity, which I rather think, because I remember to have seen at *Rome* almost the same Diadems upon the Heads of some *Ægyptian* Statues, (and, if I forget not, they were called *Tutuli,*[6] and the Idols *Tutulati*), as amongst us the Diadems of the Saints, or, as some make it, three Crowns one upon another, like the *Regno,*[7] or Pontifical Crown, of our Pope.

---

[1] A name of Siva, properly Narayana. He has various other names.

[2] See *ante*, p. 73, *note*.

[3] Literally, "crooked trunk".

[4] The name of some local deity.

[5] Probably Siva as "the Destroyer". For the attributes of this deity, see Dubois' *Mœurs des peuples de l'Inde*, vol. ii, p. 416.

[6] The word "Tutulus" was a name given to the pile of hair worn on the head by Roman women. (See *Lucian*, ii, 358, and *Juvenal*, vi, 503.) The headdress of the Egyptian Isis is made up of the serpent Thermuthes. Dubois attributes the conical shape of the headdress seen on Indian sacred statues to a "particular taste" of the Indians for a pyramidal shape. (See his *Mœurs des peuples de l'Inde*, vol. ii, p. 348.)

[7] The Pontifical crown is generally called "Tiara", consisting of three crowns, added to successively by three Popes (John XIII, Boni-

In the middle of the Temple, between the chief entrance and the inner shrine, was another darker inclosure, separated from the chief entrance, but not to the same extent as was the inner shrine, that is to say about half-way between the two, wherein stood, fastned in the ground, certain slender staves, with others across them in two rows, making a little Stockade, or Palisade, of a long form ; and these were to hang Lamps and Tapers upon, at more solemn dayes and hours. A Barber whom we had with us, an *Indian-Gentile* but a Native of the Country of *Adil-Sciàh*, who was named *Dengì*, and understood something of the *Portugal*-Tongue, could not well tell me the names of those figures and Idols of the Temple when I ask'd him ; because, he said, they were not things of his Country, where they had other things and Gods, and that every Country had particular ones of their own.

Within the circuit of this Temple, but on one side of the Court as you go in, were three other little cells, separate from the body of the great Temple, two of which were empty, perhaps not yet well prepared, but in the other was an Idol of an Ox, which our Barber knew, and said was also of his Country and that they call it *Basuanà*[1]; it was half lying, or rather sitting, upon the floor, with the Head erect ; like which Ox, or *Basuanà*, stood another in the upper part of the Temple, before the Tribunal of the Idol *Virenà*, as if it stood there for his guard.

---

face VIII, and Benedict XII), indicative of the Trinity. The word "Regno" is applied to it as indicating its signification as the badge of civil authority, the spiritual authority of the Pope being represented by the keys. The resemblance between the costumes seen in India and those of Egyptian statues is mentioned also by Mr. Elphinstone (*History of India*, p. 184).

[1] More correctly *Basav-anna.* The figure of a bull (having no doubt a symbolical meaning) is frequently represented with that of Siva. So also the Egyptian god Mitthas was represented as seated on a bull.

In the Evening the Ministers of the Temple ring a kind of Bell, or Shell,[1] which was within the Temple, striking it with a staff; and it made a tolerable sound, as if it had been a good Bell: at which sound, some from without assembling together, they begin to sound within the Temple very loudly two Drums, and two Pipes, or Flutes, of metal; after which, many Tapers being lighted, particularly at the Stockade above-mentioned, and a little quilt being put in order, with a Canopy of rich stuff above it which is alwayes ready in the Temple for carrying the Idol, they put the principal Idol *Virenà* on it, (not that one of ordinary wood in the middle of the Temple, but the other at the upper end, which was of the same bigness, about two spans round the body) and ornaments about it, but all painted with various colours, gilded, and deck'd with white Flowers. Then one of the Ministers march'd first, sounding a Bell continually as he went, and after him others, and at length two with lighted Tapers, after which follow'd the Idol in his Canopy, with a Minister before him, carrying a Vessel of Perfumes, which he burnt; and thus they carry'd him in Procession: first into the Court without the Temple, going out of it on the left Hand, as you enter, which to them as they came out was the right, and returning by the other opposite. After which, going out of the Gate of the Court into the street, they went in the same manner in Procession, (still sounding their Bells) I know not whither, but 'tis likely they went to some other Temple to perform some kind of ceremony; for in the Town there was more than one. Being at length return'd, and the Procession re-entering the Court with a great train of Men and Women of the Town, they went thrice about the inside of the Court, as they had done once, before

---

[1] As to the general use of bells in temples, see Sir J. Lubbock's *Origin of Civilization*, p. 232; and Dubois' *Mœurs des peuples de l'Inde*, quoted by Sir J. Lubbock.

they went out. But in these three Circumgyrations they observ'd this Order, that the first time they walked as they had done in the street; the second more leisurely, and those that sounded the Flutes left off and sounded another kind of shriller, sweeter, Pipe; the third time they walk'd more slowly than before, and, leaving off the second Pipes, sounded others of a far lower note. Which being done, those that carry'd and accompany'd the Canopy of the Idol stood still in the entrance of the Temple, right against the Upper End, and one of the Priests, or Ministers, standing at the Upper End, directly opposite to the Idol, (who was held standing on his Feet by help of one of the Minister's Hands, who for that purpose went alwayes on one side near him;) began to salute the Idol a far off with a dim Taper in his Hand, making a great circle[1] with the same from on high downwards, and from below upwards, directly over against the Idol, which he repeated several times; and in the end of the circles, which were alwayes terminated in the lower part, he describ'd a strait line from one side to the opposite, and that where the circle began; nor did he seem to me always to begin the circles on the same part, but sometimes on the right and sometimes on the left, with what Order I know not.

This being done within, the same Priest came to the entrance where the Idol stood, passing directly through the midst of the Palisade of Lights, (through which, I believe that, for others and at another time it is not lawful to pass; because, when any one enter'd to perform other Services other than these Ceremonies, I saw him always go without the Palisade by the side) coming along, I say, sounding a Bell, and being follow'd by a Boy who carry'd a Basin of

[1] This and the other motions of the priest, subsequently described, appear to have a distinct connection with a form of worship of the sun and other heavenly bodies.

water with *Santalus*, or *Sanders*,[1] after him, (the same wherewith, I conceive, they are wont to paint their fore-heads) and also with Drums and Flutes sounding all the while; he went in this manner three times round the Idol, beginning his circuits from the left side. When he had thus done, standing on the same side of the Idol where he began, and laying aside his Bell, he offer'd the Basin of water to the Idol, and dipping one Finger in it, lay'd the same upon the Idol's Forehead, or thereabouts ; and, if I was not mistaken, taking a little in his Hand, he also dy'd himself and the other Minister, who upheld the Idol, on the Fore-head therewith, after which he went to powre the remainder of the water in the Basin upon the ground without the Temple, but within the inclosure, or Court. Then he took a wax-Candle,[2] and therewith describ'd, within the *Palanchino*, or Carriage, before the Idol many circles with lines at the end ; and, putting out the Candle, took the Idol out of the *Palanchino*, and carrying it through the rail'd Stockade, in the middle of the Torches, plac'd it on its Tribunal at the Upper End where it usually stands.

In the mean time one of the Ministers distributed to all the by-standers a little quantity of certain Fitches,[3] mingled with small slices of Indian Nut, which, I conceive, had been offer'd to the Idol ; and they took and ate the same with signes of Devotion and Reverence. He offer'd some likewise to our people, and there wanted not such as took them ; the Drums and Fifes sounding in the mean time ; which at length ceasing, and the Candles being put out, the Ceremonies ended and the people return'd to their Houses.

---

[1] See *ante*, p. 99, note 2.

[2] Wax candles are certainly not common in India even in the present day, among natives, and were probably only used in temples.

[3] Or "vetches"; some kind of chick-pea, probably *Cicer Arietinum*.

Such Men as were not Officers of the Temple assisted at the Ceremonies at the first entrance, where we also stood ; but the Women stood more within the body of the Temple, where the rows of lights were. For the better understanding of all which description I shall here delineate the Ground-plan of the Temple with its inclosure and Porches, as well as I could do it by the Eye without measuring it.

THE GROUND-PLAN OF AN INDIAN TEMPLE.

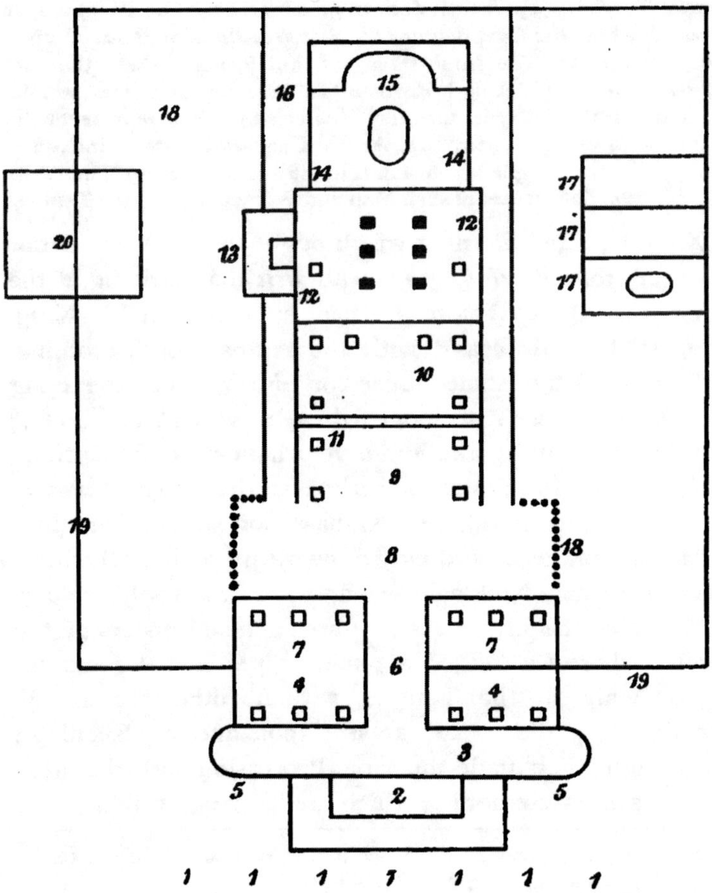

1. The Street. 2. The Stairs of the Entrance. 3. An high Wall of Earth before the Outer Porch. 4. The Outward Porch with an high Earthen Floor. 5. Two small Idols in two *Niches* on the out side of the ends of the Porch. 6. The Gate, level with the Earthen Wall No. 3. 7. The Inner Porch with an Earthen Floor higher than that of the Gate, the Wall, and the Outer Porch. 8. A Void Space between the Porch and the Temple. 9. Part of the First Entrance of the Temple, lower than the plane of the Gate and the said Void Space. 10. Part of the same, but one Step higher. 11. The said Step, dividing the first Entrance in the middle. 12. The body of the Temple, situate between the first Entrance and the Penetrale, or Chancel, the dots denoting the rows of Torches. 13. A little door to go out at. 14. The Penetrale, or Chancel, where the Oval denotes the Statue of *Boue*, or *Basava*,[1] upon the ground. 15. The Inmost Part of the Chancel, where the Idol *Virenà*[2] stands. 16. A high Earthen Wall encompassing the Temple. 17. Three little Cells; in the first of which the Oval represents the Statue of *Boue*, or *Basava*. 18. An open square-Court, or inclosure, surrounding the Temple which stands in the middle of it. 19. The Walls thereof. 20. The Houses of such Men and Women as keep the Temple.

X.—The same Evening was brought to our Ambassador a Letter from *Vitulà Sinay*,[3] who writ that, arriving at the Court on *Fryday* before, he had spoken with his King, who, being well pleas'd with the Ambassador's coming, had prepar'd the same house for him wherein the King of *Belighì*[4] was wont to lodge when he was at his Court; and that he would make him a very honorable Reception; that therefore as soon as we arriv'd at the Town *Ahinalà*,[5] (where we now were), the Ambassador should send him notice; which was accordingly done by dispatching the Messenger presently back again; and we waited for his return.

November the fifth. At day-break the Ministers of the Temple where we lodged sounded Pipes and Drums for a good while in the Temple, without other Ceremony. The like they did again about Noon and at Evening; but at night they made the same Procession with the Idol, and the same Ceremonies, which are above describ'd.

---

[1] See *ante*, p. 237, note 1. [2] See p. 235, note 2. [3] See p. 191.

[4] Or *Bilgi*, a small town near Honáwar.

[5] Previously (p. 234) called *Ahinèli*.

This day came to the Town a Captain from the King with many attendants, and, having visited the Ambassador, took divers of those Idols which stood in the first Entrance, and carry'd them away with him to be new made, because some were old and broken.

Late in the night came another Letter from *Vitulà Sinay*, which signifi'd to us that we should move towards a Town very near the Court, call'd *Badrapoor*, where some persons from the King were to meet us and accompany us to the court; although the Ambassador had writ to him before that he car'd not for being accompany'd at his Entrance, but onely when he should go to see the King.

I style him King because the *Portugals* themselves and the *Indians* do so; but, in truth, *Venk-tapà Naieka*, (not onely because his Predecessors were a few years ago Vassals and simple *Naiekas*,[1] that is feudatory Princes, or rather Provincial Gouvernours, under the King of *Vidianagher*[2]; and at this day he himself reigns absolutely by Usurpation, and is in effect no other then a Rebel; (and God know how long his House will abide in greatness); but also much more by reason of the smallness of his territory, though it be great, in respect of other Indian Gentile-Princes) deserves not the Appellation of King; and the less because he pays Tribute to *Idal-Sciàh*,[3] who although a greater Prince, is but small for a King and payes Tribute to the *Moghol*.[4] In short, *Venk-tapà Naieka*, although now absolute, should, in my opinion, be call'd a Royolet rather than a King: but the *Portugals*, to magnifie their affaires in *India*, or else to honor the persons that rule there (which is not displeasing in *Spain*, and at the Court of the Catholick King who is of the same humor), give the title of King to all these petty Indian Princes,

[1] See p. 168, note 2. [2] See *ante*, p. 109, note 1.
[3] *I.e.*, Adil Shah. See *ante*, p. 143, note 5. [4] See p. 48, note 2.

many of whom have smaller Dominions than a small feudatory Marquis in our Countries; and (which is worse) that of Emperor to some, as to him of *Japan*, of *Æthiopia* and of *Calicut*,[1] who is very inconsiderable; the quondam-Prince of *Vidianagher*, or *Bisnagà*[2] (as they speak), having in a strange and unusual manner multiply'd the number of Emperors beyond what the fabulous books of Knights Errant have done: albeit, in truth, there never was found but one Emperor in the world, the Roman *Cæsar*, who at this day retains rather the name than the substance in *Germany*.

XI.—*November* the sixth. Two hours before noon we went from *Ahinalà*, and, having travell'd through a Country like the former, but plain, about noon we came to the Town *Badrapoor;* where, according as *Vitulà Sinay* had writ us, we thought to lodge that night, and accordingly had lay'd down our baggage and withdrawn to a place of rest; but after being two hours there we found our selves surrounded by abundance of people (for 'tis a large Town, and they go almost all arm'd) who out of curiosity came to see us; whereupon the Ambassador, either having receiv'd an Answer from *Vitulà Sinay*, or not caring for a pompous entrance, rais'd us all again; and after a small journey further we arriv'd at *Ikkerì*,[3] which is the Royal City of *Venk-tapà Naieka*, where he holds his Court; having travell'd since morning from *Ahinalà* to *Ikkerì* but two Leagues.

The City is seated in a goodly Plain, and as we enter'd we pass'd through three Gates, with small Forts and Ditches, and consequently three Inclosures; the two first of which were not Walls, but made of very high Indian Canes,[4] very thick and close planted, instead of a Wall,

[1] See p. 60, note 3. [2] See *ante*, p. 109, note 1. [3] See *ante*, p. 216.

[4] Bamboo fences are a common mode of fortification in India, and are very effective against any attack except that of artillery.

and are strong against Foot and Horse in any case, hard to cut and not in danger of fire; besides that the Herbs which creep upon them, together with their own leaves, make a fair and great verdure and much shadow. The other Inclosure is a Wall, but weak and inconsiderable. But having passed these three we pass'd all. Some say there are others within, belonging to the Citadel, or Fort, where the Palace is; for *Ikkerì* is of good largeness, but the Houses stand thinly and are ill built, especially without the third Inclosure; and most of the situation is taken up by great and long streets, some of them shadow'd with high and very goodly Trees growing in Lakes of Water, of which there are many large ones, besides Fields set full of Trees, like Groves, so that it seems to consist of a City, Lakes, Fields and Woods mingled together, and makes a very delightful sight.

We were lodg'd in the House, as they said, wherein the King of *Belighì*[1] lodg'd, (I know not whether he was Kinsman, Friend, or Vassal, to *Venk-tapà Naieka*, but probably one of the above-mention'd Royolets) and to go to this House we went out of the third Inclosure, passing through the inmost part of the City by another Gate opposite to that by which we enter'd. The House indeed was such as in our Countries an ordinary Artisan would scarce have dwelt in, having very few and those small and dark Rooms, which scarce afforded light enough to read a letter; they build them so dark as a remedy for the great heat of Summer. However this must needs have been one of the best, since it was assign'd to the said King first and now to our Ambassador; although as we pass'd through the midst of the City I observ'd some that made a much better show.

XII.—At night they brought the Ambassador a couple of bed-steads to sleep upon and some stools for our use,

[1] See *ante*, p. 242.

some of them made of Canes interwoven, instead of coverings of Leather, or Cloth, being much us'd in *Goa* and other places of *India;* but some others were cover'd with Leather.

November the seventh. *Vitulà Sinay*[1] came in the morning to visit our Ambassador, and in his King's name brought him a Present of Sugar-Canes, Fruits, Sugar and other things to eat, but not any Animal; and, if I was not misinform'd (for I was not present), he excus'd his King's not sending him Sheep, or other Animals, to eat, by saying that he was of a *Lingavant*,[2] or Noble, Race, who neither eat nor kill any Creatures; as if he should have sinn'd and defil'd himself by sending any to the Ambassador who would have eaten them. With this Present he sent a piece of Tapestry, not as a Gift, but onely for the Ambassador to make use of in his House, and it was us'd in such sort that at length it had a hole in it: the Ambassador, as not prizing it, having given it to his Interpreter to sleep upon; as, indeed, he seem'd not very well pleas'd with it, or his other Donatives; for, speaking of the Reception which *Venk-tapà Naieka* made him, he would often say (according to the natural and general custom of his Nation) "Let him do me less honour, and give me something more, and it will be better." However, I believe *Venk-tapà Naieka*, who is not liberal, will abound more in Courtesie to the Ambassador than in Gifts.

Vitulà Sinay said that the next day the Ambassador should be call'd to Audience three hours after noon; wherefore Himself and all his Attendants continu'd undress'd till dinner-time. I, knowing the custom of Courts, and that Princes will not wait but be waited for, and that the hours of Audience depend upon their pleasure, not upon his who is to have it, dress'd my self in the morning

[1] See *ante*, p. 191. [2] See *ante*, p. 208, *note*.

leisurely, that I might not afterwards confound my self with haste; and though in such solemnities others cloth'd themselves in colours and with ornaments of Gold, yet I put on onely plain black Silk as mourning for my Wife.

Before we had din'd, and whilst we were at Table, they came to call us in haste to Audience, saying that *Vitulà Sinay* and other great Persons were come to conduct us to the King. The Ambassador, finding himself unready and surprised, was forc'd to desire them not to come yet, making an excuse that we were still at dinner; and, the Table being taken away, he and all the rest retir'd to dress themselves in great confusion; and greater there was in getting the Horses saddled, preparing the Presents which were to be carry'd, and providing other necessary things in haste, for nothing was ready; but the Ambassador and all his Servants were in a great hurry and confusion, calling for this and the other thing, which seem'd to me not to have too much of the Courtier. The persons who came to fetch us stay'd a good while without, but at length were brought into the Porch of the House, that is into the first Entrance within the Court, where Visits are receiv'd, without seeing the Ambassador, or any of his Attendants, who were all employ'd in the above-said confusion, at a good part of which these persons were present.

XIII.—At length the Ambassador, being dress'd, came forth with the rest and receiv'd the Visit of *Vitulà Sinay*, and another great Person sent by the King to accompany him; he was a *Moor* by Sect, but of Indian Race, very black, and Captain General in these parts of *Banghel*, from which charge he was lately return'd, and his name was *Musè Bai*.[1] With these came also a Son of his, a Youth of the same colour, but of a handsome Face, and cloth'd oddly after the Indian Fashion, that is naked from the

[1] See *ante*, p. 225, note 4.

girdle upwards, having onely a very thin and variously painted cloth[1] cast across one shoulder, and another of the same sort girt about him, and hanging down loose; he had a little Bonnet upon his Head, like those of our Galley-slaves, but wrought with divers colours; his Hands, Arms, Neck and Nose, were adorn'd with many ornaments of Gold, and he had a guilt Ponyard at his girdle, which shew'd very well. His Father was cloth'd all in white, after the manner of *India*, to wit of such as wear Clothes and go not naked from the Waste upward; upon his white vestment he had a shorter sur-coat of Velvet, guarded[2] with Gold at the bottom, loose and open before, which is the custom onely in solemnities. He had no Sword, but onely a Ponyard on the right side, the hilt and chape[3] gilded and, as I believe, of Silver; upon his Head he had a little Cap of the same form, made of Cloth of Gold; for in these Countries 'tis the fashion for Men to cover their Heads either with such Caps, or with white Turbants,[4] little and almost square.

Vitulà Sinay and some other personages, who came with them to accompany the Ambassador, were all cloth'd with white garments of very fine Silk and other rich Silken sur-coats upon the same, to honor the solemnity; and upon these they had such colour'd clothes as in *Persia* they call *Scial*,[5] and use for girdles, but the Indians wear them across

---

[1] See *ante*, p. 45, *note* 1.

[2] *I.e.*, ornamented. See Shakespeare, *Merchant of Venice*, Act ii.

"Give him a livery,
More guarded than his fellows."

[3] In the Italian *Guardia e puntale*, literally "hilt and point". "Chape" is an old word used for the metal tip to a scabbard, and also for the cross-bar below the hilt.

[4] An old English form of our word "turban", derived from the Turkish *Tulbend* or *Dulbend*, a "a turn-band", from which the word "tulip" is also derived.

[5] Or *Shâl* (Persian), our word "shawl".

the shoulders, cover'd with a piece of very fine white Silk,[1] so that the colour underneath appears; or else wear white Silk alone.

As soon as we came out of doors *Musè Bai* presented to the Ambassador one of the colour'd Skarfs[2] inclos'd in white Silk to wear about his Neck; and the Ambassador gave him a piece of, I know not what, Cloth, and in the mean time a publick Dancing-Woman, whom they had hir'd, danc'd in the presence of us all. Then we all took Horse, the Ambassador riding upon a good Horse of his own which he had brought from *Goa*, with a saddle embroider'd and adorn'd with Silver Fringe; and another Horse with trappings being led before him, both which he had brought from home, with intention, perhaps, to sell them here at his departure; for Horses here yield a good price,[3] and he had been formerly at *Ikkerì* purposely to sell Horses, and so became known to *Venk-tapà Naieka.* There was also another good led-Horse, which the Vice-Roy sent as a Present to *Venk-tapà Naieka;* that which they had given to *Vitulà Sinay* he had carry'd to his House and it appear'd not here. All the rest of us rode upon Horses of the place, which are of very small size, and were sent to us for that purpose, accoutr'd after their manner, with saddles pretty enough to look upon, but to me very inconvenient; for they have bows and cruppers[4] very high, and are all of hard wood, without any stuffing, but with sharp wreath'd edges,[5] cover'd with black or red Cloth, lay'd with bands of Gold, or yellow, or other colour;

---

[1] In the original *Bombacino*, which probably meant a mixed material of silk and worsted.

[2] In the original *panni*. The word "scarf" is derived from a German word meaning "a pocket", which was worn suspended from the neck.

[3] See *ante*, p. 194, note 5.

[4] Or, more correctly, "cantles."

[5] In the original *punte aguzze*, words which convey a vivid idea of our traveller's sufferings.

in the cruppers are many carv'd ornaments almost o. this figure (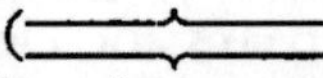), besides certain extravagant tassels hanging down to the stirrups; and, were they not so hard, they would be neither unhandsome nor unsafe to ride upon.

XIV.—The Pomp[1] proceeded in this manner: many Horsemen went formost, who were follow'd by divers Foot, arm'd with Pikes and other weapons, some of them brandishing the same as they went along; then march'd certain Musketiers with Drums, Trumpets, Pipes and Cornets sounding; these cloth'd all in one colour after the *Portugal* manner, but with coarse stuff of small value; and amongst them rode a servant of the Ambassador's, better clad after their fashion, as Captain of the Guard. Then follow'd the Ambassador in the middle, between *Vitulà Sinay* and *Musè Bai;* and after him we of his retinue, to wit the Chaplain, Sig: *Consalvo Caravaglio*, & Sig: *Francesco Monteyro*, who liv'd at *Barcelòr*,[2] and whom we found at *Ikkerì* about some affairs of his own; but because he wanted a Horse he appear'd not in the Cavalcade, but went on foot to the gate of the King. After us came the other Horse-men; but, in sum, there were but few people, a small shew and little gallantry: demonstrative signes of the smallness of this Court and Prince.

In this manner we rode to the Palace, which stands in a Fort, or Citadel, of good largeness, incompass'd with a great Ditch and certain ill built bastions. At the entrance we found two very long, but narrow, Bulwarks. Within the

---

[1] Pomp is here used in its strictly classical sense of "procession". So Milton, *Par. Lost*, Bk. VIII.

"On her, as queen,
A pomp of winning graces waited still."

[2] A town on the coast, in lat. 13° N. Written as Bracalor, Brazzalor, Bracelor, Basarur, and Abusaror (!) by other writers. It is a small city on a gulf abounding in coco-trees. (See Yule's *Cathay*, vol. ii, p. 451.)

Citadel are many Houses, and I believe there are shops also in several streets; for we pass'd through two Gates, at both of which there stood Guards, and all the distance between them was an inhabited street. We went through these two Gates on Horse-back, which, I believe, was a priviledge, for few did so besides our selves, namely such onely as entred where the King was; the rest either remaining on Horse-back at the first Gate, or alighting at the Entrance of the second. A third Gate also we enter'd, but on Foot, and came into a kind of Court, about which were sitting in Porches many prime Courtiers and other persons of quality. Then we came to a fourth Gate, guarded with Souldiers, into which onely we *Franchi*, or Christians, and some few others of the Country, were suffer'd to enter; and we presently found the King, who was seated in a kind of Porch on the opposite side of a small Court, upon a Pavement somewhat rais'd from the Earth, cover'd with a Canopy like a square Tent, but made of boards, and gilded. The Floor was cover'd with a piece of Tapistry something old, and the King sat, after the manner of the East, upon a little Quilt on the out-side of the Tent, leaning upon one of the pillars which up-held it on the right hand, having at his back two great Cushions of fine white Silk.[1] Before him lay his Sword, adorn'd with Silver, and a little on one side, almost in the middle of the Tent, was a small, eight-corner'd, Stand, painted and gilded, either to write upon, or else to hold some thing or other of his. On the right hand and behind the King, stood divers Courtiers, one of whom continually wav'd a piece of fine white linnen,[2] as if to drive away the flies from the King. Besides the King there was but one person sitting, and he the principal

[1] In the original *Bombacini*.

[2] The word translated as "linnen", here and in other passages, should probably be cotton. On this point see Heeren's *Historical Researches*, vol. i, p. 37.

Favourite of the Court, call'd *Putapaia*,[1] and he sat at a good distance from him, on the right hand, near the wall.

XV.—As soon as we saw the King afar off the Ambassador and we pull'd off our Hats and saluted him after our manner; he seem'd not to stir at all; but when we approach'd nearer the Ambassador was made to sit down within the Tent, on the left side also. *Vitulà Sinay* approach'd to a Pillar opposite to that on which the King lean'd and there serv'd as Interpreter, sometimes speaking with the King and sometimes with the Ambassador. *Musè Bai* stood also on our side, but distant from the King, and near one of the Pillars of the Porch. The King's first words were concerning the Health of the King of *Spain* and the Vice-Roy; and then the Ambassador subjoyn'd the causes of his coming, namely to visit him and continue the Amity which his Highness held with that State of the *Portugals*, (who use that style of "Highness" to these Indian Kings, as they did also to their King of *Portugal* when they had one, whence this custom first arose, and is still continu'd; although now when they name their King of *Spain*, so much a greater Lord than the King of *Portugal*, they use not the term *Highness*, but *Majesty*, after the manner of *Europe*). The Ambassador added that, in token of this Amity, the Vice-Roy sent him that Present, not as any great matter, but as a small acknowledgment; that their King had sent him a considerable Present from *Spain*, which his Highness knew was lost at Sea; that yet by the Ships which were coming this year he should receive another, as he might see in the Vice-Roy's Letter which he presented to him. And hereupon the Ambassador, arising from his Seat, went to present the same to him, almost kneeling upon one knee; and he, without moving a whit, took it and gave it to *Vitulà Sinay*, who gave it to another,

[1] "Putapaia" should be "Pratapara", or Chief Lord

probably the principal Secretary, without reading, or opening, it. The Ambassador had brought a Letter to him, likewise written in the King of *Spain's* Name, but did not present it now; because the *Portugals* say that the first time of going to Audience they are onely to make a Visit, and not to treat of Business. Then they drew forth the Present before the King, which was some pieces of cloth, within one of those wooden gilt boxes which are us'd in *India;* a Lance of the Moorish shape, to wit long and smooth like a Pike, the point of Iron gilt and the foot embellish'd with Silver, a gallant Target, and the Horse above-mention'd, cover'd with a silken Horse-cloth; which Horse was brought into the Court where the King sate.

After he had receiv'd and view'd the Present and taken the Iron of the Lance in his hand, which the Ambassador said was of *Portugal,* they caus'd the rest of us to sit down near the outer wall of the Porch on the left side, upon a rough Carpet, strip'd with white and blew,[1] (of that sort which the *Turks* and *Persians* call *Kielim*) spread upon the pavement of the Porch. The Ambassador, although he sate, yet never put on his Hat before the King, (for so the *Portugal* Nobles are wont to do before the Vice-Roy, namely to sit, but not to be cover'd) nor did the King speak to him to cover himself, but let him continue uncover'd; wherein, to my thinking, he committed an error; for, going as he did in the name of the State, which amongst them is as much as to go in the King of *Spain's* Name, why should he not be cover'd before so small a Prince? And the error seem'd the greater because he was the first that went Ambassador to *Venk-tapà Naieka* in the name of the State, and consequently hath made an ill-

[1] In the original *torchino,* allied to our word "turquoise", a colour derived from the precious stone of that name, as it was formerly supposed to come from Turkey.

precedent to such as shall come after him; and in introducing such prejudicial customs a publick Minister should have his eyes well open: but the truth is, the *Portugals* of *India* understand little, are little Courtiers and less Politicians, how exquisite soever they may be accounted here, as this Sig: *Gio: Fernandez* is esteem'd one of the most accomplish'd, and, I believe, not undeservedly.

At night I could not forbear to advertise some of his Country-men hereof in a handsome way, it not seeming fit for me, a stranger and the younger man, to offer to give him a Lesson.[1] However he never put on his Hat, and Civility oblig'd us to the same forbearance; but indeed, it was too much obsequiousness for such a Prince; as also for the Ambassador to tell him of the other times that he had been privately at that Court and kiss'd his Highnesse's Feet; with other like words little becoming an Ambassador. Nevertheless he spoke them, professing himself much the servant of *Venk-tapà Naieka*, out of hope that he, as *Vitulà Sinay* had promis'd him at *Goa*, would write to the King of *Spain* in his favor, by which means he should have some remuneration. Indeed the *Portugals* have nothing else in their Heads but Interest, and therefore their Government goes as it does.

XVI.—As we sate down, (being four of us that did so, besides the Ambassador, to wit the Chaplain, *Caravaglio*, *Monteyro*, and my self) I handsomely took the last place; because, knowing the nature of the *Portugals*, I would not have them think that I, a stranger, went about to take place and preeminence of them in their solemnities; and they, conformably to their own humor, not onely us'd no

---

[1] Here the following sentence in the original is omitted from the translation: "but only to others of his Company, and that with civility, who would not fail, as compatriots and friends, to make known to him their sentiments."

Courtesie to me, as well-bred Italians would have done, by saying to me, *Amice, ascende superiùs;* but I saw they were greatly pleas'd with my putting my self in the last place *Caravaglio* taking the first, the Chaplain the second, and *Monteyro* the third. I, little caring for this, or for shewing and making my self known in the Court of *Venk-tapà Naieka,* laugh'd within my self at their manners, and with observation of the scene satisfied my Curiosity, which alone had brought me into these parts.

The King's discourse to the Ambassador extended to divers things, and, as he was speaking, he frequently chaw'd leaves of *Betle*[1] which a Courtier reach'd to him now and then, and, when he was minded to put out a lump of the masticated leaves, another held a kind of great Cup to his Mouth for him to spit into. The King ask'd concerning the slowness of the Ships this year, as a thing which displeased him, in regard of the Money they were to bring him for Pepper. He inquir'd of several things in *India* and desir'd to know some kind of News. The Ambassador told him all the News we had at *Onòr,* which was uncertain, being onely the Relations of some vulgar persons, and therefore, in my judgement, too immaturely utter'd; affirming for certain the coming of the Fleet with a great Army, the Alliance between *Spain* and *England,* the passage of the Prince of *England* into *Spain,*[2] and moreover (Good God!) the reduction of all *England* to the Catholick Faith by the publick command of the King, with other such levities usual to the *Portugals,* who are very ignorant of the affairs of the world and of State.

---

[1] See p. 36, note 1.

[2] This, of course, refers to the journey of Prince Charles (under the name of Mr. Smith) and the Duke of Buckingham into Spain, for the purpose of arranging a marriage with the Infanta. Some amusing details of this visit will be found in an article on "Velasquez the Painter", in the *Nineteenth Century* of January 1891.

The King further spoke long concerning things transacted with him in the War of *Banghel*,[1] particularly of the Peace that concluded it; for which, it probably being disadvantageous to the *Portugals*, he said he heard that many blam'd him, the Ambassador, who negotiated it with his Ministers; and that they not onely blam'd him for it, but said he would be punished by the King of *Spain*, who was offended with it; whereat being sorry, as his Friend he had sent several times to *Goa* to inquire tidings concerning him. The Ambassador answer'd that 'twas true there had been such accusations against him and greater, some alledging that his Highness had brib'd him; but that they were the words of malevolent persons, which he had always laugh'd at, knowing he had done his duty, and onely what the Vice-Roy had appointed him; and that in *Spain* they give credit to the informations of the Vice-Roy, and not to the talk of others, as well appear'd by the event.

Venk-tapà proceeded to say that that Peace was very well made for the *Portugals*, and that much good had follow'd upon it; intimating that they would have made it with disadvantage if it had not been concluded in that manner as he concluded it; as if he would have said, "It had been otherwise ill for the *Portugals*," with manifest signes of a mind insulting toward them, and implying that the business of *Banghel* was no more to be treated of. Then he ask'd the Ambassador, How old he was? How many Children he had? putting him in mind of his being used to come, when a very Youth, to *Ikkerì* with his Father to bring Horses, and shewing himself very friendly to him. Nor did the Ambassador lose the occasion of desiring him that he would favor him with his Letters to the King of

---

[1] One of the petty contests carried on by the various chiefs of these parts after the fall of the King of Vijayanagar. (See p. 144, note 2.)

Spain, pretending to hope for much upon account of them ; a thing which I should not commend in an Ambassador, because he may thereby come to be thought by his natural Prince too partial to, and too intimate with, the Prince with whom he treats ; and also by this means disparages himself, as if he need to beg the mediation of foreign Princes with his natural Lord and of such Princes too with whom he negotiates in behalf of his own, which by no means seems well.

Then *Venk-tapà Naieka* inquir'd concerning the rest of us, and *Vitulà Sinay* answer'd his Questions ; telling him of me that I was a Roman and that I travell'd over so great a part of the World out of Curiosity and that I writ down what I saw ; with other things of the same nature. *Venk-tapà Naieka* ask'd me, Whether I understood the Language of the *Moors?* I answer'd that I did, together with *Turkish* and *Persian;* but I mention'd not the *Arabick*, because I have it not so ready as the other two to be able to make use of it before everybody. He seem'd sufficiently pleas'd in seeing me and understanding that I was born at *Rome* and came thither as a Traveller ; highly esteeming the ancient fame of *Rome* and of the Empire and its new Grandeur and the Pontificate of the Christians. These and other Discourses, which I omit for brevity, lasting for some time, he caus'd to be brought to him a piece of Silk embroider'd with Gold, such as the *Indians* wear across their shoulders, but with us may serve to cover a Table, or such like use, and, calling the Ambassador before him, whither we accompany'd him, gave it to him and caus'd it to be put upon his shoulders ; whereupon we were dismiss'd, and so, going out to Horse again, we were reconducted home with the same solemnity and company.

XVII.—After this, as we were walking through the City late in the Evening without the Ambassador we saw going along the streets several companies of young girls, well cloth'd, after their manner, with some of the above-mentioned wrought and figur'd Silk from the girdle downwards; and from thence upward either naked,[1] or else with very pure linnen, either of one colour, or strip'd and wrought with several, besides a scarf of the same work cast over the shoulder. Their heads were deck'd with yellow and white flowers form'd into a high and large Diadem, with some sticking out like Sun-beams, and others twisted together and hanging down in several fashions, which made a pretty sight. All of them carry'd in each hand a little round painted Stick, about a span long, or a little more, which they struck together after a musical measure, to the sound of Drums and other instruments, and one of the skilfullest of the company sung one verse of a song, at the end of which they all reply'd seven, or eight, times in the number of their meter with the word, *Colè, Colè, Colè,*[2] which signifies I know not what, but, I believe, 'tis a word of joy. Singing in this manner they went along the street, eight or ten together, being either friends, or neighbours, follow'd by many other women, not dress'd in the same fashion, but who were either their Mothers, or Kins-women. I imagin'd it was for some extraordinary Festival, and I was willing to have

---

[1] It is the custom of some classes of women in Southern India to wear no covering above the waist, and the attempts made to alter this custom have, as Sir R. Burton says, "been met in the same spirit which would be displayed were the converse suggested to an English woman." (*Goa and the Blue Mountains*, p. 222.)

[2] It is difficult to say positively what is the meaning of this word. It may be meant for Káli, one of the names of the goddess Gauri, in whose honour this festival was held (see Wilks' *Southern India*, vol. i, p. 22). The name Káli is said by Sir W. Hunter to be the *non-Aryan* name of the goddess Gauri. It is commonly used in Southern India, and it is possibly from this name that the word Kálſkot (Calicut) is derived (see Eastwick's *Handbook for Madras*, p. 295).

follow'd them to see whither they went and what they did; but, being in the company of others, I could not do so, nor had my Companions the same Curiosity, as indeed the *Portugals* are not at all curious. I understood afterwards that they went to the Piazza of the great Temple which is moderately large, and there danc'd in circles, singing their songs till it was late; and that this was a Festival which they keep three dayes together at the end of a certain Feast in Honor of *Gaurì*,[1] one of their Goddesses, Wife of *Mohedaca*[2]; and therefore 'tis celebrated by girls.

XVIII.—*November* the ninth. Walking about the City I saw a beam rais'd a good height, where, in certain of their Holy-dayes, some devout people are wont to hang themselves[3] by the flesh upon hooks fastned to the top of it and remain a good while so hanging, the blood running down in the mean time, and they flourishing their Sword and Buckler in the Air and singing verses in Honor of their Gods. Moreover, in a close place opposite to the Temple, I saw one of those very great Carrs,[4] or Charriots, wherein upon certain Feasts they carry their Idols in Procession, with many people on it and Dancing-women,

---

[1] Called also Dévi, Bhaváni, Dúrga, or Káli. The name of "Gauri" is generally applied to her as the "Earth-mother".

[2] So spelt in original. It should be Mahadeva, a title of Siva.

[3] This refers to the well-known festival in honour of Siva, called in some parts of India "Charak-púja" (or Swing-worship), when devotees, male and female, were suspended by hooks fixed in the muscles of the back and whirled round in the air by means of a movable lever. (See Ward's *Hindoos*, iii, p. 15, and Heber's *Journal*, i, p. 77.) This barbarous rite has now, however, happily become obsolete, except on very rare occasions.

[4] Called in the vernacular "*Raths*". The best known of these is the celebrated Car of Jagan-náth, at Púrí in Orissa, but such cars are attached to every large Vishnu temple in Southern India. They are supposed to typify the moving, active, world, over which the god presides. (See Sir Monier Williams' *Modern India*, p. 67.) That at Púrí is 45 feet in height and has 16 wheels.

who play on musical instruments, sing and dance. The four wheels of this Carr were fourteen of my spans in diameter, and the wood of the sides was one span thick. At the end of it were two great wooden Statues, painted with natural colours; one of a Man, the other of a Woman, naked, in dishonest postures; and upon the Carr, which was very high, was room for abundance of people to stand; and, in brief, it was so large that scarce any but the widest streets in *Rome*, as *Strada Giulia*, or *Babuino*, would be capable for it to pass in.

I saw also certain Indian Fryers, whom in their Language they call *Giangàma*[1] and who, perhaps, are the same with the Sages seen by me elsewhere; but they have Wives, and go with their faces smear'd with ashes, yet not naked, but clad in certain extravagant habits, with a kind of peaked hood, or cowl, upon their heads, of dy'd linnen, of that colour which is generally used amongst them, namely a reddish brick-colour,[2] with many bracelets upon their arms and legs, fill'd with something within that makes a jangling as they walk. But the prettiest and oddest thing was to see certain Souldiers on Horse-back, and considerable Captains too, as I was inform'd, who for ornament of their Horses wore hanging behind the saddle-bow two very large tassels of certain white, long and fine skins (they told me they were the tails of certain wild Oxen,[3] found in India[4] and highly esteemed), which tassels were about two

---

[1] Or Jangama, the same as the Lingavats, or Lingáyats, mentioned *ante*, p. 208.

[2] Or saffron colour.

[3] *I.e.* of the Yak (*Poephagus grunniens*, or *Bos poephagus*).

[4] They are not found in *India*, but in Thibet, and their tails are thence imported. In the mountains to the north of India this animal is commonly used as a beast of burden. The tail is in great request in India as a weapon against flies and also as a mark of honour. There is an amusing account of the animal in the *Topographia Christiana*, by Cosmas the monk (written about A.D. 545), given in Sir H. Yule's

yards in compass[1] and so long as to reach from the saddle-bow to the ground; two, I say, hung behind the saddle-bow and two before of equal height and two others higher at the head stall; so that there were six in all: between which the Horse-man was seen upon the saddle, half naked and riding upon a Horse which leap'd and curvetted all the way; by which motion those six great tassels of skin, being very light and not at all troublesome, but flying up and down, seem'd so many great wings; which, indeed, made a pretty spectacle, and made me think I saw so many *Bellerophons* upon severall *Pegasuses*.

The same Evening I saw the companies of girls again, and, following them, I found that they did not go to the Piazza of the Temple, as they had done the two nights before, but into one of the King's Gardens, which for this purpose stood open for every body and is nothing but a great field, planted confusedly with shady and fruit bearing Trees, Sugar Canes and other Garden plants. Hither almost the whole City flock'd, Men and Women and all the companies of the flower'd Virgins, who, putting themselves into circles, here and there danc'd and sung; yet their dancing was nothing else but an easie walking round, their sticks alwayes sounding; onely sometimes they would stretch forth their legs, and now and then cowre down as if they were going to sit, one constantly singing, and the rest repeating, the word *Colè*, *Colè*. There wanted not other Dancing-women, who exceeded the

---

Cathay and the Way Thither (I, clxxiv), in which he says: "They tell of this beast that, if his tail catches in a tree, he will not budge, but stands stock still, being horribly vexed at losing a single hair of his tail, so the natives come and cut his tail off, and then, when he has lost it altogether, he makes his escape! Such is the nature of the animal."

[1] In the original, "perhaps more than the size of a barrel at Rome".

former in skill and dexterity. In conclusion, they gather'd into several companies to supper, with the other Women that accompany'd them; so did the Men also, some with their Wives, and some alone, of which there wanted not some who invited us, not to eat with them (for they communicate not with strangers at the Table) but to take some of their fare; which we thank'd them for, but accepted not, being delighted onely to see them feast so together, dispers'd in several places of the Garden, this being the night that the Feast ended.

XIX.—The same night a Post from *Goa* brought the Ambassador a Letter from the Vice-Roy, with another for *Vitulà Sinay*[1] and a third from the Captain of *Onòr*.[2] The Ambassador imparted his intelligence to none, and forbad the Post to let it be known that he had brought Letters; whence I conceiv'd that the News was not good, otherwise it would have been presently publish'd; onely I heard some obscure talk of the *Malabaris*,[3] but I would not inquire further into the matter, as that which did not belong to me; especially amongst the *Portugals*, who are very close and reserv'd towards strangers.

November the tenth. I saw passing along the street a Nephew of *Venk-tapà Naieka*, his Sister's Son, a handsome youth and fair for that Country; he was one of those who aspire to the succession of this State, and was now returning from the fields without the Town, whither he uses to go every morning. He is called *Sedàsiva Naieka*, and was attended with a great number of Souldiers, both Horse and Foot, marching before him and behind, with many Cavaliers and Captains of quality, himself riding alone with great gravity. He had before him Drums, Cornets and every sort of their barbarous instruments. Moreover both in the Front and in the rear of the Caval-

[1] See p. 191. [2] See p. 190, note 3. [3] See p. 121, note 4.

cade were (I know not whether for magnificence, or for guard) several Elephants carrying their guides upon their backs, and amongst them was also carried his *Palanchino*.

November the eleventh. The Ambassador went again to Audience to present to *Venk-tapà Naieka* the letter writ to him in the King of Spain's Name and declare what that King requir'd of him. He went alone without any of us, or of the *Portugals* his Companions, either not willing that we should be present at the debating of business, or because he went in a *Palanchino* and had his two Horses led before him, but there were neither *Palanchinos* in the house nor Horses enough for the rest of us. With those that came to fetch him came also a publick Dancing-woman, who perform'd a pretty piece of agility in his presence; for, standing upon one foot, when the Drums and other instruments sounded, with the other she swiftly turned round in the Air a large Iron Ring, about a span in Diametre, without letting it fall off her great Toe, and at the same time with one hand toss'd two hollow brass balls, catching one in her Hand whilst the other was aloft, and so alternately and very nimbly without ever letting them fall; which indeed was great dexterity, to be imploy'd at the same time with the foot and the hand, standing firm all the while on the other foot without support and yet attending to the Musick and this for a good space together: during which an old Man with a white beard and bald head who brought her stood behind her, crying all the while, *Abùd, Abùd, Abùd,* which in their language signifies "Yes", and in this instance as much as *Good, Good, Good.*

The Ambassador return'd quickly from audience, but said not a word of anything. The King frequently sent him things to eat; particularly fruits out of season, brought to him from far distant places, amongst which we had *Ziacche*,[1] (which I take to be the same with *Zdtte*,[2] which is a kind of gourd) a fruit very rare at this time; and also Indian Melons, which how good soever are worth nothing[3] at any time, the Climate not being fit for such fruits.

On *November* the twelfth I took the height of the Sun at *Ikkeri* and found the Meridian Altitude 31 degrees. He was now in the 19th degree of *Scorpio* and consequently declined from the Æquinoctial toward the South 17 gr. 29′ 23″, which being subtracted from the 31 degrees in which I found the Sun there remain 13° 30′ 37″, and such is the Elevation of the Pole at *Ikkeri*; which must also be as many degrees, to wit 13° 30′ 37″, distant from the Æquinoctial towards the North.[4]

At dinner the Ambassador told us that the King of

---

[1] The Jack-fruit (*Artocarpus integrifolia*). The original name is *Ciaka*, or *Tsjaka*, a Malay word, written also as *Jaca*. It is common in India and has the peculiarity of growing from the *trunk* of the tree. It is thus described by John de Marignolli, who visited China in 1342: "There is again another wonderful tree, called *Chakebaruhe*, as big as an oak. Its fruit is produced from the trunk and not from the branches, and is something marvellous to see, being as big as a great lamb, or a child of three years old. It has a hard rind like that of our pine cones, so that you have to cut it open with an axe; inside it has a pulp of surpassing flavour, with the sweetness of honey and of the best Italian melon; and this also contains some five hundred chesnuts of like flavour, which are capital eating when roasted." It is called *Shaki Barki* by Ibn Batuta, and *Giacha Barca* by P. Vincenzo Maria (*Viag.*, p. 355). The second name as given by these writers is said to stand for *Waracha*, a Singhalese name of the fruit. (See Sir H. Yule's *Cathay and the Way Thither*, ii, p. 362.) The fruit weighs sometimes as much as sixty, or seventy, pounds. A curious superstition is said to prevail in some parts of India that this fruit will not ripen unless a stick, covered with lime, be passed through it.

[2] The words in parenthesis are interpolated by the translator.

[3] This refers probably to the common water-melon. Some melons of good quality are certainly grown in India in the present day.

[4] The latitude of Ikkeri is stated in Hunter's *Gazetteer of India* to be 14° 7′ 20″ N.

Spain's letter, which he had presented the day before to *Venk-tapà Naieka*, concern'd not any business but was onely one of compliment and particularly to give him much thanks for having of late years refus'd to sell Pepper to the English and Dutch, who had been at his Court to buy it; and also for the good Amity he held with the *Portugals*, which he desir'd might encrease every day. That of the affairs of *Banghel*,[1] or any others, he said nothing, referring all to the Vice-Roy and the Ambassador whom the Vice-Roy had sent to him. Wherewith *Venk-tapà Naieka* was very well pleas'd, and he had reason; for during the present State of the *Portugals* affairs I certainly think they will not speak a word to him of *Banghel*, nor of anything else that may be disgustful to him.

XX.—The same day the Ambassador went to Court, being invited to see solemn Wrestling at the Palace. We did not accompany him for want of Horses and *Palanchinoes;* but at night he told us that *Vitulà Sinay* asked much for me, wishing I had been present at this Wrestling, which was performed by Persons very stout and expert therein; because he had heard that I writ down what I saw remarkable. However *Carvaglio*, *Monteyro* and myself, not going thither, went out of *Ikkerì* half a League Northwards, to see another new City which *Venk-tapà* hath begun to build there. 'Tis called *Saghèr* and is already pretty well inhabited, with Houses all made of Earth[2] after their manner. The Palace is finish'd and *Venk-tapà* frequently goes to it; as also a Temple built upon a great Artificial Lake, and a house for his Nephews and other Grandees with all conveniencies thereunto, particularly great Stalls for Elephants, of which he keeps above eighty; we saw many of them here, some for War, large and handsome.

---

[1] See *ante*, p. 212.

[2] That is, of mud, or of sun-dried bricks.

A Market was kept this day in *Saghèr*, as 'tis the custom every *Sunday* and at *Ikkerì* every *Fryday*. There was a great concourse of people, but nothing to sell besides necessaries for food and clothing after their manner. The way between *Ikkerì* and *Saghèr* is very handsome, plain, broad, and almost always direct, here and there beset with great and thick Trees which make a shadow and a delightful verdure.

As we return'd home at night we met a Woman in the City of *Ikkerì*, who, her husband being dead, was resolv'd to burn herself, as 'tis the custom with many Indian Women. She rode on Horse-back about the City with face uncovered, holding a Looking-glass in one hand and a Lemon in the other,[1] I know not for what purpose; and beholding herself in the Glass, with a lamentable tone sufficiently pittiful to hear, went along I know not whither, speaking, or singing, certain words, which I understood not; but they told me they were a kind of Farewell to the

[1] The mirror and lemon may, or may not, have had a symbolical meaning. In the *Percy Anecdotes* (vol. iv, p. 393) is an account of a woman who, intending to immolate herself, "held in her right hand a cocoa-nut, and in the left a knife and a small looking-glass, into which she continued to look." A mirror has always been regarded among Oriental nations as an emblem of the soul, and has been credited with various magical powers. It was one of the sacred objects carried in an ark in the Eleusinian mysteries, and in the processions in honour of Bacchus. In the *Arabian Nights* it is called the "touchstone of virtue", and it is used as an emblem of the Deity in Japanese temples. Even at the present day a mirror is regarded by many with superstitious reverence, and its fracture dreaded as an unlucky event. As to the use of a mirror in arriving at a knowledge of the true self in man, see Max Müller's *Hibbert Lectures*, p. 318.

Dubois (*Mœurs des peuples de l'Inde*, vol. ii, p. 259) states that he saw a man who was on his way to self-immolation carrying a lemon on the point of a dagger. The lemon may have been an emblem of purity.

Cases of widow-burning in *Southern* India are not common. Mr. Elphinstone (*Hist. of India*, p. 190) goes so far as to say that "the practice never occurs south of the river Kistna (or Krishna)".

World and herself; and indeed, being uttered with that passionateness which the Case requir'd and might produce they mov'd pity in all that heard them, even in us who understood not the Language. She was follow'd by many other Women and Men on foot, who, perhaps, were her Relations; they carry'd a great Umbrella over her, as all Persons of quality in *India* are wont to have, thereby to keep off the Sun, whose heat is hurtful and troublesome.[1] Before her certain Drums were sounded, whose noise she never ceas'd to accompany with her sad Ditties, or Songs; yet with a calm and constant Countenance, without tears, evidencing more grief for her Husband's death than her own, and more desire to go to him in the other world than regret for her own departure out of this: a Custom, indeed, cruel and barbarous, but, withall, of great generosity and virtue in such Women and therefore worthy of no small praise. They said she was to pass in this manner about the City I know not how many dayes, at the end of which she was to go out of the City and be burnt, with more company and solemnity. If I can know when it will be I will not fail to go to see her and by my presence honor her Funeral with that compassionate affection which so great Conjugal Fidelity and Love seem to me to deserve.

XXI.—On *November* the thirteenth I took the Altitude of the Sun at *Ikkeri*, and found it 31° 40′. The Sun was now in the 20th degree of *Scorpio* and declin'd Southwards 17° 45′ 40″, which taken from 31° 40′ leave

---

[1] In Coryat's *Crudities* (vol. i, p. 134) reference is made to the custom of carrying "Umbrellaes" as "things that minister shadow for shelter against the scorching heat of the sun". Fynes Morison also mentions the custom, and adds, "a learned physician told me that the use of them was dangerous, because they gather the heat into a pyramidale point and thence cast it down perpendicularly upon the head, except they know how to carry them for avoyding that danger."

13° 54′ 20″. The former time I found *Ikkerì* to be in 13° 30′ 31″;[1] but now I found it to be in 13° 54′ 20″, between which there is onely the difference of 23′ 43″, which is a small matter: and therefore I count my observation right; for the small variation between the two times is no great matter, inasmuch as the declination of the Sun not being exactly known may cause the difference.

At night, walking in the City, I saw in the Piazza of the great Temple (which I understood was dedicated to an Idol call'd *Agore Scuarà*,[2] who, they say, is the same with *Mahadeù*,[3] although they represent him not in the same shape as that I saw of *Mahadeù* in *Cambaia*, but in the shape of a Man, with but one Head and Face and sixteen Arms on each side (in all thirty-two); which is not strange, since our Antients call'd many of their Idols by names sufficiently different and pourtray'd them in several shapes; and wherein also I understood there was an Idol of *Parveti*,[4] who is the wife of *Mahadeù*, though the Temple be not dedicated to her): I saw, I say, in the Piazza one of their Fryers, or *Giangami*,[5] clad all in white, sitting in an handsome *Palanchino*, with two great white Umbrellas[6] held over him, one on each side, (which two were for the

---

[1] So in the original, but it should be 37″.

[2] For "Aghoreswāra", a name of Siva. See *ante*, p. 216.

[3] See *ante*, p. 72, note 1.

[4] See *ante*, p. 35, note 3.

[5] Or *Jangami*, so called from the word *Jangam*, "movable". See *ante*, p. 208, note. They are the same as the Lingavants.

[6] Umbrellas are, and were even in the time of Arrian, regarded in the East as marks of dignity. The Emperor of China has twenty-four umbrellas carried before him, and other dignitaries have a lesser quantity in proportion to their rank. Speaking of some of these Indian sects Mr. Elphinstone says (*Hist. of India*, p. 104): "Some of them maintain a good deal of state, especially on their circuits, where they are accompanied by elephants, flags, etc., like temporal dignitaries."

more gravity) and a Horse led behind, being follow'd by a great train of other *Giangami*, clad in their ordinary habits. Before the *Palanchino* march'd a numerous company of Souldiers and other people, many Drums and Fifes, two strait long Trumpets and such brass Timbrels as are used in *Persia*, Bells and divers other Instruments, which sounded as loud as possible, and amongst them was a troop of Dancing-women adorn'd with Girdles, Rings upon their Legs, Neck-laces and other ornaments of Gold, and with certain Pectorals, or Breast-plates, almost round, in the fashion of a Shield and butting out with a sharp ridge before, embroyder'd with Gold and stuck either with Jewels, or some such things, which reflected the Sun-beams with marvellous splendor; as to the rest of their bodies they were uncover'd, without any Veil, or Head-tire. When they came to the Piazza the *Palanchino* stood still, and, the multitude having made a ring, the Dancing-women fell to dance after their manner; which was much like the Moris-dance[1] of *Italy*, onely the Dancers sung as they danc'd, which seem'd much better. One of them who, perhaps, was the Mistress of the rest danc'd along by her self, with extravagant and high jumpings, but always looking towards the *Palanchino*. Sometimes she cower'd down with her haunches almost to the ground, sometimes, leaping up, she struck them with her feet backwards, (as *Cœlius Rhodiginus*[2] relates of the ancient dance call'd *Bibasi*)[3] continually singing and making several gestures with her Hands; but after a barbarous manner and such

---

[1] In original *Morescha*, or Moorish dance. See Shakespeare :

"I have seen him caper upright like a wild *morisco*."

[2] A learned Venetian, born 1450, died 1525.

[3] Or Bibasis, a Spartan dance, described by Aristophanes (*Lysist.*, 28), and by Pollux (iv, 102).

as amongst us would not be thought handsome.[1] The Dance being ended, the *Palanchino* with all the train went forward, the Instruments continually playing before them. I follow'd to see the end, and found that they went into the chief street and so out of the City by the Gate which leads to *Saghèr*, stopping in divers places of the street to act the same, or the like, dances over again; and particularly in the Entrance of the said Gate, where, amongst many Trees and Indian Canes which make the City-Wall, there is a small Piazza, very even and shaded about like a Pastoral Scene and very handsome. At last the *Giangamo* with his *Palanchino* and train enter'd into certain Gardens without the Gate where his House stood; and after the last dance he remain'd there and the rest went away. They told me this honor was done him because they had then cast water upon his Head and perform'd some other Ceremony, equivalent to our ordaining one *in Sacris*, or creating a Doctor.

As I was going along the streets to behold this Pomp I saw many persons come with much devotion to kiss the Feet of all those *Giangami*, who on Foot follow'd the principal *Giangamo* who was in the *Palanchino;* and, because they were many and it took up much time to kiss the feet of them all, therefore when any one came to do it they stood still all in a rank to give him time; and, whilst such persons were kissing them and, for more reverence, touching their Feet with their Fore-heads, these *Giangami* stood firm with a seeming severity and without taking notice of it, as if they had been abstracted from the things of the World; just as our Fryers used to do when any devout persons come out of reverence to

---

[1] As to religious dances, see Sir J. Lubbock's *Origin of Civilization*, p. 257 *et seq.*, and Sir Monier Williams' *Modern India*, p. 198, and Dubois' *Mœurs des peuples de l'Inde*, vol. ii, p. 354 *et seq.*

kiss their Habit; but with Hypocrisie conformable to their superstitious Religion.

XXII.—Returning home I met a corpse going to be burn'd without the City, with Drums sounding before it; it was carry'd sitting in a Chair, whereunto it was ty'd that it might not fall, cloth'd in its ordinary attire, exactly as if it had been alive. The seat was cover'd behind and on the sides with red and other colours, I know not whether Silk or no. It was open onely before, and there the dead person was to be seen. By the company, which was small, I conjectur'd him to be one of mean quality. But they told me that all dead people are carry'd thus, as well such as are buried (as the *Lingavani*,[1] whom they also put into the Earth sitting) as those that are burn'd; and that he whom I saw was to be burn'd we gather'd from the Fire and Oyle which they carry'd after him in vessels.

The night following there was a great solemnity in all the Temples by lighting of Candles, singing, Musick and dancing, about twenty Dancing-women, who went in procession with the Idol into the Piazza, dancing before the great Temple; but, as I was told, they began very late, namely at the rising of the Moon, which was about an hour before mid-night; so that I was gone to bed before I knew of it, although in the Evening I saw the lights in the Temple. But though I saw nothing yet I heard of it as I was in bed, being awaken'd by the noise; and, hearing the same was to be acted over again the next night, I purpos'd with myself to see it.

November the fourteenth. I went at night to the Temple to see whether there was any extraordinary solemnity; but there was nothing more than usual, nor did the Idol come forth; onely in the great Temple and its Inclosure, or

---

[1] As to *Lingavani*, see *ante*, p. 208. Burial in a sitting posture is peculiar to more than one religious sect in India.

Court, into which they suffer not strangers to enter, they made their accustom'd Processions with musical instruments, singing and other ceremonies, which, I conceive, were the same with those I saw in *Ahinelì*[1]: onely they are celebrated here every night, because as 'tis a more eminent Church so, consequently, the service is more pompous; besides that they told me *Venk-tapà Naieka* had a great and particular devotion to the Idol *Agoresuàr*,[2] who is here worship'd.

On the fifteenth of the same month came first in the day-time and afterwards at night to our House twelve, or fifteen, publick Dancing-women, who, by consequence, are also publick Strumpets, although very young, being conducted by certain of their men. In the day time they did nothing but talkt a little; and some of them made themselves drunk with a certain Wine made of dry'd Raisins, or a sort of *Aqua Vitæ* and other mixtures, call'd in *India Nippa*[3]; I say some of them, because certain others of less ignoble Race as they are more abstinent in eating so they drink not any thing that inebriates. At night they entertain'd us a good while with Dancing after their mode, accompany'd with singing, not unpleasant to behold; for they consist of a numerous company of Women, all well cloth'd and adorn'd with Gold, Jewels and Tresses[4] of several fashions, who sing and strike their wooden instruments.[5] They begin all their dances slowly and, by degrees growing to a heat, at last end with furious and quick

[1] See *ante*, p. 238.

[2] See *ante*, p. 216, *note*.

[3] A name of the juice of a palm (*Nipa fruticans*), thence applied to other spirituous concoctions and probably the origin of our word "nip for a drink. (See Sir H. Yule's *Hobson-Jobson*.)

[4] In the original *Intrecciature*, which might mean also "garlands", or "wreaths".

[5] In the original *legnetti*, or "pieces of wood", a kind of castanet. See *ante*, p. 261.

motions which appear well enough. Amongst their other Dances two pleas'd me well, one in which they continually repeated these words, ...[1] and another wherein they represented a Battel and the actions of slaughter. In the conclusion, the Master of the Ballet, who directs all, and was one of those that brought them, danced in the midst of them with a naked Ponyard, wherewith he represented the actions of slaughter as the Women did with their short sticks. But the end of this shew was most ridiculous: for when they were dismiss'd they not onely were not contented with the largess of the Ambassador, although I added as much of my own to it, but went away very ill satisfi'd, testifying the same by cholerick yellings, which to me was a new Comedy.

November the sixteenth. I was told that the aforemention'd Woman,[2] who had resolv'd to burn her self for her Husband's death, was to dye this Evening. But upon further enquiry at the Woman's House I understood that it would not be till after a few dayes more, and there I saw her sitting in a Court, or Yard, and other persons beating Drums about her. She was cloth'd all in white and deck'd with many Neck-laces, Bracelets and other ornaments of Gold; on her Head she had a Garland of Flowers, spreading forth like the rayes of the Sun; in brief she was wholly in a Nuptial Dress and held a Lemon in her Hand, which is the usual Ceremony.[3] She seem'd to be pleasant enough,[4] talking and laughing in conversation, as a Bride would do in our Countries. She and those with her took notice of my standing there to behold her, and, conjecturing by my foreign Habit who I

---

[1] This hiatus occurs in the original.

[2] See *ante*, p. 266.

[3] See *ante*, p. 266, note 1.

[4] In the original, "di buonissima voglia".

was, some of them came towards me. I told them by an Interpreter that I was a Person of a very remote Country, where we had heard by Fame that some Women in *India* love their Husbands so vehemently as when they dye to resolve to dye with them; and that now, having intelligence that this Woman was such a one, I was come to see her, that so I might relate in my own Country that I had seen such a thing with my own Eyes. These people were well pleas'd with my coming, and she her self, having heard what I said, rose up from her seat and came to speak to me.

We discours'd together, standing, for a good while. She told me that her name was *Giaccamà*, of the Race *Terlengà*,[1] that her Husband was a Drummer; whence I wonder'd the more; seeing that Heroical Actions, as this undoubtedly ought to be judg'd, are very rare in people of low quality. That it was about nineteen dayes since her Husband's death, that he had left two other Wives elder then she, whom he had married before her, (both which were present at this discourse) yet neither of them was willing to dye, but alledg'd for excuse that they had many Children. This argument gave me occasion to ask *Giaccamà*, (who shew'd me a little Son of her own, about six or seven years old, besides a little Daughter she had) how she could perswade her self to leave her own little Children; and I told her, that she ought likewise to live rather than to abandon them at that age. She answer'd me that she left them well recommended to the care of an Uncle of hers there present, who also talk'd with us very cheerfully, as if rejoycing that his Kins-woman should do such an

[1] Properly Telinga (see Wilks' *S. India*, p. 34, *note*). As part of Telingana lies to the north of the river Krishna this fact may perhaps explain the apparent anomaly, according to Mr. Elphinstone, of a case of widow-burning occurring to the south of that river. See *ante*, p. 266, note 1.

action; and that her Husband's other two remaining Wives would also take care of them. I insisted much upon the tender age of her Children, to avert her from her purpose by moving her to compassion for them, well knowing that no argument is more prevalent with Mothers than their Love and Affection towards their Children. But all my speaking was in vain, and she still answer'd me to all my Reasons, with a Countenance not onely undismay'd and constant, but even cheerful, and spoke in such a manner as shew'd that she had not the least fear of death. She told me also, upon my asking her, that she did this of her own accord, was at her own liberty and not forc'd nor perswaded by any one. Whereupon, I inquiring whether force were at any time us'd in this matter, they told me that ordinarily it was not, but onely sometimes amongst Persons of quality, when some Widow was left young, handsome, and so in danger of marrying again (which amongst them is very ignominious),[1] or committing a worse fault; in such Cases the Friends of the deceas'd Husband were very strict, and would constrain her to burn her self even against her own will, for preventing the disorders possible to happen in case she should live (a barbarous, indeed, and too cruel Law[2]); but that neither force nor persuasion was used to *Giaccamà*, and that she did it of her own free will; in which, as a magnanimous action, (as indeed it was) and amongst them of great honor, both her Relations and herself much glory'd. I ask'd concerning the Ornaments and Flowers she wore, and they told me that such was the Custom, in token of the *Masti's*[3] joy (they call the Woman, who intends to burn her self for the death of her Husband, *Masti*) in that she was very shortly to go to him and therefore had reason to rejoyce; whereas

---

[1] See *ante*, p. 83. [2] See *ante*, pp. 85, 86.

[3] *Máhá-sati*, or "Very virtuous". Hence the Anglo-Indian word "*Suttee*".

such Widows as will not dye remain in continual sadness and lamentations, shave their Heads and live in perpetual mourning for the death of their Husbands.[1]

At last *Giaccamà* caus'd one to tell me that she accounted my coming to see her a great fortune, and held her self much honour'd, as well by my visit and presence as by the Fame which I should carry of her to my own Country; and that before she dy'd she would come to visit me at my House, and also to ask me, as their custom is, that I would favour her with some thing by way of Alms towards the buying of fewel for the fire wherewith she was to be burnt. I answer'd her that I should esteem her visit and very willingly give her something; not for wood and fire wherein to burn her self, (for her death much displeas'd me, and I would gladly have disswaded her from it, if I could) but to do something else therewith that her self most lik'd; and I promis'd her that, so far as my weak pen could contribute, her Name should remain immortal in the World. Thus I took leave of her, more sad for her death than she was, cursing the custom of *India* which is so unmerciful to Women.[2] *Giaccamà* was a

---

[1] As to the miserable fate of a Hindú widow see Sir Monier Williams' *Modern India*, p. 318, where it is truly said that she "suffers a living death". Not only does she live in perpetual mourning, but she is "a household drudge, and must eat only one meal a day". See also Dubois (*Mœurs des peuples de l'Inde*, vol. ii, p. 14 *et seq.*), who concludes his description of a Hindú widow with the melancholy words: "Elle ne peut trouver d'idées consolantes que dans le souvenir des chagrins qu'elle a eus à endurer lorsqu'elle était sous le joug conjugal."

[2] This assertion is somewhat dogmatic. The conclusion at which Mr. Elphinstone arrives in regard to the motives of this custom is that "it is more probable that the hopes of immediately entering on the enjoyment of heaven, and of entitling the husband to the same felicity, as well as the glory attending such a voluntary sacrifice, are sufficient to excite the few enthusiastic spirits who go through this awful trial." (See *Hist. of India*, p. 189.) Be this as it may, it is not improbable that the misery of a Hindú widow's life may tempt a woman to prefer death as the better alternative. One ingenious theory on the subject is

Woman of about thirty years of age, of a Complexion very brown for an Indian and almost black, but of a good aspect, tall of stature, well shap'd and proportion'd. My Muse could not forbear from chanting her in a Sonnet which I made upon her death, and reserve among my Poetical Papers.[1]

XXIV.—The same Evening Lights being set up in all the Temples, and the usual Musick of Drums and Pipes sounding, I saw in one Temple, which was none of the greatest, a Minister, or Priest, dance before the Idol all naked, saving that he had a small piece of Linnen over his Privities, as many of them continually go; he had a drawn Sword in his Hand, which he flourish'd as if he had

---

that propounded by Thevenot, who says that the custom is owing to "the tyranny of the Bráhmins, because, these ladies never being burnt without all their ornaments of gold and silver about them, and none but they (the Brahmins) having power to touch their ashes, they fail not to pick up all that is precious amongst them."

Dr. Schrader, in his *Sprachvergleichung und Urgeschichte*, as translated by Mr. F. Byron Jevons, says: "It is no longer possible to doubt that ancient Aryan custom ordained that the wife should die with her husband." This opinion appears to be opposed to that of Sir Monier Williams (*Modern India*, p. 315) and of Prof. Max Müller (*Hibbert Lectures* of 1878, p. 83), who both regard widow-burning as a comparatively modern custom.

[1] It is not within the editor's knowledge whether this sonnet was ever published. But in its place the following "noble language", as it is truly styled by Sir Monier Williams (*Modern India*, p. 313), translated from the address of *Sita* to her husband, in the *Rámáyana*, may be quoted:

"Thou art my king, my guide, my only refuge, my divinity.
. . . . . To me the shelter of thy presence
Is better far than stately palaces, and paradise itself.
Protected by thy arm, gods, demons, men, shall have no power to harm me.
Roaming with thee in desert wastes a thousand years will be a day;
Dwelling with thee, e'en hell itself would be to me a heaven of bliss."

been fencing; but his motions were nothing but lascivious gestures. And, indeed, the greatest part of their Worship of their Gods consists in nothing but Musick, Songs & Dances, not only pleasant but lascivious, and in serving their Idols as if they were living Persons; namely in presenting to them things to eat, washing them, perfuming them, giving them *Betle*-leaves,[1] dying them with Sanders,[2] carrying them abroad in Procession, and such other things as the Country-people account delights and observances. In rehearsing Prayers I think they are little employ'd and as little in Learning. I once ask'd an old Priest, who was held more knowing than others, grey, and clad all in white, carrying a staff like a Shepherds crook in his Hand, What Books he had read, and what he had studied? adding that I myself delighted in reading, and that if he would speak to me about any thing I would answer him. He told me that all Books were made onely that Men might by means thereof know God, and, God being known, to what purpose were Books?[3] as if he knew God very well. I reply'd that all thought they knew God, but yet few knew him aright; and therefore he should beware that himself were not one of those.

November the seventeenth. By Letters brought from *Barselòr*,[4] with News from *Goa*, we heard that the Prince of *England* was gone *incognito* into *Spain* to accomplish his Marriage with the *Infanta;* and that his arrival being known, and the King having seen him, preparations were making for his publick Reception. That the Fleet was not yet arriv'd at *Goa*, except one Galeon; and that the

---

[1] See p. 36, note 1.

[2] See p. 99, note 2.

[3] This question will remind the reader of the answer made by the Khálif Omar to his lieutenant Amrou, which led to the burning of the library at Alexandria. (See Gibbon's *Roman Empire*, vol. v, p. 136.)

[4] See *ante*, p. 168, note 1.

News from *Ormùz*[1] was that *Ruy Freyra*[2] was landed in that Island and, having entrench'd himself under the Fort, held the same besieg'd with that small *Armado* he had with him: whence 'twas hop'd that, great supplies being about to be sent to him from *Goa*, and the enmity of the English ceasing in consideration of the Marriage between the two Crowns, and consequently also their assistance of the *Persians*, *Ormùz* would shortly be recover'd; and indeed, in respect of the above-said circumstances, I account it no hard matter.

November the twentieth. In the Evening, either because it was the next night after *Monday*, or that 'twas their weekly custom, or, perhaps, for some extraordinary solemnity, Tapers were lighted up in all the Temples of *Ikkerì;* a great noise was made with Drums and Pipes, together with the Dancings of the Ministers of some Temples before the Gates, as is above describ'd.

XXV.—Wherefore I went to the great Temple, where, as it is the principal, I thought to see the greatest and most solemn Ceremonies. After the people were call'd together by the sounding of several Trumpets a good while without the Temple they began to make the usual Procession within the Yard, or Inclosure, with many noises of their barbarous instruments, as they are wont to do here every evening: which after they had done as often as they pleas'd they went forth into the street, where much people expected them, carrying two Idols in Procession, both in one *Palanchino*, one at each end, small and so deck'd with Flowers and other Ornaments that I could scarce know what they were. Yet I think that in the back-end was *Agoresouer*, to whom the Temple is dedicated,[3] and the other *Parveti*,[4] or some other Wife of his. First march'd

---

[1] See *ante*, p. 2.

[2] See *ante*, p. 187.

[3] See *ante*, p. 216, note 1.

[4] See *ante*, p. 35, note 3.

the Trumpets and other instruments of divers sorts, continually sounding, then follow'd amongst many Torches a long train of Dancing-women, two and two, bare-headed, in their dancing dress and deck'd with many Ornaments of Gold and Jewels. After them came the *Palanchino* of the Idols, behind which were carry'd many Lances, Spears with silken Streamers, and many Umbrellas garnish'd with silken tufts and fringes round about, more stately than those used by others, even the King himself; for these are commonly the Ensignes of Grandeur.[1] On each side of the *Palanchino* went many rows of Women, either publick Dancers, or prostitutes; but because these were not to dance they went bare-fac'd indeed, (as the Pagan Women here little care for covering their Faces[2]) but with a cloth bound about their Heads and hanging down behind upon their Shoulders and before upon their Breasts. Some of them next the *Palanchino* carryed in their Hands certain little Staves, either of Silver, or Silver'd over; at the end of which hung thick, long and white tufts of the hair of Horses tails,[3] with which (as 'tis the custom of great Persons in India to use them) they went fanning the Air, and either drove away the Flies from the Idols in the *Palanchino*, or at least performed this Office as a piece of Grandeur, as with us the same is done to the Pope,[4] with fans made of the tails of white Peacocks, when he goes

---

[1] See *ante*, p. 268, *note*.

[2] See *ante*, p. 46, *note*. As to the history of the custom of covering the face adopted by women in India, see Sir Monier Williams' *Modern India*, p. 312. Many of the women in these parts uncover not only the face, but the body above the waist also. See *ante*, p. 258, *note*.

[3] The tails here referred to were probably not those of horses, but of the Yak (see *ante*, p. 260), which were and are used in India, and China also, as a mark of dignity. By a resolution of the Dutch Government the Director of the Factory at Surat was specially authorised to have four fans "made after the fashion of the country, with feathers of birds of paradise and *cow hair*" (*i.e.*, yaks' tails).

[4] The fan used by the Pope is called *Flabellum*.

abroad in *Pontificalibus*. Neither were there wanting about the Idols many of their Priests, or Ministers, of the Temple who accompany'd them; particularly one who seem'd the chief and *Archimandrita* of the rest; besides abundance of Torches whose light dispell'd the darkness of the Moon-less night. In this order they came into the Piazza, and there, after they had made a large ring, the dancing began; first two Dancing-women, one from one side of the circle, and another from another, yet both with their Faces always turn'd towards the Idols, walk'd three steps forward and then three backward[1]; and this they did innumerable times. I suppose it was a way of saluting the Idols. After the said two Dancers alone had done thus two others from the several sides joyn'd with them, and they did the same again, three and three. This Salutation, or Preamble of the Ballet, being many times repeated, they began to dance, namely two that danc'd better than the rest, one on the right side of the circle, and the other on the left, both with their Faces, never with their backs, towards the *Palanchino* of the Idols, though often in the Dance they retir'd backwards as well as went forwards. Their dancing was high, with frequent leapings and odd motions, sometimes inclining their haunches as if they meant to sit down, sometimes rising very high and causing the skirt wherewith they are cover'd from the girdle downwards to fly out, and always holding one Arm stretch'd out before them, wherewith they now and then made as if they were thrusting, or fencing; besides other mad gestures which were all accompany'd with words which they sang, and sometimes with cries more apt to give horror than delight. Hence, while all the other Dancing-women (that is those who were uncover'd and loosed for dancing)

---

1 These steps may have been originally symbolical of the three strides of Vishnu as the Sun (viz., morning, midday and evening). See Prof. M. Müller s *Hibbert Lectures* of 1878, p. 263.

danced all in a company together further distant from the Idols, striking their little sticks and singing, being guided by a Man who danced with them and was their Master, the other Dancers who were cloth'd stood about the Idols, but danced not, nor ever moved from their place; onely they accompany'd the Show, very fine with Ornaments of Gold and Jewels, and some of them having Flowers, others leaves of *Betle*,[1] or other Odoriferous Herb, in their Hands.

This Dance being ended, the Procession went forwards with the same Pomp and a numerous Train of Men and Women of all sorts. They went not round the great Piazza in front of the Temple but within the outermost walls of the Temple, which is surrounded by very large streets, inhabited for the most part by the said Dancers, or publick Strumpets. The circuit of the Procession began from the right Hand as you come out of the Temple, which comes to be the left as you enter in; and in the same manner I saw the Procession begin at the Temple of the Town *Ahinelà*, which I have described above[2]; so that it must needs be one of their usual Ceremonies. This procession stop'd at several places in the streets through which it past; and at every such stopping, the above-mention'd Dancings, Perambulations and other performances were again repeated; whence the Show lasted a good while and concluded at length with the last Dance in the Piazza before the Temple-Gate; which ended, the Procession with the Idols re-entered the Temple, where it being replaced according to their accustomed Ceremonies, the solemnity ended and all the people departed.

XXVI.—I was told by one of the spectators that this Ceremony was practised every *Monday* at night and at

---

[1] See *ante*, p. 36, note 1.
[2] See *ante*, p. 238.

every New and Full Moon,[1] as also upon certain other extraordinary solemnities, with more or less Pomp proportionably to the Festivals: and he added that the night following there would be a greater solemnity than this, because the New Moon and another of their Feasts were then co-incident, and that the King himself would be there; wherefore I resolved with my self to see it.

November the one and twentieth. This night an infinite number of Torches and Candles were lighted, not onely in all the Temples but also in all the Streets, Houses and Shops of *Ikkeri*, which made a kind of splendour over all the City. In each of the Temples was its Idol, which in some was a Serpent[2]; and they had adorned the outward Porches not onely with lights, but also with certain contrivances of paper, on which were painted Men on Horseback, Elephants, people fighting and other odd figures; behind which papers lights were placed in certain little Arches, like those which we make in our Sepulchres; these with other gay Ornaments of Silk hung round about made a sufficiently prety Show. In the great Temple not onely the inside, in the middle whereof is a very high and slender Cupola, (which appears without too) but also all the outer walls and all those round about the Piazza which lies before it, as also the Houses on the adjacent sides, were

---

[1] As to the prevalence of moon worship, see Sir J. Lubbock's *Origin of Civilization*, pp. 319 to 322, and Prof. Max Müller's *Hibbert Lectures* of 1878, p. 181 *et seq.* Most of the religious festivals in India are regulated by the phases of the moon. See Dubois, *Mœurs des peuples de l'Inde*, vol. ii, p. 327 *et seq.*

[2] Serpent-worship, as is well known, was formerly very prevalent in India and is not yet extinct. See Sir M. Williams' *Religious Life in India*, p. 321, and Sir J. Lubbock's *Origin of Civilization*, p. 270 *et seq.*, and Prof. Max Müller's *Hibbert Lectures* of 1878, p. 115, and Dubois, *Mœurs des peuples de l'Inde*, vol. ii, p. 435 *et seq.*, and especially Fergusson's *Tree and Serpent Worship*. In many temples in Southern India not only serpent idols, but living serpents, are worshipped.

all full of lights. The concourse of people of all sorts and degrees, both Men and Women, was very great; and they appeared to go about visiting all the Temples. When it was very late the King came to the great Temple, accompanied onely by his two grandsons, to wit *Seda-Siva Naieka*, (whom I had formerly seen) Son of one of his Daughters, and *Vira-badrà Naieka*, a young boy, his Son's Son, whom he designs for his Successor, if his other kindred elder than he, to wit the above-said *Seda-Siva* and two of *Venk-tapà's* Nephews by one of his Brothers whom he keeps prisoner, do not disturb him. The King came in a *Palanchino* at a great pace, his two Nephews on Horse-back, and so did *Vitulà Sinay*,[1] who rode by the King's side with appearance of a great Favourite. Likewise *Putapaia*[2] came in a *Palanchino* and other of his Grandees, some in *Palanchinos*, and some on Horse-back, following him at a great distance, with some number of Souldiers and Servants on Foot; but, in summ, the whole train was not very considerable. The King stay'd in the Temple about an hour, being entertain'd with Musick, Dancing and other things which I could not see because I was without. At length he came forth, and with the same company, and running in as much haste as he came return'd home; the like did all the other people of whom the Piazza was full, some on one side, some on the other.

After the King was come out of the Temple they carry'd the Idols a while in Procession about the Piazza, but with small pomp and company; so that I car'd not for staying to see them, but went to another Temple standing at the end of the *Bazar*, or market, facing a large and goodly street, where the show of lights was gallant, and there I stay'd a good while with my Companions,

---

[1] See *ante*, p. 191.

[2] See *ante*, p. 252.

(for all the Ambassador's party was come abroad this night to see the solemnities; even the Chaplain himself, but disguis'd) to see two great companies of Dancing-women dance, they all being sent for thither by a great Captain, (who, perhaps, had the care of the solemnities of this Temple) after the King was gone from the great Temple; they danc'd here a good while in numerous companies; after which we return'd home, it being after mid-night.

November the two and twentieth. *Venk-tapà Naieka* had already given our Ambassador an answer concerning the affairs which he negotiated, and the Ambassador had prepared a dispatch to be sent to the King of *Banghel*,[1] also another for the Vice-Roy of *Goa*, giving him an account of his negotiation, when a Currier arriv'd from *Banghel* with new Letters, both for *Venk-tapà Naieka* and the Ambassador; whereupon consultation was held as to what answer to return him, which was soon concluded on the part of *Venk-tapà Naieka* to this effect, (being no other than what I have already mentioned) namely that he would pay the King of *Banghel* 7000 Pagods[2] yearly, according to the Treaty of Peace, provided the said King would come and live in his[3] Court, or in some other place of his Country, (excepting such Lands as were formerly his, for fear he might make new insurrections) or else in *Goa*, or any of the adjacent places, namely in the Island of *Salsette*,[4] or some place there without the City; but in any case such wherein he may be subject to the Vice-Roy of *Goa;* so that *Venk-tapà* might be secure that the said King of *Banghel* would live peaceably without making new commotions. But in case (as he seem'd to intend) he

---

[1] See *ante*, pp. 212 and 213.

[2] See *ante*, p. 209, note 1.

[3] *I.e.*, Venk-tapa's.

[4] See *ante*, p. 139, note 2.

would live neither in *Venk-tapà's* Country, nor in that of *Goa*, but would continue in *Cagnoroto*,[1] where he was at present (which is a place beyond *Mangalòr*[2] Eastwards,[3] and belongs to another small but free Prince, alli'd to *Banghel*, whither, being near his quondam-Territories, he had betaken himself) or else would wander here and there like a Fugitive and Invader, disquieting these Countries, then *Venk-tapà* was resolv'd not to give him any thing at all. Therefore let him either accept the above-said Offer, or never speak more to him, for he would not hear him; that he hath been mov'd to make this offer of paying the said summ by the instance of the *Portugals*, who had interpos'd in his behalf by this Embassie: and for the king of *Banghel's* assurance that he would perform this, he would give the Ambassador (and accordingly he did so) a Copy of the Letter containing these promises, which he writ to the said King of *Banghel*, to the end the Ambassador might send it to the Vice-Roy, and be a witness of what he promis'd and was to observe.

He has further told the Ambassador that this King had formerly writ to him that he would come and live in his Dominion, and repented of what he had done heretofore through evil counsel; and that for the future he would be at his devotion, receiving that Pension which he had promis'd him and the like: nevertheless he had now chang'd his mind, and refus'd both to come into his Dominion and to go to *Goa*: that therefore, seeing him so unconstant, he had much reason not to trust him, and, in short, would neither trust him nor give him any thing, saving upon the

---

[1] It is not clear what place is here referred to, but it seems probable that it is Cánara (or Kánara). In the map accompanying these letters the place is marked as lying on the coast due S. of Mangalúr. No such name appears in modern maps. As to Cánara, see *ante*, p. 168, note 1.

[2] See *ante*, p. 212, note 2.

[3] In the original, "Ostro", *i.e.* South-west.

above-said terms; and that not for his own sake, but in regard of the intercession which the *Portugals* made for him: that this was his last Answer, and that nothing more was to be expected, or hoped, from him.

From *Spain*, they say, Orders are sent to the Vice-Roy to re-establish the king of *Banghel* by all means in his State, and to make war upon *Venk-tapà* unless he restore the King intirely. However, being[1] that country is remote, and in the time that is spent in the going and coming of dispatches many things may happen which may render it necessary for the Vice-Roy in the present conjuncture to proceed in sundry particulars differently from the Orders he receives from *Spain*, and to have authority in this business of *Banghel* to deliberate as to Peace or War, as shall to him seem most expedient, endeavouring to comply no less with the times and the State of affairs than with the instructions from *Spain:* therefore the King of *Spain* in the Letter which he writ to *Venk-tapà Naieka*, making onely general complements to him, refers all matters of business to the Vice-Roy to guide himself therein as he shall think most fit.

Accordingly the Vice-Roy, though he knows the King of *Spain's* intention and order to make war upon *Venk-tapà*, yet, not deeming it a fit time, whilst the *Portugals* are engag'd in the war of *Ormùz*[2] and also in *Malacca*, (which is reported to be besieg'd either by the King of *Acem*,[3] which is *Sumatra*, or by him and the Dutch together) and being much perplex'd in a thousand other intricacies in *India*, hath therefore given Order to the Ambassador to seem satisfi'd with whatever Answer *Venk-tapà Naieka* gives, and to return without making further

---

[1] For "since"; see *ante*, p. 27, *note*.

[2] See Introduction, p. xxvii.

[3] That is, Achin (Atcheh), a town on the northernmost point of Sumatra, in Lat. 5 N. and Long. 95 E. (See Yule's *Cathay*, vol. i, p. 101.)

instance; it sufficing the Vice-Roy to have made this compliment for the service of the King of *Banghel* and to have shown that he hath done therein what was in his power; he well knowing that *Venk-tapà* would not be moved by the Embassie alone, and that the conditions he requires of the King of *Banghel* upon which to give him what he had promis'd are but excuses, and being certain that this King will not venture himself in his[1] Dominions, (as neither is it reasonable) much less go and subject himself in the Territories of *Goa*, and so will not consent to the proposals. Wherefore, seeing 'tis not time now to constrain *Venk-tapà Naieka* to greater things by war, he dissembles till a better occasion, for fear of drawing this new Enemy upon him at an unseasonable conjuncture, and orders the Ambassador to depart with a show of good Friendship.

The Ambassador hath accordingly done so, and, seeming satisfi'd with *Venk-tapà's* Answer, hath added other Letters to those formerly written to the King of *Banghel*, certifying him of *Venk-tapà's* resolute Mind; that either he must accept of the Agreement, or must speak no more of any; and that he onely expects at *Ikkerì* this his last Resolution before returning to *Goa*. He hath written the same to the Vice-Roy of *Goa;* and, the dispatches being seal'd, he hath order'd both Curriers to depart, and also a *Brachman* call'd *Nangasà* together with the Currier to the King of *Banghel*, sending likewise with them a Christian of *Barselòr*[2] nam'd *Lorenzo Pessoa*, who was at *Ikkerì* with *Monteyro*, that he might, either in *Mangalòr*,[3] *Banghel*, or other places thereabouts, procure Mariners for a Ship remaining at *Barselòr* unprovided of Men; giving the said *Pessoa* a License to hire some, which license he had obtain'd of the

---

[1] *I.e.* Venk-tapa's.

[2] See *ante*, p. 250, note 2.

[3] See *ante*, p. 212, note 2.

Ministers of *Venk-tapà Naieka* to levy mariners in his Territories if need were.

Being by this time sufficiently inform'd of remarkable things in *Ikkerì* I am desirous of divers others, especially to see the person of the Queen of *Olala,*[1] whose History and many valiant exploits[2] I read of when I was in *Persia;* for which I have a fair opportunity by accompanying these Men sent from the Ambassador, of whom when I have taken leave I shall (God Willing) depart tomorrow.

[1] Marked "Oolaul" and "Ulala" in modern maps. It is a small place of no importance on the coast near Mangalur, about three miles to S.W. (See Brookes' *Gazetteer.*) It is near the village of Manjeshwaram described in Eastwick's *Handbook of Madras*, p. 301.

[2] The history and exploits here referred to are described in the next letter at pp. 313, 314.

LETTER VI.

From Mangalòr, Decemb. 9, 1623.

HAVING already seen in *Ikkerì* as much as there was remarkable, and being very desirous of seeing *Barselòr*,[1] *Mangalòr*,[2] and also principally the Queen of *Olala*,[3] whose Dominion and Residence are contiguous to *Mangalòr*, as well because she is Sovereign of those parts, (a thing not ordinary in other Countries) and a Princess famous in our dayes, even in the Indian Histories of the *Portugals*, as because she is a *Gentile* in Religion, as likewise all her Subjects are, (whence, I conceiv'd, I might possibly see some considerable curiosity there) I lay'd hold of the occasion of going thither in company of these Men who are sent by the Ambassador, by whose favour being provided of a good Horse (in regard that there were no *Palanchinos* to be hir'd in *Ikkerì*) and a Man to carry my baggage upon his Head I prepar'd to set forth the next Morning.

November the three and twentieth. Before my departure from *Ikkerì* I was presented by *Vitulà Sinay*[4] (of whom I had before taken leave) with a little Book, written in the

---

[1] See p. 250, note 2.
[2] See p. 212, note 2.
[3] See *ante*, p. 289.
[4] See *ante*, p. 191.

Canara[1] language, which is the vulgar tongue in *Ikkerì* and all that State. It is made after the custom of the Country, not of paper, (which they seldom use) but of Palm-leaves, to wit of that Palm which the *Portugals* call *Palmum brama*,[2] *i.e.*, *Wild-palm*, and is of that sort which produces the Indian Nut; for such are those commonly found in *India*, where Palms that produce Dates are very rare.[3] On the leaves of these Palms they write, or rather ingrave, the Letters with an Iron style made for the purpose, of an uncouth form; and, that the writing may be more apparent, they streak it over with a coal,[4] and tye the leaves together to make a Book of them after a manner sufficiently strange. I, being desirous to have one of these Books, to carry as a curiosity to my own Country for ornament of my Library, and not finding any to be sold in the City, had entreated *Vitulà Sinay* to help me to one, but he, not finding any one vendible therein, caus'd a small one to be purposely transcrib'd for me, (there being not time enough for a greater) and sent it to me as a gift just as I was ready to take Horse.

What the Book contains I know not, but I imagine 'tis Verses in their Language, and I carry it with me, as I do also (to show to the curious) divers leaves not written upon, and a style, or Iron Pen, such as they use, together with one

[1] See *ante*, p. 168, note 1.

[2] Probably *brabo*, "wild" (Port.). If by this name the coco-nut palm (*Cocos nucifera*) is referred to the statement here made is not quite correct, for the palm-leaves used for writing on in India are *generally* those of the Palmyra (*Borassus flabelliformis*), and of the *Corypha umbraculifera*, or *Talipat* (which means "palm-leaf") tree in Ceylon and the adjacent parts of India (Yule's *Cathay*, *etc.*, ii, 449), though the coco-nut palm is *sometimes* used. The leaf of *Licuala Spinosa* is also used for this purpose.

[3] Even in the present day fruit-bearing date-trees (*Phœnix dactylifera*) are not common in India. Date-trees (*Phœnix sylvestris*) are there generally grown for the purpose of making sugar from their sap. It is said that Bengal alone formerly furnished annually 100,000 cwt. of this sugar. (See Lindley's *Vegetable Kingdom*, p. 137.)

[4] Or rather "with charcoal".

leaf containing a Letter Missive after their manner, which was written, by I know not whom, to our Ambassador; of whom taking leave with many compliments, as also of Sig: *Carvaglio*, the Chaplain, *Monteyro* and all the company, I departed from *Ikkerì* a little before noon, going out at the same Gate whereat I had enter'd; and having no other company but a *Vetturino*[1] and a *Pulià*[2] who carry'd my luggage, without any other servant; for as for *Galàl* the Persian, aliàs *Cacciàtur*,[3] I was constrain'd to dismiss him for some uncommendable actions and to send him back from *Ikkerì* to *Goa*.

I will not omit to tell you that this my brave God-son, (whom I had brought so carefully out of *Persia* and trusted so much, and who alone of all my old servants remain'd with me) one day cunningly open'd a light box, or basket, (*Canestri* the *Portugals* call them) wherein I kept my Clothes, and which, after the fashion of the Country, was not made of wood, but of hoops lin'd with leather, and clos'd with little Padlocks, like those which are us'd at *Rome* for Plate; and they are thus contriv'd that they may be of little weight, because in these parts goods and baggage for travel are more frequently transported upon Men's shoulders than upon beasts' backs; and one of these baskets, or *Canestri*, is just a Man's load. Now the good Cacciàtur having open'd mine, without hurting the lock, or meddling with the linnen which he found therein, took out onely all the little money which I then had and had

---

[1] *I.e.*, a man from whom the horse had been hired (literally "one who lets on hire')

[2] The name o an outcast tribe, perhaps derived from the word *pulai*, "flesh", such tribes eating flesh forbidden to other persons. There is a good description of this tribe, called by him *Puler*, in Barbosa's (?Magellan's) account of the Malabar coast, p. 142. He says: "These people are great charmers, thieves and very vile people." See also Dubois, *Mœurs des peuples de l'Inde*, vol. i, p. 66.

[3] See *ante*, pp. 126 12 .

put into it, to avoid carrying its weight about me; it was in one of those long leathern purses, which are made to wear round the waist like a girdle, full of Spanish Rials,[1] a Coin in these parts, and almost in all the world, current enough. His intention, I conceive, was to leave me (as we say) naked in the Mountains in the center of *India*, and, peradventure, to go into some Territory of the *Gentiles*, or *Mahometans*, there to pass a jovial life at my expence. But as it pleas'd God, the theft being done in my Chamber where none but he resorted, we had vehement suspicion of him; and therefore the Ambassador, making use of his Authority, caus'd him to be laid hold on, and we found the theft[2] in his breeches ty'd to his naked flesh; and thus I recover'd my money. I was unwilling that any hurt should be done to him, and, withall, to keep him any longer; nevertheless, that he might not go into the Infidel-Countries, lest thereby he should lose his Religion and turn to his native errors, I sent him away with some trusty persons to *Goa*, giving him Letters also to Signora *Maria*,[3] but such as whereby they might know that I had dismiss'd him and that he was not to be entertain'd there, though not otherwise punished. By this Story you may see how much a Man may be deceiv'd in his trusting; how little benefits prevail upon an unworthy nature; and, withall, you may consider to what misfortunes a Stranger is subject in strange Countries; so that, if I had nothing else, being thus depriv'd of all, I should have been left to perish miserably amongst *Barbarians*.

II.—But, leaving him to his Voyage, I departed from *Ikkeri*, and having pass'd the Town *Badrapor*,[4] I left the

---

[1] Or "Real", a coin equal to about 15*s*. of English money in the 17th century.

[2] See Exodus, chap. xxii, v. 4, for an instance of the use of this word to signify the thing stolen.

[3] See *ante*, p. 24, note 1.

[4] See *ante*, pp. 243, 244.

road of *Ahinelì*[1] and by another way, more towards the left hand, went to dine under certain Trees near a small Village of four Houses, which they call *Bamanen coppa.*[2] After dinner we continued our way and forded a River call'd *Irihalè*,[3] not without being wet, by reason of the small size of my Horse; and having travell'd near two *Gaus*[4] (one *Gau* consists of two *Cos*, and is equivalent to two *Portugal* Leagues) we lodg'd at night in a competent Town the name whereof is *Dermapora.*[5] In these Towns I endeavor'd to procure a servant, as well because I understood not the Language of the Country, (for though he that carry'd my Goods could speak *Portugal* yet he could not well serve me for an Interpreter, because, he being by Race a *Pulià*,[6] which amongst them is accounted vile and unclean, they would not suffer him to come into their Houses nor touch their things; though they were not shie of me, albeit of a different Religion, because they look'd upon me as a Man of noble Race), as because I found much trouble in reference to my diet: for, as these Indians are extremely fastidious in edibles, there is neither flesh nor fish to be had amongst them; one must be contented onely with Rice, Butter, or Milk, and other such inanimate things, wherewith, nevertheless, they make no ill-tasted dishes; but, which is worse, they will cook every thing themselves and will not let others either eat, or drink, in their vessels; wherefore, instead of dishes, they give us our victuals in great Palm[7] leaves, which yet are smooth

---

[1] See *ante*, p. 234, note 3.

[2] Or "Brahman's grove".

[3] A small stream not marked in modern maps, but erroneously marked "Trishale" in the map accompanying these letters.

[4] See *ante*, p. 230, note 1.

[5] Or "Dharmapoor" (City of Virtue), a small town not marked in ordinary maps.

[6] See *ante*, p. 292, note 2.

[7] Or, probably, "Plantain".

enough, and the Indians themselves eat more frequently in them than in any other vessels. Besides, one must entreat them three hours for this, and account it a great favor; so that, in brief, to travel in these Countries requires a very large stock of patience. The truth is 'tis a most crafty invention of the Devil against the Charity so much preach'd by our Lord Jesus Christ to put it so in the heads of these people that they are polluted and become unclean, even by touching others of a different Religion; of which superstition they are so rigorous observers that they will sooner see a person, whom they account vile and unclean, (though a *Gentile*) dye, than go near him to relieve him.

November the four and twentieth. In the Morning, before day, the Brachman *Nangasà*[1] and the Ambassador's other Men, being in haste, went on before; but I, desirous to go more at my own ease, remain'd alone with my *Pulià*[2] and the horse keeper; as I might well enough do, since the High-ways of *Venk-tapà Naieka's* Country are very secure. The road lay over pleasant peaks of Hills and through Woods, many great streams likewise occurring. I descended the Mountain *Gat*[3] by a long precipice, some of which I was fain to walk on foot, my Horse having fallen twice without any disaster, and by a third fall almost broke my knee to pieces. I din'd, after I had travell'd one *Gau*[4] and a half, in a good Town called *Colùr*,[5] where there is a great Temple, the Idol whereof, if I mis-understood not, is the Image of a Woman[6]; the place is much venerated, and many resort to it from several parts in Pilgrimage.

---

[1] See *ante*, p. 288.

[2] See *ante*, p. 292, note 2.

[3] See *ante*, p. 185, note 2.

[4] See p. 230, note 1.

[5] Marked as "Colloor" in Wyld's map of India, to N.E. of Mangalur.

[6] Probably an image of the goddess Kálì. (See *ante*, p. 258, note 2.)

After dinner, my Horse being tired, I travelled not above half another *Gau*,[1] and, having gone in all this day but two *Gaus*, went to lodge at a certain little village, which, they said, was called *Nalcàl*. Certain Women, who dwelt there alone in absence of their Husbands, courteously gave us lodging in the uncovered Porches of their Houses and prepared supper for us. This Country is inhabited not onely with great Towns, but, like the *Mazandran*[2] in *Persia*, with abundance of Houses, scattered here and there in several places amongst the woods. The people live for the most part by sowing of Rice; their way of Husbandry is to overflow the soil with water, which abounds in all places; but they pay, as they told me, very large Tribute to the King, so that they have nothing but the labour for themselves and live in great Poverty.

November the twenty fifth. I travelled over great Mountains and Woods like the former and forded many deep Rivers. Having gone three *Cos*[3] we din'd in two Houses of those people who sow Rice, whereof the whole Country is full, at a place call'd *Kelidì*.[4] In the Evening my *Pulià*[5] being very weary and unable to carry the heavy load of my baggage further, we stay'd at some of the like Houses which they call'd *Kabndr*,[6] about a mile forwards; so that the journey of this whole day amounted not to a full *Gau*.

November the twenty sixth. I pass'd over peaks of Hills, and uneven and woody places. At noon I came to a great River,[7] on the Northern bank whereof stands a little

---

[1] See *ante*, p. 230, note 1.

[2] The province forming the southern shore of the Caspian Sea.

[3] See *ante*, p. 22.

[4] Probably Keladi, a town in the Shimóga district, the cradle of the family who reigned at Ikkeri. See *ante*, p. 168, note 2, and p. 216, note 1.

[5] See p. 292, note 2.

[6] A small village of no importance.

[7] Or rather an estuary of the sea.

village nam'd *Gulvàn*,[1] near which the River makes a little Island. We went to this Island by boat and forded over the other stream to the far side. Thence we came by a short cut to *Barselòr*,[2] call'd the Higher, *i.e.* within Land, belonging to the Indians and subject to *Venk-tapà Naieka*, to distinguish it from the Lower *Barselòr* on the Sea-coast belonging to the *Portugals*. For in almost all Territories of *India* near the Sea-coast there happen to be two places of the same Name, one call'd the Higher, or In-land, belonging to the natives, the other the Lower, near the Sea, to the *Portugals*, wherever they have footing. Entring the Higher *Barselòr* on this side, I came into a fair, long, broad and straight Street, having abundance of Palmetos[3] and Gardens on either hand. The soil is fruitful and well peopled, encompass'd with weak walls and ditches, which are pass'd over by bridges of one, or two, very great stones, which shew that there is good and fair Marble here, whether they were digg'd thus out of the Quarry, or are the remains of ancient Fabricks.[4] It stands on the South side of the River, which from the Town *Gulvàn* fetches a great circuit, seeming to return backwards; and many Travellers, without touching at the Upper *Barselòr*, are wont to go to the Lower *Barselòr* by boat, which is soon done; but I was desirous to see both places and therefore came hither.

III.—Having din'd and rested a good while in Higher *Barselòr*, I took boat and row'd down the more Southern stream; for a little below the said Town it is divided into many branches and forms divers little fruitful Islands. About an hour and half before night I arriv'd at the Lower *Barselòr* of the *Portugals*, which also stands on the

---

[1] A place of no importance.

[2] See *ante*, p. 250, note 2.

[3] See *ante*, p. 182, note 3.

[4] A kind of black marble is plentiful in these districts.

Southern bank of the River, distant two good Cannon-shot from its mouth; having travell'd this day in all one *Gau*[1] and a half. The Fort of the *Portugals* is very small, built almost in form of a Star, having not bad walls, but wanting ditches, in a Plain and much expos'd to all sorts of assaults. Such *Portugals* as are married have Houses without the Fort in the Town, which is pretty large and hath good buildings.

I went directly to the House of Sig: *Antonio Borges*, a former acquaintance, who came from *Goa* to *Onòr*,[2] together with us, and to whom the Ambassador at *Ikkeri*[3] had recommended me. I found, sitting before his House in the street, the Captain of *Barselòr*, call'd Sig: *Luis Mondes Vas Conti*.[4] We discours'd together for a good while and he seem'd a gallant man, though but young. Here were an Armada and a *Cafila*[5] of Ships, which came from *Goa* and were going to *Mangalòr*[6] and *Cocin*,[7] or further; they were to depart the next day, and therefore I prepar'd my self to go with them to *Mangalòr*. This night I supp'd at the House of Sig: *Antonio Borges* with some other *Portugals* that came in the Fleet, and went to lodge by his direction in another good House, together with some Souldiers of the same Fleet who were friends of his, as he had not room in his own House.

November the seven and twentieth. That I might not go alone, without any body to serve me in the Ship, I took into my service a Christian of *Barselòr*,[8] recommended to me by Sig: *Antonio* and nam'd *Manoel de Matos*, with whom alone I went aboard about noon, having first din'd with many *Portugals* of the Fleet in the House of Sig: *Rocco Gomes*, the chief *Portugal* in *Barselòr*, who enter-

---

1 See *ante*, p. 230, note 1.
2 See *ante*, p. 190, note 3.
3 See *ante*, p. 216, note 1.
4 In original, "Consigliero
5 See *ante*, p. 121, note 3.
6 See *ante*, p. 212, note 2.
7 See *ante*, p. 199, note 1.
8 See *ante*, p. 250, note 2.

tain'd us at his Gate[1] in the street very well. Among others that din'd with us there was one Sig: *Hettor Fernandez*, by me elsewhere mention'd,[2] who came from *Goa* to *Onòr* with us; & the Captain Major of the whole Armada, Sig: *Francesco de Lobo Faria*, who commanded a Galley and six other Ships, besides the *Cafila* of Merchants.

I imbarqu'd in the Ship of Sig: *Hettor Fernandez*, who in the street express'd much courtesie to me. Being gone a good way upon the Sea, and it being now night, the Captain Major of the Galleys sent our Ship back to fetch certain of his Men and the other Ships which were not yet got out of the Port of *Barselòr;* whereinto we designing to enter in the dark, and not hitting the narrow channel which was to be kept, we struck upon land, and, the wind growing pretty stiff, were in great danger of being over-set and lost; and the more because when we perceiv'd it and went to strike sail we could not for a good while, because the ropes, either through moistness, or some other fault, would not slip; so that the Ship, being driven forcibly against the ground, not onely became very leaky, but gave two or three such violent knocks that, had she not been new, without doubt she had been split. The Sea-men were not onely confounded but all amaz'd; nothing was heard but disorderly cries; the voice of him that commanded could not be heard; every one was more intent upon his own than the common safety; many of the Souldiers had already strip'd themselves to leap into the Sea: some ty'd their Money at their backs, to endeavour to save the same together with their lives, making little account of their other goods; divers made vows and promises of Alms; all heartily recommended themselves to God; one embrac'd

---

[1] In the original *porta*, probably a covered portico.

[2] See *ante*, pp. 194 and 205.

the Image of our Lady and plac'd his hope in that alone. I could not induce my self to believe that God had reserv'd me after so many dangers to such a wretched and ignoble end, so that I had, I know not what, secure confidence in my heart; nevertheless, seeing the danger extreamly great, I fail'd not to commend my self to God, his most Holy Mother and all the Saints. By whose favour, at length, the sail being let down by the cutting of the rope, and the Sea not being rough, (for, if it had, it would have done us greater mischief) the Mariners freed the Ship, having cast themselves into the Sea and drawn her off from the ground by strength of Arm; the remainder of the night we spent in the mouth of the Haven, lying at anchor and calling to the other Ships to come out.

IV.—The whole Fleet being set forth before day, we return'd to where the Captain General with the Galley and the rest of the Ships stay'd at Anchor for us; and thence we set sail all together.

November the eight and twentieth. We sail'd constantly Southwards, coasting along the Land which lay on the left hand of us. Half way to *Mangalòr*,[1] to wit six Leagues from *Barselòr*,[2] we found certain Rocks, or little desert Islands, which the *Portugals* call *Scogli di Santa Maria*[3]; one of which we approach'd with our Ship, and many of our Men landed upon it to take wild Pigeons, (of whose nests there is great abundance) wherewith we made a good supper. Afterwards, continuing our course, we pass'd by *Carnate*,[4] and at night safely enter'd the Port of *Mangalòr*.

---

[1] See *ante*, p. 212, note 2.

[2] See *ante*, p. 250, note 2.

[3] These are marked as the "Premeira rocks" in Black's Atlas.

[4] No such place is to be found in modern maps. The name may be used to denote the southern limit of Kánara, also called Cárnata, or Kárnata. See *ante*, p. 168, note 1.

This Port is in the mouth of two Rivers,[1] one more Northern runs from the Lands of *Banghel*[2]; the other more Southern from those of *Olala*,[3] which stands beyond the River Southwards, or rather beyond the bay of salt-water, which is form'd round and large, like a great Haven, by the two Rivers before their entrance into the Sea, whose flowing fills the same with salt water. *Mangalòr* stands between *Olala* and *Banghel* and in the middle of the bay right against the Mouth of the Harbor, into which the Fort extends itself, being almost encompass'd with water on three sides. 'Tis but small, the worst built of any I have seen in *India*, and, as the Captain told me one day when I visited him, may rather be termed the House of a Gentleman than a Fort. The City is but little neither, contiguous to the Fort and encompass'd with weak walls; within which the Houses of the inhabitants are inclos'd. There are three Churches, namely the See,[4] or Cathedral, of our Lady *Del Rosario*, within the Fort, *La Misericordia*, and *San Francesco* without. Yet in *Mangalòr* there are but three Ecclesiastical Persons in all; two Franciscan Fryers in *San Francesco* and one Vicar Priest, to whose charge, with very small revenues, belong all the other Churches. I went not ashore because it was night, but slept in the Ship.

November the nine and twentieth. Early in the Morning I landed at *Mangalòr* and went, together with Sig: *Hettor Fernandez*, and others of our Ship, to dine in the House of Sig: *Ascentio Veira*, a Notary of the City. After which I was provided with an empty House, belonging to a Kins-man of his, by Sig: *Paolo Sodrino*, who was married in *Mangalòr* and came from *Goa* in our Ship. The next

---

[1] These are the Bolúr (also called Netrawati) and the Balure, of which the former runs to S. of the latter. (See Eastwick's *Handbook of Madras*, p. 301.)

[2] See *ante*, p. 212.

[3] See *ante*, p. 289, note 1.

[4] See *ante*, p. 133, note 4.

night the Fleet departed for *Cocin*,[1] but I remain'd in *Mangalòr* with intention to go and see the Queen of *Olala*.

November the thirtieth. After hearing Mass in the Church *Del Rosario* I visited the Captain of *Mangalòr*, not in the Fort, but in a cover'd place without the Gate, which is built to receive the cool Air of the Sea, and where he was then in conversation. He was an old Man all gray, by Name Sig: *Pero Gomes Pasagna.*

V.—The first of *December*, in the Morning I went to see *Banghel*, by the Indians more correctly call'd *Bangher*, or *Banghervan;* 'tis a mile, or little more, distant from *Mangalòr*, towards the South[2] and upon the Sea; and, the King that rul'd there and in the circumjacent lands being at this day driven out, 'tis subject to *Venk-tapà Naieka*.[3] A musket-shot without *Mangalòr*, on that side, is a small River which is pass'd over by a ruinous stone bridge and may likewise be forded; 'tis the boundary of the *Portugal's* jurisdiction. The above-said mile is through cultivated fields, and then you come to *Banghel*, which is of a rich soil, and sometime better peopled than at present; whence the Houses are poor Cottages of earth and straw. It hath but one straight street, of good length, of Houses and Shops continu'd on both sides, and many other sheds dispers'd among the Palmetoes.[4] The King's House stood upon a rais'd ground, almost like a Fort, but is now wholly destroy'd, so that there is nothing left standing but the posts of the Gate; for when *Venk-tapà Naieka* took this Territory he demolish'd whatever was strong in it. The *Bazàr*, or market-place, remains, although not so stor'd with goods as it was in the time of its own King; yet it

---

[1] See *ante*, p. 199, note 1.

[2] "Towards the south" is a mistranslation for "towards the north".

[3] See *ante*, p. 212.

[4] See *ante*, p. 182, note 3.

affords what is necessary, and much *Areca*,[1] or *Fofel*, whereof they make Merchandise, sending the same into divers parts, that of this place being better then others; here are also in the *Bazàr* some Gold-smiths who make knives and cizzers,[2] adorn'd with Silver, very cheap, and other like toys, of which I bought some, and, having seen all that was to be seen, return'd on foot, as I came, though somewhat late, to *Mangalòr*.

December the second. This Morning I went to see *Olala*, which is about the same distance from *Mangalòr* as *Banghel* is, but the contrary way towards the South, and stands on the other side of a great River, which was to be pass'd over by boat. The Queen was not here, and seldom is, but keeps her Court commonly in another place more within land; yet I would not omit to see *Olala*, the rather because in the *Portugal* Histories it gives name to that Queen, as being that Land of hers which is nearest and best known to the *Portugals*, and, perhaps, the richest and fruitfullest which she now enjoyes. I found it to be a fat soil, the City lying between two Seas, to wit the Main-sea and the Bay, upon an arm of Land which the Port incloses; so that the situation is not onely pleasant, but might also be made very strong if it were in the hands of people that knew how to do it. It is all open, saving on one side towards the mouth of the Haven between the one Sea and the other, where there is drawn a weak wall with a ditch and two inconsiderable bastions.

The *Bazàr* is fairly good, and, besides necessaries for provisions, affords abundance of white and strip'd linnen cloth, which is made in *Olala*, but coarse, such as the people of that Country use. At the Town's end is a very pleasant Grove, and at the end thereof a great Temple,

---

[1] See *ante*, p. 36, note 2.

[2] This mode of spelling is unusual. The word is spelt "Cizar" by Beaumont and Fletcher and by Swift.

handsomely built for this Country and much esteem'd. *Olala* is inhabited confusedly, both by *Gentiles* who burn themselves[1] and also by *Malabar Moors.* About a mile off, Southwards, stands the Royal House, or Palace, amongst the aforesaid Groves, where the Queen resides when she comes hither sometimes. 'Tis large, enclos'd with a wall and trench, but of little moment. In the first entrance it hath a Gate with an open Porch, where the Guard is to stand; and within that a great void place, like a very large Court, on the far side whereof stands the House, whose inside I saw not, because the Court was not there; yet for this place it seem'd to have something of wild Majesty; behind it joyns to a very thick wood, serving both for delight and security in time of necessity. The way from the Palace to the City is almost wholly beset with Houses. Having seen as much as I desir'd I stay'd not to dine, but return'd to *Mangalòr;* there being always a passage-boat ready to carry people backwards and forwards.

VI.—*December* the third. Arriving not timely enough to hear Mass in the Church *Del Rosario* I went to *San Francesco*, where I heard Mass and a tolerably good Sermon, preached by an old Father call'd *Francesco dos Neves.* In the Evening I prepar'd to go to see the Queen of *Olala* at her Court, which was the design of this little peregrination. And, not finding Sig: *Paolo Sodrino* my friend at *Mangalòr*, by the aid of Sig: *Luis Gomes*, an unattached soldier, a Native of *Canandr*, but who had liv'd long at *Mangalòr*, and showed me much courtesy, I engaged a boat which should take me to the court of the said Queen, not by the Southern River which comes from the Territories of *Olala*, but by another more Northern River, (different from, and larger than, the before-mention'd little and swift one, over which I pass'd by a bridge to

---

[1] Or rather their (dead) friends and relations.

Banghel) above which large river lies the state of the said Queen and the place where she holds her Court, and which winds round a good extent of country at the back of *Mangalòr* towards the East, and falls into the Port of *Mangalòr*. I took with me also a *Brachman* call'd *Narsù*, a Native of *Mangalòr*, to serve me for an Interpreter with the Queen, (although my Christian Servant spoke the Language well) partly that I might have more persons with me to serve me, and partly because the *Brachman*, being a *Gentile*, known to, and vers'd in the ways of, this Court, might be more serviceable to me in many things than my own Servant; so, having provided what was needful, and prepar'd victuals to dine with upon the River by the way, which is somewhat long, I determin'd to set forth the next Morning.

On *December* the fourth, before daylight I took boat at *Mangalòr*, in which there were three Water-men, two of whom row'd at the Prow and one at the Poop, with a broad Oar which serv'd both for an Oar and a Helm. Having pass'd by *Banghel*[1] we enter'd into the great Northern River, in which on the left hand is a place where passage-boats laden with Merchandize pay a Toll[2] to the Ministers of *Venk-tapà Naieka*,[3] to whom the circumjacent Region is subject. Rowing a great way against the stream, the water whereof for a good space is salt, at length we stay'd to dine at a Town call'd *Salè*,[4] inhabited for the most part by *Moors*, and situate on the right bank as you go up the River.

This Town, with others round it, is subject to an Indian

---

[1] See p. 302.

[2] Transit dues on merchandise formerly prevailed everywhere in India, but they have, by the efforts of the British Government, been abolished to a great extent.

[3] See *ante*, p. 168, note 2, and p. 216.

[4] A small town of no importance.

Gentile Lord, call'd *Ramo Rau*,[1] who in all hath not above 2000 Paygods[2] of yearly Revenew, of which he payes about 800 to *Venk-tapà Naieka*, to whom he is Tributary. Nevertheless he wears the Title of King, and they call him *Omgiu Arsù*,[3] that is King of *Omgiù*,[4] which is his chief place. Having din'd and rested a while we continu'd our Voyage, and after a good space enter'd into the State of the Queen of *Olala*, to whom the Country on either side of the River belongs. The River is here very shallow, so that though our boat was but small yet in many places we stuck against the ground; at length about Evening we arriv'd at *Manèl*,[5] so they call the place where the Queen of *Olala* now resides, which is onely a Street of a few Cottages, or Sheds, rather than Houses; but the Country is open, fair and fruitful, inhabited by abundance of little Houses and Cottages, here and there, of Husband-men, besides those united to the great Street above-mentioned, call'd the *Bazàr*, or Market; all which are comprehended under the name of *Manèl*, which lies on the left bank of the River as you go against the stream.

VII.—Having landed, and going towards the *Bazàr* to get a Lodging in some House, we beheld the Queen coming alone in the same way without any other Woman, on foot, accompany'd onely with four, or six, foot Souldiers before her, who all were naked after their manner, saving that they had a cloth over their shame, and another like a sheet, worn across the shoulders like a belt; each of them had a Sword in his hand, or at most a Sword and Buckler; there were also as many behind her of the same

---

[1] More correctly *Rao*, a chief.

[2] See *ante*, p. 209, note 1.

[3] *I.e.*, *Arasu*, "King" (Tamil).

[4] A small town not marked in modern maps.

[5] A village which is not marked in maps of India.

sort, one of whom carry'd over her a very ordinary Umbrella made of Palm-leaves. Her Complexion was as black as that of a natural Æthiopian; she was corpulent and gross, but not heavy, for she seem'd to walk nimbly enough; her Age may be about forty years, although the Portugals had describ'd her to me as much older. She was cloth'd, or rather girded at the waist, with a plain piece of thick white Cotton, and bare-foot, which is the custom of the Indian *Gentile* Women, both high and low, in the house and abroad; and of Men too the most, and all the most ordinary, go unshod; some of the more grand wear Sandals, or Slippers; very few use whole Shoes covering all the Foot. From the waist upwards the Queen was naked, saving that she had a cloth ty'd round about her Head, and hanging a little down upon her Breast and Shoulders. In brief, her aspect and habit represented rather a dirty Kitchen-wench, or Laundress, than a delicate and noble Queen; whereupon I said within myself, Behold by whom are routed in *India* the Armies of the King of *Spain*, which in *Europe* is so great a matter! Yet the Queen shew'd her quality much more in speaking than by her presence; for her voice was very graceful in comparison with her Person, and she spoke like a prudent and judicious Woman. They had told me that she had no teeth, and therefore was wont to go with half her Face cover'd; yet I could not discover any such defect in her, either by my Eye, or by my Ear; and I rather believe that this covering of the Mouth, or half the Face, as she sometimes doth, is agreeable to the modest custom which I know to be common to almost all Women in the East.[1] I will not omit to state that though she was so corpulent, as I have mention'd, yet she seems not deform'd, but I imagine she was handsome in her Youth; and, indeed, the Report is

---

[1] See *ante*, p. 280, note 2.

that she hath been much of a Lady, of majestic beauty; though stern rather than gentle.[1]

As soon as we saw her coming we stood still, lay'd down our baggage upon the ground and went on one side to leave her the way to pass. Which she taking notice of, and of my strange habit, presently ask'd, Whether there was any among us that could speak the Language? Whereupon my Brachman, *Narsù*, step'd forth and answer'd, Yes; and I, after I had saluted her according to our manner, went near to speak to her, she standing still in the way with all her people to give us Audience.

She ask'd who I was, (being already inform'd, as one of her Souldiers told me, by a *Portugal* who was come about his business before me from *Mangalòr* to *Manèl*, that I was come thither to see her). I caus'd my Interpreter to tell her that I was "*Un Cavaliero Ponentino*", (*A Gentleman of the West*), who came from very far Countries; and, because other *Europeans* than *Portugals* were not usually seen in her Dominions, I caus'd her to be told that I was not a *Portugal* but a *Roman*, specifying too that I was not of the *Turks* of *Constantinople*, who in all the East are styl'd and known by the Name of *Rumi*[2]; but a Christian of *Rome*, where is the See of the Pope who is the Head of the Christians. That it was almost ten years since my first coming from home and wandering about the world, and seeing divers Countries and Courts of great Princes; and that being mov'd by the fame of her worth, which had long ago come to my Ears, I was come into this place purposely to see her and offer her my service. She ask'd, What Countries and Courts of Princes I had seen? I gave her a brief account of all; and she, hearing the Great

---

[1] In original: "particularly in regard to her person below the waist, where her corpulence, owing to the cotton cloth which she wears, which, accord ng to Indian fashion, is worn very tight, is very evident."

[2] See Yule's *Cathay and the Way Thither*, vol. ii, p. 427.

Turk, the Persian, the Moghol, and *Venk-tapà Naieka*[1] nam'd, ask'd, What then I came to see in these Woods of hers? intimating that her State was not worth seeing, after so many other great things as I said I had seen. I reply'd to her that it was enough for me to see her Person, which I knew to be of great worth; for which purpose alone I had taken the pains to come thither, and accounted the same very well imploy'd.

After some courteous words of thanks she ask'd me, If any sickness, or other disaster, had hapned to me in so remote and strange Countries, how I could have done, being alone, without any to take care of me? (a tender affection, and natural to the compassion of Women). I answer'd that in every place I went into I had God with me, and that I trusted in him. She ask'd me, Whether I left my Country upon any disgust, the death of any kindred, or beloved person, and therefore wander'd so about the world, (for in *India* and all the East some are wont to do so upon discontents, either of Love, or for the death of some dear persons, or for other unfortunate accidents; and, if *Gentiles*, they become *Gioghies*[2]; if *Mahometans*, *Dervisci* and *Abdali*[3]; all which are a sort of vagabonds, or despisers of the world, going almost naked, onely with a skin upon their Shoulders and a staff in their Hands, through divers Countries, like our Pilgrims; living upon Alms, little caring what befalls them, and leading a Life suitable to the bad disposition of their hearts).[4] I conceal'd my first

---

[1] See *ante*, pp. 168 and 216.

[2] See *ante*, p. 37, note 5.

[3] *I.e.*, *Darwesh* (from two words, meaning "one who waits at the door" (of God), and *Abd-Allah* (from *Abd*, "slave", and *Allah*, "God").

[4] See Elphinstone's *History of India*, pp. 14 and 60, 61. He says: "Many are decent and inoffensive religionists, but many are also shameless and importunate beggars, and worthless vagabonds of all descriptions." See also Dubois' *Mœurs des peuples de l'Inde*, vol. ii, p. 269.

misfortunes, and told the Queen that I left not my Country upon any such cause, but onely out of a desire to see divers Countries and customs, and to learn many things which are learnt by travelling the World; men who had seen and convers'd with many several Nations being much esteem'd in our parts; that indeed for some time since, upon the death of my Wife whom I lov'd much, though I were not in habit, yet in mind I was more than a *Gioghi* and little car'd what could betide me in the World. She ask'd me, What my design was now, and whither I directed my way? I answer'd that I thought of returning to my Country, if it should please God to give me life to arrive there. Many other questions she ask'd, which I do not now remember, talking with me, standing, a good while; to all which I answer'd the best I could. At length she bid me go and lodge in some house, and afterwards she would talk with me again at more convenience. Whereupon I took my leave, and she proceeded on her way, and, as I was afterwards told, she went about a mile off to see a work which she had in hand of certain Trenches to convey water to certain places whereby to improve them. I spoke to the Queen with my head uncover'd all the while; which courtesie, it being my custom to use it to all Ladies my equals, onely upon account of being such, I thought ought much rather to be us'd to this one who was a Queen and in her own Dominions, where I was come to visit her and to do her Honour.

VIII.—After she was gone her way, I with my people enter'd into a little village and there took a lodging in an empty house, belonging to a *Moor* of the Country and near the Palace; but I caus'd my diet to be prepar'd in an other house of a *Moorish* neighbour, that so I might have the convenience of eating flesh, or what I pleas'd, which in the houses of *Gentiles* would not be suffer'd, and as the inhabitants of *Manèl* are partly *Gentiles* and partly *Mala-*

bar Moors, who have also their *Meschitas*[1] there, I was not in want of good accommodation.

The name of the Queen of *Olala* is *Abag-devì-Ciautrù;* of which words *Abag* is her proper Name; *Devì*[2] signifies as much as Lady, and with this word they are also wont to signifie all their gods; nor have they any other in their Language to denote God but *Deù*, or *Deurù*, which are both one, and are equally applied to Princes; whereby it appears that the Gods of the *Gentiles* are for the most part nothing else but such Princes as have been famous in the world,[3] and deserv'd that Honor after their deaths; as likewise (which is my ancient opinion) that the word "God" wherewith we, by an introduc'd custom, denote the Supreme Creator, doth not properly signifie that First Cause, who alone ought to be ador'd by the World, but signifi'd at first either Great Lord, or the like[4]; whence it was attributed to Heroes and noted persons in the world, similar to the words of the Holy Scripture, *Filii Deorum*, *Filii Hominum;* and, consequently, that the gods of the *Gentiles*, though ador'd and worship'd both in ancient and modern

---

[1] Masjid, or Mosque. See p. 228, note 1.

[2] Literally, "bright". From Sanskrit root, *div*, "to shine". See Prof. M. Müller's *Hibbert Lectures of* 1878, p. 4, where it is said: "'Deva', as 'Deus' in Latin, came to mean 'God', because it originally meant 'bright', and we cannot doubt that something beyond the meaning of brightness had attached itself to the word 'Deva' before the ancestors of the Indians and Italians broke up from their common home."

[3] This statement is no doubt true to a certain extent. See Sir J. Lubbock's *Origin of Civilization*, p. 353 *et seq.*, where he quotes the following passage from the "Wisdom of Solomon": "And so the multitude took him now for a god, which a little before was but honoured as a man." See also Dubois, *Mœurs des peuples de l'Inde*, vol. ii, p. 292.

[4] The word translated here as "God" is, of course, *Dio*, and is no doubt derived (as already stated) from the Sanskrit *div*. Hence came the name *Dyaus* (Illuminator), and the Latin *Deus*. (See Prof. Max Müller, *Hibbert Lectures of* 1878, p. 144). The English word "God" has of course a quite different history.

times, were never held by them in that degree wherein we hold God, the Creator of the Universe, and wherein almost all Nations of the world always held and do hold him; (some calling him *Causa Prima;* others *Anima Mundi;* others *Perabrahmi*,[1] as the *Gentiles* do at this day in *India:*) but that the other gods are, and were always, rather but as Saints are amongst us; of the truth whereof I have great Arguments, at least amongst the Indian *Gentiles;* or if more than Saints, yet at least only Deifi'd by favour, and made afterwards *Divi*, as *Hercules*, *Romulus*, *Augustus*, etc., were amongst the *Romans*.[2]

But to return to our purpose, they told me the word *Ciautrù*,[3] (the last in the Queen of *Olala's* Name) was a Title of Honour peculiar to all the Kings and Queens of *Olala*, and therefore possibly signifies either Prince, or King and Queen, or the like. As to this Country being subject to a Woman, I understood from intelligent persons of the Country, that in *Olala* Men were, and are always, wont to reign, and that 'tis a custom receiv'd in *India* amongst the greatest part of the *Gentiles*,[4] that the Sons do not succeed their Fathers, but the Sons of their Sisters; they accounting the Female-line more certain, as indeed

---

[1] *I.e.*, *Param*, or *Para*, *Brahma*, the chief *Brahma* (or Pervader) (see *ante*, p. 73, note 1), from the Sanskrit root, *brih*.

[2] For a comparison of the Hindu deities with those worshipped by Greeks and Romans, see Dubois' *Mœurs des peuples de l'Inde*, vol. ii, p. 293. In the consideration of the question here raised the distinction (pointed out by Sir Monier Williams in *Modern India*, pp. 155 and 191) between Brahmanism and Hindúism must be borne in mind.

[3] Probably meant for *Kshatrya*, the name of the second, or warlike, caste, from which kings are selected. Queens and princesses of the Malabar royal families are restricted in their choice of paramours to men of either the Kshatrya (military) caste, or Brahmans, and hence the descendants of the former caste style themselves "Kshatryas" (see Sir R. Burton's *Goa and the Blue Mountains*, p. 210).

[4] This applies in India to some of the Southern races only. See *ante*, p. 218, note 2.

it is, than the Male. Yet the last King of *Olala* having neither Nephews nor other Legitimate Heirs, his Wife succeeded him; and she, also dying without other Heirs, left this *Abag-devi*, who was her Sister, to succeed her. To whom, because she is a Woman and the descent is certain, is to succeed a Son of hers, of whom I shall hereafter make mention; but to him, being a Man, not his own Sons, but the Son of one of his Sisters, hereafter likewise mention'd, is to succeed.[1]

IX.—Not to conceal what I know of the History of this Queen, I shall add that, after her Assumption of the Throne upon the death of her Sister, she was married for many years to the King of *Banghel*, who now is a fugitive, depriv'd of his Dominions, but then reign'd in his own Country which borders upon hers. Yet, though they were Husband and Wife, (more for Honor's sake than any thing else) they liv'd not together, but apart, each in their own Lands: on the confines whereof, either upon Rivers, where they caus'd Tents to be erected over boats, or in other places of delight, they came to see and converse with one another; the King of *Banghel* wanting not other Wives and Women who accompany'd him wherever he went. 'Tis reported that this Queen had the Children, which she hath, by this King of *Banghel*, if they were not by some other secret and more intimate Lover; for, they say, she wants not such.

The Matrimony and good Friendship having lasted many years between the King of *Banghel* and the Queen, I know not upon what occasion discord arose between them, and such discord that the Queen divorc'd him, sending back to him, (as the custom is in such case) all the Jewels which he had given her as his Wife. For this, and perhaps for other

---

1 For observations on this custom see Wilks' *Hist. of Mysore*, pp. 121 and 122, and Lubbock's *Origin of Civilization*, p. 151 *et seq.*

causes, he became much offended with the Queen, and the rupture proceeded to a War: during which it so fortun'd that one day as she was going in a boat upon one of those Rivers, not very well guarded, he, sending his people with other boats in better order, took her and had her in his power: yet with fair carriage and good words she prevail'd so far that he let her go free and return to her Country. In revenge of this injury she forthwith rais'd War against the King of *Banghel*, who relied upon the aid of the neighbouring *Portugals* because he was confederate with them, and (as they say of many Royolets of *India*) Brother in Arms to the King of *Portugal.* The Queen, to counterpoise that force, call'd to her assistance against the King of *Banghel*, and the *Portugals* who favour'd him, the neighbouring King *Venk-tapà Naieka*,[1] who was already become very potent and fear'd by all his Neighbours, and under his protection and obedience she put her self. *Venk-tapà Naieka* sent a powerful Army in favour of the Queen, took all the King of *Banghel's* Territories and made them his own, destroying the Fort which was there; he also made prey of divers other petty Lords thereabouts, demolishing their strength, and rendering them his Tributaries; one of whom was the Queen of *Curnat*,[2] who was also confederate with the *Portugals*, and no friend to her of *Olala:* he came against *Mangalòr*,[3] where in a battle rashly undertaken by the *Portugals* he defeated a great number; and, (in short) the flower and strength of *India*,[4] carrying the Ensigns, Arms and Heads of the slain to *Ikkerì*[5] in triumph. He did not take *Mangalòr*, because he would not, answering the Queen of *Olala* who urg'd

[1] See *ante*, pp. 168 and 216.

[2] *I.e.*, Karnáta, or the Kanarese country. See *ante*, p. 168, note 1.

[3] See *ante*, p. 212, note 2.

[4] This statement must be accepted *cum grano*.

[5] See *ante*, p. 216, note 1.

him to it; That they could do that any time with much facility, and that 'twas best to let those Portugals remain in that small place, (which was rather a House than a Fortress) in respect of the Traffick and Wares which they brought to the benefit of their Countries. After which he came to a Treaty with the *Portugals*, by which he restor'd the Ensigns he had taken from them, and by their means the King of *Banghel* surrendered the Fort, which *Venk-tapà*, as I said before, demolish'd; besides making other conditions which are now under consideration, according as is above-mention'd in my Relation of the Embassie to *Ikkerì*.[1]

This was the War of *Banghel*, in which the Queen got the better of the King and the *Portugals*, of which she was very proud; yet, withall, her Protector, *Venk-tapà Naieka*, who is very rapacious and little faithful, sufficiently humbled her, and she got not much benefit by him, saving quiet living; for, besides his subjecting her to his obedience in a manner, she was necessitated, whether by agreement, or violence, I know not, to resign to him *Berdrete*,[2] which is the best and richest City she had, together with much Land on the confines of *Venk-tapà*, and of the inner part of her Country, which amounted to a good part of her Dominions; however at present she lives and governs her Country in Peace, being respected by all her Neighbours. This Queen had an elder Son than he who now lives; he was call'd *Cic-Rau-Ciauerù*,[3] and dy'd a while since. The *Portugals* say that she herself caus'd poyson to be given him because the young man, being grown up and of much spirit, aspir'd to deprive her of the Government and make

---

[1] See *ante*, pp. 285-86.

[2] Not traceable in modern maps.

[3] Probably meant for "Chikka-Rao", or "Junior Chief". "Ciauerù" seems to be a misprint for "Ciautru", the title already mentioned at p. 312, *quod vide*.

himself Master: which is possible enough; for divers other Princes in the world have procur'd the death of their own Children upon jealousie of State; so prevalent is that cursed, enormous, ambition of ruling. Yet, such an impiety not being evident to me concerning the Queen, I will not wrongfully defame her, but rather believe that the young man dy'd a natural death, and with regret to her. So neither do I believe what the *Portugals*, incens'd against her, further report, namely that she hath attempted to poyson this second Son, but that it succeeded not, he being advertis'd thereof by his Nurse who was to give him the poyson; since I see that this Son lives with her, in the same place and house, peaceably, which would not be if there were any such matter: nor can I conceive why she should go about to extinguish all her own Issue in this manner, having now no other Heir born of herself.

X.—*December* the fifth. The Queen of *Olala's* Son, who, though he govern not, (for the Mother administers all alone, and will do so as long as she lives) yet for honor's sake is styl'd King, and call'd *Celuuà Rairù*,[1] (of which words Celuuà is his proper name, and Rairù his title) sent for the Brachman, my Interpreter, in the Morning, and, discoursing long with him, made particular inquiry about me, telling him that he understood I was much whiter than the *Portugals* who us'd to trade in that Country and of a very good presence and consequently must needs be a person of quality. In conclusion he bid him bring me to him when my convenience serv'd; for he was very desirous to see me and speak with me. This Message being related to me, I let pass the hour of dinner, (because, having no appetite, and finding my stomack heavy, I would not dine this day) and, when it seem'd a convenient time, I went

[1] Probably meant for "Saluva Rairu", or King Saluva. Unknown to fame, so far as has been ascertained.

(with my Interpreter) cloth'd in black, after my custom; yet not with such wide and long Breeches down to the heels, as the *Portugals* for the most part are wont to wear in *India*,[1] in regard of the heat, (for they are very commodious, covering all the Leg and saving the wearing of Stockings, so that the Leg is naked and free) but with Stockings and Garters and ordinary Breeches, without a Cloak, (though it is us'd by the *Portugal* Souldiers in *India*, even of greatest quality) but with a large Coat, or Cassock,[2] open at the sides, after the Country fashion.

The Palace, which may rather be call'd *Capanna Reale* (a *Royal Lodge*), is entered by a Gate like the grate, or lattice,[3] of our Vine-yards at *Rome*, ordinary enough, placed in the midst of a field, which like them is divided by a small hedge from the neighbouring fields. Within the Gate is a broad Walk, or Alley, on the right side whereof is a spacious cultivated plot, at the end of which the Walk turns to the right hand, and there, upon the same plot, stands the Royal Mansion, having a prospect over all the said great green field. In the middle of this second turn of the Walk you enter into the House, ascending seven, or eight, wooden stairs, which lead into a large Porch, the length of which is equal to the whole fore-part of the House. This Porch was smeared with cow-dung after their manner, the walls about shining, and being painted with a bad red colour much us'd by them. The fore-part of it, which is all open, is upheld by great square posts, of no great height, for 'tis their custom to make all buildings, especially Porches, low in respect of their breadth and length, with very broad eaves; which is, I believe, by reason of the great heat of the Country, where they have more need of shade and coolness, than of air, or light. Directly opposite to the

[1] *I.e.*, Paijámas, or loose trousers.
[2] See *ante*, p. 43, note 4.
[3] In original, "Cancello".

stairs, in the middle of the Porch, was another small Porch, which was the only entrance into the inner part of the building.

Within the little Porch was a small room, long and narrow, where the King sate near the wall on the left side; and he sate upon the ground after the Eastern manner, upon one of those coarse cloths, which in *Persia* and *Turkie* are call'd *Kielim*[1] and serve for poor people; nor was it large, but onely so much as to contain the Person of the King, the rest of the room being bare, saving that it was smoothed over with Cow-dung.[2] Beside the King, but a little farther on his left hand, sate upon a little mat, sufficient onely to contain him, a Youth of about fifteen, or eighteen, years of age, call'd *Balè Rairù*,[3] who is his nephew, and is to succeed him, being the Son of his deceased Sister, who was daughter of the present Queen.[4] The Father of this Youth was a neighbouring *Gentile* Prince, whom they call the King of *Cumbià*,[5] (or perhaps more correctly, *Kunblè*) call'd by his proper name *Ramò-Nàto-Ari*[6]; of which words *Ramò-Nàto* is the proper name, and *Ari*[7] the title. They said he was still living, though others at *Goa* told me afterwards that he was dead. But being[8] this young *Balè Rairù* was not to succeed his Father, but had Right of Inheritance in *Olala*, therefore he liv'd not in his Father's Country, but here at *Manèl* with his Grand-

---

1 See *ante*, p. 253. An interesting article on Turkish and Persian carpets, by Mr. Church, will be found in *The Portfolio* of April 1892.

2 As to this use of cow-dung, see *ante*, pp. 87, 230, and 231.

3 See *ante*, p. 316, note 1.

4 As to this rule of succession, see *ante*, p. 218, note 2.

5 Marked "Coombla" in Wyld's map of India. It is a small town on the coast, of no importance.

6 More correctly "Rámnáth Adi".

7 *I.e.*, Rám, or Ráma, an incarnation of Vishnu (see *ante*, p. 223), *Nath*, "Lord", and *Adi*, or *Ari*, "First" or "Chief".

8 For "since"; see *ante*, p. 27, note 1.

mother and his Uncle. None other sate with the King, but three, or four, of his more considerable servants stood in the room, talking with him; and in the great Porch, outside the little one, stood in files on either side other servants of inferior degree, two of whom nearest the entrance fanned the Air with fans of green Taffeta[1] in their Hands, as if to drive away the flyes from the King, or from the entrance, a Ceremony us'd, as I have said elsewhere, by Indian Princes for Grandeur[2]; and they told me the use of a green colour was a ceremony too, and the proper badge of the King of *Olala*, for the King of *Banghel* uses Crimson; other Princes white, as I saw us'd by *Venk-tapà Naieka*[3]; and others, perhaps, other colours. A small company indeed, and a poor appearance for a King; which call'd to my remembrance those ancient Kings, *Latinus*, *Turnus* and *Evander*,[4] who, 'tis likely, were Princes of the same sort.[5]

Such persons as came to speak with the King stood without in the Porch, either on one side, or in the middle of the little Porch; either because the room was very small and not sufficient for many people; or rather, as I believe, for more State. The King was young, not above seventeen

---

[1] In the original *Zendado*, which means a thin kind of silk cloth. "Taffeta" is so called from the Persian word *Taftan*, "to weave". A remarkable instance of the rapid naturalization of a foreign word is found in the use of the word "Taffata" as early as in Shakespeare's time, to denote flimsy, or frivolous talk. (See *Love's Labour's Lost*, Act v, Sc. 2):

> "Taffata phrases, silken terms precise,
> Three-pil'd hyperboles, spruce affectation,
> Figures pedantical."

See also *Love's Labour's Lost*, Act v, Sc. 2:

> "Beauties no richer than rich taffata."

[2] See *ante*, p. 251.

[3] See *ante*, p. 251.

[4] See Virgil's *Æneid*, vii, viii, and ix. The last name is written as "Austè" in the original.

[5] "Tum res inopes Evandrus habebat." (Virg., *Æn.*, viii, 100.)

years of age, as they told me, yet his aspect showed him to be older; for he was very fat and lusty, as far as I could conjecture of him while sitting, and, besides, he had long hairs of a beard upon his face, which he suffer'd to grow without cutting, though they appeared to be but the first down. In complexion he was dusky,[1] not black, as his Mother is, but rather of an earthy colour, as almost all the *Malabaris*[2] generally are. He had a louder and bigger voice than Youths of his age use to have, and in his speaking, gestures and all other things he shew'd Judgment and manly gravity. From the girdle upwards he was all naked, saving that he had a thin cloth painted with several colours[3] cast across his shoulders. The hair of his head was long after their manner, and ty'd in one great knot, which hung on one side wrapt up in a little plain piece of linnen, which looked like a night-cap fallen on one side. From the girdle downwards I saw not what he wore, because he never rose from his seat, and the Chamber was somewhat dark; besides that the painted cloth on his shoulders hung down very low. His Nephew who sate beside him was not naked, but clad in a wholly white garment; and his Head was wrapt up in a greater fold of white cloth, like a little Turban.[4]

XI.—When I came before the King his Men made me come near to the little Porch in the midst of them, where standing by myself, after the first salutations, the King presently bid me cover my head; which I forthwith did without further intreaty; though with his Mother, being a Lady, I was willing to superabound in Courtesie, speaking to her all the time uncover'd. But with the Son, who was a Man, I was minded to enjoy the priviledge of my

[1] In original, "basso".
[2] See *ante*, p. 121, note 4.
[3] *I.e.*, chintz. See *ante*, p. 45, note 1.
[4] See *ante*, p. 248, note 4.

descent, and to receive the favour which he did me as due to my quality. At first they offer'd me nothing to sit upon, nor was it fitting to sit down upon the bare ground. Yet, to shew some difference between my self and the by-standers, after I had put on my Hat I lean'd upon my Sword and so talk'd as long as I was standing, which was not long, the King, who at first sat side-wise, turning himself directly towards me, although by so doing he turn'd his back to his Nephew. He ask'd me almost all the same questions as his Mother had done[1]; Whence I came? What Countries I had travell'd through? What Princes I had seen? Whether I had left my own Country upon any misfortune? Or why? How I would have done thus alone in strange Countries, in case of sickness or other accidents? To all which I answer'd as I had done to his Mother; and upon my saying that I wander'd thus alone, up and down, trusting in the help of God, he ask'd me, Who was my God? I answer'd him, (pointing upwards) "The God of Heaven, the Creator of the Universe"; whereupon certain Souldiers there present, (in all likelyhood *Moors*) as if applauding me, said, *Ah! Chodia, Chodia*,[2] which in the Persian Tongue signifies *Lord*, and is meant for God; inferring that I worship'd the true God, whom the *Moors* pretend to know, in opposition to the Idols of the *Gentiles* of the Country; and they us'd the Persian word *Chodia*, because that probably the Sect of Mahomet came into these parts from *Persia*,[3] (which is not very remote from *India*) as also from *Arabia;* or, perhaps,

---

[1] See *ante*, pp. 308-10.

[2] For *Khúda*, "Lord" or "God" (Arabic).

[3] The first invasion of India by Muhammadans (A.D. 664) was made by Arabs. But they only penetrated as far as Multán. The first invasion of the western coast of India, to which P. della Valle probably refers in this passage, was by a Persian army sent from Shiráz in A.D. 711. (See Elphinstone's *Hist. of India*, pp. 259-61.)

because the Indians of the Territory of *Idal-Sciàh*[1] and *Dacàn*,[2] being in great part *Moors*, use much the Persian Tongue, which is spoken in the Courts of those Princes no less than their natural Language[3]; with whom these other Indians more inland to the South have, by reason of neighbourhood, communication both in Religion and Speech.

The King told me several times that he had very great contentment in seeing me and that no European of any quality had ever been in his Country; that my person well shew'd of what quality I was. Nor was he mistaken herein; for what other person would ever go out of *Europe* into his Country? unless some *Portugal* Merchant, one of those who come hither for the most part to seek wood to make masts and yards for Ships; these Woods abounding with very goodly Trees. I told him I was sorry I had nothing worthy to present to him; that in my Country there wanted not gallant things for his Highness; but, it being so many years since my departure thence, and my Travels extending so far, I had nothing left as I desir'd; yet, as a memorial of my service, I should venture to give him a small trifle from my Country. Whereupon I caus'd my Interpreter, who carried it, to offer him a little Map of the World which I had brought with me out of *Italy;* telling him what it was, and how all the Countries, Lands, Seas and Islands of the world were exactly delineated in it, with their Names set to each place in our Tongue, and all that was necessary to make him understand what it was. The King was greatly pleas'd with it and desir'd to see several Countries, where they lay, and how great they were, asking me sundry questions about them; but, being[4] he understood

---

[1] See *ante*, p. 143, note 5, and p. 149.
[2] See *ante*, p. 141, note 1.
[3] See *ante*, p. 150, note 2.
[4] For "since"; see p. 28, note 1.

not our letters written therein, he satisfi'd himself with the sight onely and with shewing it to all the by-standers as a curious and ingenious Work of Art. Then he ask'd me whether I could eat in their Houses, or of their meats; for he desir'd to give me something to eat. I answer'd that I could, and that the purity of our Religion consisted not in the eating, or touching, of things, but in doing good works. He earnestly desir'd of me that I would stay awhile till some meat were prepar'd for me; for by all means he would have me eat something in his House, and would himself see me eating. I told him that, if his intention were onely to give me meat, the time was already past, nor was I dispos'd to eat; but if it were to see me eat, I could not eat in that place after the fashion of my Country, not having there the preparations necessary thereunto, so that his Highness[1] would not see what, perhaps, he desir'd; and therefore I besought him to excuse me. Nevertheless he was so urgent for it, that not to appear discourteous, I consented to obey him. And, till the meat came, the King commanded some of his Servants to conduct me to sit down by them in the Porch, where I might sit after our manner, but not in the King's sight.

Hereupon I with-drew with some of his Men to entertain me, and in the mean time the King remain'd talking with the rest of them concerning me, commending me much for several things, but, above all, for a good presence, for speaking truly and discreetly like a Gentleman, and for my civil deportment. But, before I proceed further, I will here present you with a rough and unmeasur'd draught of the King's House and the place wherein he was; so far as may suffice for the better understanding of what is already said and is to follow after.

[1] As to this title of "Highness" (and other titles), see Selden's *Titles of Honour*, Part I, p. 140, and D'Israeli's *Curiosities of Literature*, p. 66.

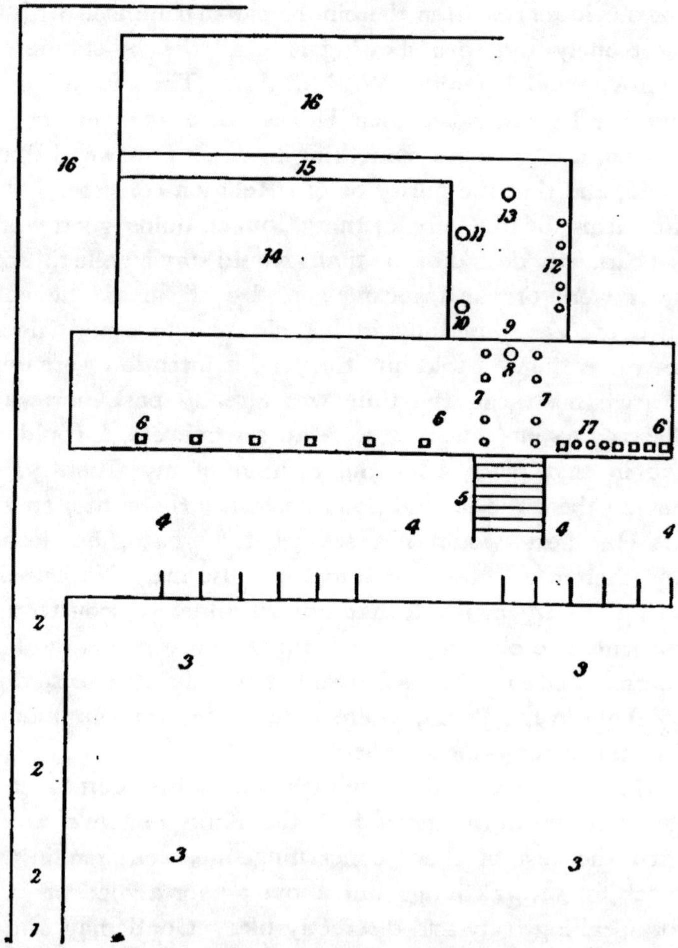

1. At the foot of this design is the Gate of the Palace.

2. The Walk leading to it, and included within the enclosure of the palace.

3. A great plain and sown field.

4. The turning of the Walk before the House, where the short lines, intersecting the outward line towards the field, represent the Trees planted at equal distances and in order.

5. Seven or eight wooden Stairs leading up to the Porch.

6. The Porch of the House, in which the little squares, near the

outer lines, are the wooden pillars which support it, and the surrounding lines are the walls.

7. The King's Servants, standing on either side without the little Porch of the Chamber.

8. I, *Pietro Della Valle*, when I first talk'd with the King, standing.

9. The Room wherein the King was.

10. The King, sitting on the ground upon a little coarse cloth.

11. The King's Nephew, sitting on the ground upon a little mat.

12. The King's Servants standing.

13. I, *Pietro Della Valle*, sitting in the said room on the ground upon a little low Table, whilst I ate and discours'd with the King a very long time together; the place mark'd with the number 13 being that where they set the meat before me.

14. A small open Court.

15. A small slope, or bank, in the said Court, leading from the more inward Chambers to that where the King was.

16. Inner Chambers and Lodgings, which what they were I saw not; but they were of very bad earthen buildings, low and covered with thatch, like Cottages, that is with Palm-leaves; which are always to be understood when I speak of Cottages, or Houses, cover'd with thatch in *India*.

17. I, *Pietro Della Valle*, sitting between two of the King's Servants upon the side of the Porch, (after having spoken the first time with the King) entertaining me while the meat was preparing.

XII.—The meat was not long in preparing, and, it being now in order, the King call'd for me again to enter into the room where it stood ready; and one of the *Brachmans*, who spoke *Portugal* and was wont to accompany me, ask'd me Whether it would not be more convenient for me to ungird my Sword and put off my Cassack[1]? I answer'd, that my Cassack gave me no trouble, nor was there occasion to lay it off; but my Sword might be laid aside, and, therewith ungirding it, I gave it him to hold: which I did the rather because, all Princes being commonly suspicious, I imagin'd the King would not like my entring in with Arms; and he that goes into another's House, to visit him and do him honour, is not to disgust, but to comply with, him in all points. So I enter'd without a Sword, but yet

[1] See *ante*, p. 43, *note*.

with shoes and stockings on, though with them it be unusual to do so; for none should enter into that place but bare-foot, and the King himself is so there, according to their custom: nor did I scruple[1] as to their taxing me with uncleanliness, as undoubtedly they would have done in *Turkie* and *Persia* if I had enter'd into their rooms with shoes, or slippers, on, because there all the rooms are cover'd with Carpets, but there was not any in these of the King, onely the pavement was gloss'd with Cow-dung.[2] Wherefore, as to have put off my shoes, (besides that they are not so easily slip'd off as Pantofles, nor does it shew well to do so) would have been an exorbitant and unnecessary humility, so to enter with them on was to me convenient and decorous, without any liableness to be accus'd of uncleanliness, being[3] the floore was not cover'd; if it had been so with Carpets, or the like, as 'tis usual in *Turkie* and *Persia*, then, (to avoid seeming slovenly by soiling the place with my dirty shoes and my self by sitting upon them,[4] which indeed is not handsome) I should have caus'd my shoes to be pull'd off; for which purpose I had accordingly caus'd a pair of slippers of our fashion to be brought along with me, in case there should have been need of them; our kind of shoes being not so easie to be put off, by shaking the foot alone without the help of the hand, as those which for this end are us'd by all the Eastern people.[5]

Entering in this manner and saluting the King as I pass'd I went to sit down at the upper end of the Chamber, (as 'tis above describ'd) where they had prepar'd a little

---

[1] So Milton: "He scrupled not to eat against his better knowledge" (*Par. Lost*, ix, 997).

[2] See *ante*, p. 231.

[3] For "since"; see *ante*, p. 28, *note*.

[4] This result would follow from the adoption of the usual deferential posture of kneeling and sitting on the heels.

[5] Shoes, or slippers, open at the heels being usually worn by Oriental nations.

square board of the bigness of an ordinary stool, which might serve for a single person, but rais'd no more than four fingers above the ground; upon this I sat down, crossing my Legs one over the other; and that little elevation help'd me to keep them out from under me, with such decency as I desir'd. Right before the seat, upon the bare floor, (the Indians not using any Tables) they had spread, instead of a dish, (as their custom is, especially with us Christians, with whom they will not defile their own vessels; it not being lawful for them ever to eat again in those wherein we have eaten) a great Leaf of that Tree which the *Arabians* and *Persians* call *Mouz*,[1] the *Portugals* in *India Fichi d' India*, *Indian Fig-trees;* and upon the said Leaf they had lay'd a good quantity of Rice, boyl'd, after their manner, onely with water and salt; but for sauce to it there stood on one side a little vessel made of Palm-leaves, full of very good butter melted. There lay also upon another Leaf one of those Indian Figgs, clean and pared; and hard by it a quantity of a certain red herb,[2] commonly eaten in *India*, and call'd by the *Portugals Brèdo*, (which yet is the general appellation of all sort of herbs). In another place lay several fruits us'd by them, and, amongst the rest, slices of the *Bambù*,[3] or *great Indian Cane;* all of them preserv'd in no bad manner, which they call *Acciaò*,[4] besides one sort pickled with Vinegar, as our Olives are. Bread there was none, because they use none, but the Rice is instead of it; which was no great defect to me, because I am now accustom'd to do without it, and eat

---

1 For *Mouzah*, the Arabic name of *Musa Paradisiaca*, the "plantain"; or *Musa sapientum*, usually called *banana*.

2 Perhaps the tomato (*Lycopersicum esculentum*).

3 See p. 220, note 3.

4 Properly *Achár*, a native word for any kind of pickle. Mandelslo, speaking of mangoes, says: "They (*i.e.*, the natives of India) get them while they are green, and put them up in salt, vinegar and garlick, and then they call them 'Mangas d'Achar'."

very little. The King very earnestly pray'd me to eat, excusing himself often that he gave me so small an entertainment on the sudden; for if he had known my coming beforehand he would have prepar'd many *Carils*[1] and divers other more pleasing meats.

Caril is a name which in *India* they give to certain Broths made with Butter, the Pulp of Indian Nuts, (instead of which in our Countries Almond Milk may be us'd, being equally good and of the same virtue) and all sorts of Spices, particularly Cardamoms[2] and Ginger, (which we use but little) besides herbs, fruits and a thousand other condiments. The Christians, who eat everything, add Flesh, or Fish, of all sorts, especially Hens, or Chickens, cut in small pieces, sometimes Eggs, which, without doubt, make it more savory: with all which things is made a kind of Broth, like our *Guazetti*, or *Pottages*, and it may be made in many several ways; this Broth, with all the abovesaid ingredients, is afterwards poured in good quantity upon the boyled Rice, whereby is made a well-tasted mixture, of much substance and light digestion, as also with very little pains; for it is quickly boyled, and serves both for meat and bread together. I found it very good for me, and used it often, as also the *Pilào* elsewhere spoken of,[3] and made of Rice and butter boyled with it and flesh fryed therein, besides a thousand other preparations of several sorts which are so common to everybody in *Asia;* and I account it one of the best and wholesomest meats that can be eaten in the world, without so many Artificial Inventions as our gutlings of *Europe* (withall procuring to themselves a thousand infirmities of Gouts, Catarrhs and other Maladies, little

---

[1] This is our well-known "curry" in disguise. The word is derived from the Persian *Khúrdi.*

[2] *Cardamomum repens.* (See Eastwick's *Handbook*, p. 299.)

[3] In one of the Letters from Persia.

known to the Orientals[1]) daily devise to the publick damage.

But to return to my Relation, the King told me he would have given me a better entertainment, but yet desired me to receive this small extemporary one, and eat without any respect, or shyness of those that were present; for thereby he should understand that I liked it. I answer'd that the Favour and Courtesie which his Highness shew'd me was sufficient: but as for eating, the time being now past, I did it onely to obey him; and so, to comply with him, although I had little will to eat, I tasted lightly here and there of those fruits and herbs, wherewith my Hand was a little soiled, which upon occasion I wiped with my handkerchief, being[2] they use no other Table-linnen, nor had any laid for me. The King, seeing that I touched not the Rice, spoke to me several times to eat of it, and to pour upon it some of that butter which stood by it prepared. I did not, because I would not grease my self, there being no Spoon; for the *Indians* eat every thing with the Hand alone and so do the *Portugals;* I know not whether as having learnt so to do in *India* of the *Indians*, or whether it be their own natural custom; but they too, for the most part, eat with the Hand alone, using no spoon, and that very ill-favouredly; for with the same Hand, if need be, they mingle together the Rice, the Butter, the *Caril*[3] and all other things how greasie soever, daubing themselves up to the wrist, or rather washing their Hands in their meat before they eat it; (a fashion indeed sufficiently coarse for people of *Europe*): and though at

---

1. Gout is certainly not prevalent in India, even if known there. By some physicians gout is attributed to the eating of animal food, and this theory, if true, may account for the exemption of natives of India from the disease.

2. For "since"; see *ante*, p. 28, *note*.

3. See *ante*, p. 328, *note* 1.

their Tables, which are handsome enough, there want not knives, spoons and silver forks, and some few sometimes make use thereof, yet the universal custom is such that few use them, even when they lie before them. The truth is they wash their Hands many times during one dinner, to wit as often as they grease them, but they wipe them not first; for neither do they make use of napkins, whether they have any before them (as for the most part they have) or not; but, besides the trouble of washing so often, in my judgment there is but little neatnesse in washing their greasy Hands after that manner; and I know not whether the washing cleanses, or defiles more. I, being accustomed to the neatness of *Italy*,[1] could not conform to slovenliness; and, let them cover this barbarous custom with what pretence they please, either of military manners, or what else they think fit, 'tis little trouble for a civil Man to carry even in the Warr and Travels, amongst other necessary things, a spoon, knife and fork, wherewith to eat handsomely. The Turks themselves, barbarous as they are, yet are so much observers of this that amongst them there is not the meanest Souldier, but who, if he hath not other better convenience, at least carries his spoon[2] ty'd to the belt of his sword.

---

[1] On this point, a curious passage from Coryat's *Crudities*, vol. i, p. 106, may be quoted: "I observed a custom in all those Italian cities and towns, through the which I passed, that is not used in any other country that I saw in my travels, neither do I think that any other nation of Christendom doth use it, but only Italy. The Italians, and also most other strangers that are commorant in Italy, do always at their meals use a little fork when they cut their meat." Then he describes how they use the fork and continues: "The reason of this their curiosity is because the Italian cannot by any means endure to have his dish touched with fingers, seeing all men's fingers are not alike clean." And then he proceeds to tell how he himself adopted the custom, and, when he made use of his fork in England, was called "Furcifer" by his friends.

[2] This is not the custom among the Turks at the present day.

In short the King frequently urg'd me to eat of the Rice, and I as often refused with several excuses; at last he was so importunate that I was fain to tell him I could not eat that meat in that manner because I had not my Instruments. The King told me I might eat after my own way and take what Instruments I would, which should be fetch'd from my House. I reply'd divers times that there was no need, and that my tasting of it was enough to testifie my obedience. However by all means he would have what was necessary fetch'd from my House. So I sent my *Brachman* and my Christian Servant with my key, and they, the King so enjoyning, went and return'd in a moment, for my House was directly over against the Palace. They brought me a spoon, a silver fork and a clean and fine napkin, very handsomely folded in small plaits; this I spread upon my knees which it cover'd down to my feet, and so I began to eat Rice, pouring the butter upon it with a spoon, and the other things with the fork, after a very cleanly manner, without greasing my self, or touching any thing with my Hands, as 'tis my custom. The King and all the rest admir'd these exquisite, and to them unusual, modes; crying out with wonder *Deuru*, *Deuru*, that I was a *Deuru*, that is a great Man, a God, as they speak. I told the King that for eating according to my custom there needed much preparation of a table, linnen, plates, dishes, cups and other things; but I was now travelling through strange Countries, and treated my self "*alla Soldatesca*", after the Souldiers' fashion, leading the life of a *Gioghi*, and consequently had not with me such things as were necessary. The King answer'd that it suffic'd him to see thus much, since thereby he easily imagin'd how all my other things would be, and that, in brief, he had never seen any European like me, and that it was a great contentment to him to see me. He desir'd me several times to eat more, perceiving that I rather tasted of things to please him than to satiate my self. He caus'd divers other Fruits, pickled with Vinegar and Salt, to be brought me by a Woman who came from the inner rooms through the little Court; as also for my drink (in a cup made likewise of Palm-leaves[1]) a kind of warm Milk, to which they are accustom'd, and which seem'd to me very good.

XIII.—Both before and after and whilst I was eating I had much discourse with the King, who entertain'd me, sitting there, above two long hours; but, not remembring it all, I shall onely set down some of the most remarkable particulars. He ask'd me concerning our Countries, all the Christian Princes, with the other *Moors* and Pagan Princes whom I had seen; concerning the power and Armies of each and their Grandeur in comparison of others.[2] On which occasion I told him that amongst us Christians the prime Prince was the Pope, my Lord, the Head of the Church and the High-Priest, to whom all others gave Obedience; the next was the Emperor, in dignity the first of Souldiers, or secular Princes; that the first Nation was *France;* and that for Territory and Riches *Spain* had most of all; with many other circumstances too long to be rehearsed. Which discourse led me to tell him, as I did, that the King of *Portugal*, as they call him, that is the King of *Spain*, so much esteem'd in *India*, pay'd Tribute to our Lord the Pope for the Kingdom of *Naples*, which he held of His Holiness in homage; for which he had a great conceit of the Pope. As to the Moorish Princes I said concerning the *Moghòl*,[3] whom he much cryed up to me, that we held him indeed for the richest in treasure, but otherwise had greater esteem of the Turk and the Persian, because, though the *Moghòl* hath an

---

[1] See *ante*, p. 294, note 7.

[2] "The usual exchange of questions and answers which compose the small-talk of an Oriental visit" (Burton, *Goa, etc.*, p. 179).

[3] See *ante*, p. 48, note 2.

infinite number of people, and, without doubt, more than others, yet they were not people fit for war; and that the *Sciàh*,[1] among the rest, did not value him at all, as manifestly appear'd in the late war.

As to *Sciàh Abbas* the King profess'd to account him a great Prince, a great Souldier and a great Captain; and I related to him how I had been for a great while together very familiar with him, and that he had done me many favours, having me with him on divers notable occasions: whereto he answer'd that he did not doubt it, and that being such a person as I was there was no Prince but would highly favour me. He ask'd me also concerning the commodities of our Countries and of those which are brought from thence into these Oriental parts; and (being[2] that in *India* they are accustom'd to the *Portugals*, who, how great Personages soever they be, are all Merchants, nor is it any disparagement amongst them) he ask'd me whether I had brought from my Country any thing to bargain withall, either Pearls, or Jewels, for he knew very good ones came from thence? I answer'd him that in my Country the Nobles of my rank never practis'd Merchandize, but onely used Arms, or Books, and that I addicted myself to the latter and meddled not with the former. He ask'd me how I was supply'd with Money for my Travels in so remote Countries? I answer'd that I had brought some along with me and more was sent me from time to time by my Agents, either in Bills, or in ready Money, according as was most expedient in reference to the diversity of places. He ask'd me whether I had either a Father, or a Mother, Brothers, or Sisters, Wife, or Children remaining by that Wife, who, I said, was pass'd to a better life? I answer'd that I had not; whereupon he said it was no wonder then that I pleas'd myself in

---

[1] That is, the Sháh of Persia. See *ante*, p. 150.

[2] For "since"; see *ante*, p. 28, *note*.

wandering thus about the World, being so much alone and destitute of all kindred. And, indeed, the King did not ill inferr; for had any of my dearest Relations been living, as they are not, perhaps I should not have gone from home, nor even seen *Manèl*, or *Olala;* but since 'tis God's Will to have it so I must have patience.

The King told me that if I could procure a good Horse out of my Country he would pay very well for it, for the Indians have none good of their own breed[1]; and the good ones they have are brought to them either from *Arabia*, or *Persia*, and the *Portugals* make a Trade of carrying them thither to sell, even the greatest Persons, as Governours of places and Captains General, not disdaining to do the same. I, standing upon the point of my Italian Nobility, which allows not such things, answer'd the King that to sell Horses was the Office of Merchants, not my profession; that I might present some good one to his Highness, there being in my Country very good ones, and would gladly do it if it were possible. The King was much pleas'd with this Answer of mine and said to his Men that I spoke like a right Gentleman, plainly and truly; and did not like many, who promise and say they will do many things, which afterwards they perform not, nor are able to do.

He ask'd me concerning Saffron,[2] which is much esteemed among them; they use it, mix'd with Sanders,[3] to paint their foreheads withal,[4] as also for Perfumes, for Meats,

---

[1] Sir R. Burton (*Goa and the Blue Mountains*, p. 174) says, "Arab and other valuable horses cannot stand the climate." See also Yule's *Cathay*, vol. i, p. 219; and *ante*, p. 194, note 5.

[2] It is curious that the saffron plant (*Crocus sativa*), though a native of Greece and Asia Minor, should be known (and was so, even in the time of Chaucer) by a name derived from the Arabic word *safra*, "to be yellow".

[3] See *ante*, p. 99, note 2.

[4] See *ante*, pp. 75, 99 (note 1), 104 (note 2), and 105.

and for a thousand other uses. I answer'd that I might be able to serve his Highness, that it was a thing that might be transported; and that in my Country there was enough, and that, if it pleas'd God I arrived there alive, I would send him a Present of it, with other fine things of my Country, which perhaps would be acceptable to him. And indeed, if I arrive in *Italy*, I intend to make many compliments to this and divers other Princes, whom I know in these parts; for, by what I have seen, I may get myself a great deal of Honour amongst them with no great charge. Every now and then the King would talk with his Servants, and all was in commendation of me and my discreet speaking, and especially of my white complexion, which they much admired, although in *Italy* I was never counted one of the fair, and, after so many Travels and so many sufferings both of Body and Mind, I am so changed that I can scarce acknowledge my self an Italian any longer. He prayed me once with much earnestness and courtesie, (out of a juvenile curiosity) to unbrace one of my sleeves a little and my breast, that he might see whether my body were correspondent to my face. I laughed, and, to please him, did so. When they saw that I was whiter under my clothes (where the Air and Sun had not so much injured me) than in the face they all remained astonished and began to cry out again that I was a *Deurù*, that I was a Hero, a god, and that blessed was the hour when I entered into their House, (I took my self to be *Hercules*, lodged in the Country of *Evander*[1]) and the King, being much satisfied with my courtesie, said that he knew me to be a Noble Man by my civil compliance with his demands; that if I had been some coarser person I would not have done so, but, perhaps, have taken ill, and been offended with, their curious Questions.

---

[1] See Virg., *Æneis*, Lib. viii, 100 *et seq.*

XIV.—As for the Ceremonies of eating, I must not omit to say that after he saw that I had done eating, notwithstanding his many instances to me to eat more, he was contented that I should make an end; and because most of the meat remained untouch'd, and it was not lawful for them to touch it, or keep it in the House, they caused my Christian Servant to come in and carry it all away (that he might eat it); which he did in the napkin which I had us'd before; for to fling it away, in regard of the discourtesie it would be to me, they judged not convenient. At length, when I rose up from my seat and took leave of the King, they caused my said Servant to strew a little Cow-dung, (which they had got ready for the purpose) upon the place where I had sat, which, according to their Religion, was to be purified. In the mean time, as I was taking leave of the King, he caused to be presented to me, (for they were ready prepared in the Chamber) and delivered to my Servants to carry home, four *Lagné*,[1] (so they in *India*, especially the *Portugals*, call the Indian Nuts before they be ripe, when, instead of Pulp, they contain a sweet refreshing water which is drunk for delight; and if the Pulp (for of this water it is made) be begun to be congealed yet that little is very tender and is eaten with much delight and is accounted cooling; whereas when it is hard and fully congealed, the Nut, remaining without water within and in the inner part somewhat empty, that matter of the Nut which is used more for sauce than to eat alone is, in my opinion, heating, and not of so good taste as before when it was more tender). Of these *Lagné* he caus'd four to be given me, besides I know not how

---

1 The name *Lanha* is applied on the Malabar coast to the coconut when ripe but still soft. "Sometimes they gather the cocoa fruit before it comes to perfect maturity, and then it is called 'Lanho'." (*Mandelslo.*)

many great bunches of *Moùl*,[1] or *Indian Figs*, which, though a small matter, are nevertheless the delights of this Country; wherefore as such I received them, and, thanking the King for them, (who also thank'd me much for my visit, testifying several times that he had had very great contentment in seeing me) at length taking my leave I departed about an hour, or little more, before night.

XV.—I intended to have visited the Queen also at the same time, but I understood she was gone abroad, whilst I was with her Son, to the before-mention'd place of her Works. Wherefore, being desirous to make but little stay in *Manèl*, both that I might dispatch as soon as possible, and, withall, not shew any dis-esteem of the Queen by visiting her not only after her Son but also on a different day, I resolv'd to go and find her where she was, although it were late; being also persuaded so to do by that *Brachman* to whom I gave my Sword when I went to eat, and who sometimes waited upon the Queen; and the rather because they told me she was little at home, but, rising at break of day, went forthwith to her Works and there stayed till dinner; and as soon as dinner was done return'd thither again and remain'd there till night. By which action I observ'd something in her of the spirit of *Sciàh Abbas* King of *Persia*,[2] and concluded it no wonder that she hath alwayes shew'd herself like him, that is, active and vigorous in actions of war and weighty affairs. Moreover they said that at night she was employ'd a good while in giving Audience[3] and doing Justice to her Subjects; so that it was better to go and speak to her in

---

[1] So spelt in original. A misprint for *mouz*. See *ante*, p. 327.

[2] Described in Letter IV from Persia.

[3] It is a common practice with princes and chief landowners in India to give audiences and transact business at night, in consequence of the heat prevailing while the sun is above the horizon.

the field, while she was viewing her Workmen, than in the house.

Accordingly I went and, drawing near, saw her standing in the field, with a few Servants about her, clad as at the other time, and talking to the Labourers that were digging the Trenches. When she saw us she sent to know wherefore I came, whether it were about any business? And the Messenger, being answer'd that it was onely to visit her, brought me word again that it was late and time to go home; and therefore I should do so, and when she came home she would send for me. I did as she commanded, and return'd to my house, expecting to be call'd when she thought fit; but she call'd not for me this night, the cause whereof I attributed to her returning very late home, as I understood she did.

December the sixth. I understood that the Queen was gone abroad very early to her Works, before I was up, without sending for me. Wherefore, desiring to dispatch, I sent the *Brachman*, my Interpreter, to her, to remind her that I desir'd to do her Reverence, having come into her Country onely for that purpose, and to know when she pleas'd the time should be. The *Brachman* gave the Message, and she answer'd that I should not wonder at this delay, being[1] that she was employ'd all day at those works; but, however, she would send for me when she came home. She ask'd the *Brachman* many questions concerning me; and, because some of her people extolled me much, and particularly for Liberality, saying that I had given so much for a House, so much for Hens, so much for other things, she, wondering thereat, said, "Do we here toil and moil so much for a *fano*,[2] (which is a small piece of Money) and does he spend in this manner?" The *Brachman* re-

[1] For "since"; see p. 28, *note*.

[2] Or *fanam*, of which the value varies in different localities from 1½*d*. to 15*d*. (See Yule's *Cathay*, *etc*., vol. ii, p. 344.)

turned with this Answer, and I waited all this day for the Queen's sending, but in vain.

In the mean while, not to lose time, I went to see a Temple at the end of the Town, standing on a high place and reached by some ill-favour'd stairs; they told me it was dedicated to *Nardina*,[1] yet it is very ill built, like the rest of the Edifices, being cover'd with Palm-leaves for the roof; and, in short, such as suited with such a Town. Then, descending the street which leads to the neighbouring River, I saw likewise upon another Hill a little square Chappel, which, instead of walls, was inclosed with pales of wood and cover'd with a roof. My interpreter told me it was built by this Queen, and that there was in it an Idol dedicated to the Devil, to whom, out of their fear of him, that he may do them no evil, these wretched people do reverence. I, hearing of a thing so strange though not new to my ears, said I would go see it, that I might affirm with truth I had with my own eyes seen the Devil worship'd. The *Brachman*, my Interpreter, dissuaded me as much as he could, alledging that many Devils dwelt in that place and might do me some mischief. I told him that I was not afraid of the Devil, who had no power over me; that himself needed to fear him as little as I; and therefore I desired him to go along with me cheerfully. When he saw me resolute he accompany'd me to the foot of the Hill and shew'd me the way; but it was not possible for me to get him further; he remain'd at a distance and said he would by no means approach near that place, for he was afraid of the Devil. Wherefore I went forward alone and said, If that Caitif, the

[1] See p. 236, note 1. From *Nara* and *Ayana*, "moving on the water". See Sir W. Jones' *Asiatic Researches*, who thus quotes from the *Mánava Shástra:* "The waters are called 'Nara' since they are the offspring of *Nera*, or *Ishwar*, and thence was *Narayana* named because his first *ayana*, or moving, was on them."

Devil, could do anything, let him hurt me; for I was his Enemy and did not value him; and that if he did not it was a sign he had no power. Speaking thus and invoking the Name of Jesus, (at which Heaven, Earth and Hell ought to bow the knee) I mounted up the Hill, and, being come to the Chappel, and finding nobody there, I opened the door and went in.

I saw the Idol standing in the middle upon the plain ground, made of white unpolish'd stone, exceeding a human stature, and not of that shape as we paint the Devil, but like a handsome Young Man,[1] with a high round Diadem upon his Head after their fashion. From each Arm issu'd two Hands, one of which was stretch'd out, the other bent towards the body. In the anterior right Hand he had a kind of weapon, which, I believe was one of those Indian Ponyards of this form[2]  of which I keep one by me. In the anterior left Hand he had a round thing which I know not what it was, and in the other two Hands I cannot tell what. Between the Legs was another Statue of a naked Man with a long beard, and his Hands upon the ground, as if he had been going upon them like an Animal; and upon this Image the Devil seem'd to ride. On the right Hand of the Idol was a great trunk of a Tree, dead but adhering to the root, low and seeming to be the remains of a great Tree that had grown there. I imagine that this Tree was the habitation of the Devils, who are wont to be in this place, and to do much mis-

---

[1] This was probably a figure of a *Daitya*, or Demon, though it might be intended to represent *Siva* as "The Destroyer". The "round thing" held in one hand was probably intended for a skull, or for a *discus*, or quoit, which is sometimes represented as held by *Siva*. See *ante*, p. 72, *note*.

[2] The sketch is intended to represent a form of dagger common in India. The shaded part represents the blade, the two horizontal lines form a guard for the wrist, the two vertical lines being handles grasped by the hand.

chief; to remedy which the Queen founded this Chappel here and dedicated this Idol to *Brimòr*,[1] (which they say is the name of a great Devil, King of many thousands of Devils) who dwelt here. The same conjecture was afterwards confirm'd to me by others of the Country, all confessing that it was *Buto*,[2] *i.e.*, the Devil; for so they term him in their Language.

When I had seen all, and spit several times in the Idol's face, I came away and return'd home, upbraiding the *Brachman* with his Cowardice, and telling him that he might see whether my Religion were good or no; since so powerful and fear'd a Devil could not hurt me when I went to his very house and did him such injuries. Whereunto the *Brachman* knew not what to answer.

Concerning Idols they told me at *Manèl* that the Queen of *Olala* and all her Family, as 'twere upon an Hereditary Account, ador'd and held for her principal God an Idol call'd *Putià Somnàta*,[3] which they said was the same with *Mahadeù*,[4] and which they delineated also as of a round figure, like the little pillar[5] of a Land-mark, circular at the top after this manner , as I have elsewhere noted that they pourtray *Mahadeù* in *Cambaia*, and the Sun in other places.

The same day, *December* the sixth, being return'd home before noon I took the Altitude of the Sun at *Manèl*

---

[1] A local deity, of whom hundreds are worshipped in their respective villages.

[2] That is, *Bhūta*, a malevolent spirit, or ghost. Demon worship is still common on the S.W. coast of India, particularly among the Shánárs (palm cultivators) of Tinnevelli. For a theory as to its origin, and an account of the ceremonies connected with it, see Sir M. Williams' *Modern India*, p. 195 *et seq.*

[3] A title of Siva. Literally, "Lord of the Moon".

[4] See *ante*, p. 72, *note*. Literally "Great God".

[5] This was, of course, a *Lingam*, the usual emblem of Siva. See *ante*, pp. 93, 100, 208 and 235.

with an Astrolabe. I found him to decline from the Zenith 35 degrees; he was this day in the fourteenth degree of *Sagittary*. His Southern Declination was 22 degrees 30′ 24″, which subtracted from 35 degrees, (the Altitude which I took) leave 12 degrees 29′ 36″, which is the Declination of the Æquinoctial Southwards from the Zenith of *Manèl*, and also the height of the Northern Pole in that place. So that *Manèl*, where the Queen of *Olala* now resides, lies 12 degrees 29′ 36″ distant from the Æquinoctial towards the North.

At night, having waited all the day and not hearing of the Queen's sending for me, as she had promis'd, I thought it not good to importune her further, but imagin'd she was not willing to be visited more by me. Wherefore I gave Order for a Boat to carry me back to *Mangalòr* the next day. Of the Queen's not suffering herself to be visited more by me certain Men of the Country who convers'd with me gave sundry Reasons. Some said the Queen imagin'd I would have given her some Present, as indeed I should, which would require a requital; but, perhaps, she had nothing fit to requite me with in these wretched places, or was loath to give: so that to avoid the shame she thought best to decline the visit. Others said there was no other decent place to give Audience in but that where her Son was; and for her to come thither did not shew well; as neither to send for me into some other unhandsome place, nor yet to give me Audience in the Street, when it was no unexpected meeting but design'd, for which reason she avoided speaking with me. The *Brachman*, not my Interpreter but the other who held my Sword, had a more extravagant and (in my opinion) impertinent conceit, to wit that there was spread such a Fame of my good presence, fairness and handsome manner of conversation, that the Queen would not speak with me for fear she should become enamor'd of me and be guilty of some unbecoming action, at which I heartily laugh'd. 'Twas more probable that she intended to avoid giving people occasion to talk of her for conversing privately with a stranger that was of such Reputation[1] amongst them. But, let the Cause be what it will, I perceiv'd she declin'd my visit and therefore caus'd a Boat to be provided, which (there being no other) was not row'd with Oars, but guided by two Men with Poles of Indian Cane, or *Bambù*,[2] which serv'd well enough for that shallow River.

The next day, *December* the seventh, a little before Noon, without having seen the Queen, or any other person, I departed from *Manèl*.[3] In a place somewhat lower, on the left bank of the River, where the Queen receives a Toll[4] of the Wares that pass by, (which for the most part are only Rice, which is carried out of, and Salt which is brought into, her Country) I stay'd a while to dine. Then, continuing my way, I arriv'd very late at *Mangalòr*, where, the Shops being shut up, and nothing to be got, I was fain to go supperless to bed. Occasion being offer'd for sending this Letter to *Goa*, whence the Fleet will depart next *January*, I would not lose it; so that, wherever I may happen to reside, the Letter may at least arrive safe to you, whose Hands I kiss with my old Affection.

---

[1] *I.e.*, so inferior in the eyes of the native Hindús.

[2] See *ante*, p. 220, note 3.

[3] *Manel* is perhaps another form of *Manjeshwarám*. See Eastwick's *Handbook of Madras*, p. 301.

[4] Called *Soonka*. The amount is specified at from 2½ to 10 per cent. (See Burton's *Goa and the Blue Mountains*, p. 199, who gives a list of twenty-seven different tolls or taxes, including two on cattle born with peculiar marks on them, and one on pigs fallen into wells.)

LETTER VII.

From Goa, January 31, 1624.

IN this my excursion and absence from *Goa*, (which was short, but the pleasantest three Moneth's Travel that ever I had) besides the Royal Seats of *Ikkerì* and *Manèl*, describ'd in my last letter to you, I had the fortune to go as far as *Calecut*,[1] to the other Royal Seat of

---

[1] See *ante*, p. 60, note 3. Properly "Kálíkot". This well-known town is described by Ibn Batuta (A.D. 1342) as one of the finest ports in the world. Here Vasco da Gama freighted his first ships for Europe in 1498. The name is also sometimes written as "Colicodu", and is said to be derived from two words, meaning "cock-crow", owing to the fact that the territory granted to the first King of Kálíkot was limited to the extent over which a cock could be heard to crow. (See Buchanan's *Journey through Malabar*, vol. ii, p. 474.) But this etymology is open to great doubt. It seems more probable that the derivation is as stated at p. 258, note 2. This town occupies an important place in the history of Southern India. In 1502 and 1510 it was attacked by the Portuguese. (See *Commentaries of Dalboquerque*, vol. II, pp. xxi and lxiv.) A fortified factory was built here by the Portuguese in 1513 (see *Commentaries of Dalboquerque*, vol. iv, p. 73), which was destroyed by the Portuguese Governor in 1525, in fear of its falling into the hands of the enemy. In 1616 an English factory was established here. It was taken by Haidar Ali in 1766 (see Wilks' *History of Maisúr*, vol. i, p. 292), but was occupied by the British forces in 1782. (See Wilks, vol. ii, p. 27.) It was sub-

Vikirà,[1] call'd by his proper Title, *il Samorino*,[2] where I have erected the Pillars of my utmost peregrination towards the South. Now on my Return, before I describe to you the Court of this *Samorino* and his Princesses, following the order of my Journeys I shall first inform you of my going to the famous Hermitage of *Cadiri*,[3] and visiting *Batinato*,[4] call'd King of the *Gioghi*,[5] who lives at this day

---

sequently taken by Tipú Sáhib, but recaptured by the British in 1790. (See Wilks, vol. ii, p. 180.) The surrounding territory was ceded to the British Government in 1792. The town is said to have been built about A.D. 1300 (see Eastwick's *Handbook of Madras*, p. 297, and Hunter's *Gazetteer, sub verb.*), but an earlier date (A.D. 805) is assigned to it by D'Anville. For an account of Kálíkot as it is (and the adjacent country), see Sir R. Burton's *Goa and the Blue Mountains*, chaps. x and xi. See also Barbosa, p. 103 *et seq.* (Hakluyt ed.).

[1] Or *Mana Vikrama*, "valiant", the dynastical name of the *Tâmurins* of Kálíkot, and said to be derived from Manicham and Vikram, two of the brothers on whom dominion was originally conferred.

[2] Properly *Tamurin*. See *ante*, p. xxiii. This word is said by some to be a modification of the Sanskrit word *Samunri*, or "Sea-king", and is one of the titles by which the kings of Kálíkot were known in former days, sometimes spelt "Zamorin" or "Zomodri", or "Zamorine" and (by Ibn Batuta) "Samari". The death of the last independent "Zamorine", in 1766, by self-immolation, owing to the cruelty of Haidar Ali, is described by Forbes (*Oriental Memoirs*, vol. iv, p. 207) and by Wilks (*History of Maisúr*, vol. i, p. 292.) By his own people the King was called "Támuri Rájá". His family pretended to far higher rank than even that of the Bráhmans. He was of the "Nair" or "Nayar" race. In *Ibn Batuta's Travels* there is an account of his honourable reception (A.D. 1342) by the "Samari" (or King) of Kálíkot. (See Yule's *Cathay and the Way Thither*, vol. ii, p. 416. See also *Comm. of Dalboquerque*, vol. i, p. 1.)

[3] The hill of Kádiri is about two miles distant from Mangalúr. On it is a Jain temple and (which is probably the "Hermitage" here mentioned) the residence of a *Mahant*, or Abbot, of the *Kánphattis* (Split-ears), a sect of Hindú ascetics, distinguished by their split ears. It is a pretty spot, shaded with trees, and rich in a spring of the clearest and most delicious water. (See Eastwick's *Handbook of Madras*, p. 302.)

[4] Probably *Bhát Náth*, or "Lord of the Bháts". See p. 80, note 1.

[5] See *ante*, p. 37, note 5.

in his narrow limits of that Hermitage, impoverish'd by *Venk-tapà Naieka*.[1]

December the tenth. Being yet in *Mangalòr* I took the Altitude of the Sun, whom I found to decline from the Zenith 35 degrees and 20 minutes. He was now in the 18th degree of *Sagittary* and declined towards the South 22 degrees 55′ 28″, which being subtracted from the 35 degrees 20′ wherein I found him, there remain 12 degrees 24′ 32″, and so far is *Mangalòr* distant from the Æquinoctial towards the North and hath the Northern Pole so much elevated. At this time the heat at *Mangalòr* is such as it is at *Rome* in the moneth of June, or the end of August.

On *December* the eleventh I went in the Morning about half a League from *Mangalòr* to see the Hermitage, where lives and reigns the *Archimandrita*[2] of the Indian *Gioghi*, whom the *Portugals* (usually liberal of the Royal Title) style " King of the *Gioghi*", perhaps because the Indians term him so in their Language ; and in effect he is Lord of a little circuit of Land, wherein, besides the Hermitage and the habitations of the *Gioghi*, are some few Houses of the Country people and a few very small Villages subject to his Government. The Hermitage stands on the side of a Hill in this manner.

II.—On the edge of the Plain, where the ascent of the Hill begins, is a great Cistern, or Lake, from which ascending a flight of stairs, with the face turn'd towards the North, you enter into a Gate, which hath a cover'd Porch, and is the first of the whole inclosure, which is surrounded with a wall and a ditch like a Fort. Having enter'd the said Gate, and going straight forward through a handsome broad Walk, beset on either side with sundry fruit trees, you come to another Gate, where there are stairs and a Porch higher than the former. This opens into a square *Piazza*,

---

[1] See *ante*, p. 168.

[2] Or chief of a Monastery.

or great Court, in the middle whereof stands a Temple of indifferent greatness, and for Architecture like the other Temples of the Indian *Gentiles;* onely the Front looks towards the East, where the Hill riseth higher, and the South side of the Temple stands towards the Gate which leads into the Court. Behind the Temple, on the side of the Court, is a kind of Shed, or Pent-house, with a Charriot in it, which serves to carry the Idol in Procession upon certain Festivals.[1] Also in two, or three, other places of the side of the Court, there are little square Chappels for other Idols. On the North Side of the Court is another Gate opposite to the former, by which going out and ascending some steps you see a great Cistern, or Lake, of a long form built about with black stone, and stairs leading down to the surface of the water; in one place next the Wall 'tis divided into many little Cisterns, and it serves for the Ministers of the Temple to wash themselves in and to perform their Ceremonies.

The Gate of the Temple, as I said, looks Eastward, where the Hill begins to rise very high and steep. From the Front of the Temple to the top of the Hill are long and broad stairs of the same black stone,[2] which lead up to it, and there the place is afterwards plain. Where the stairs begin stands a high, strait and round brazen Pillar,[3] ty'd about in several places with little fillets; 'tis about 60 Palms high, and one and a half thick from the bottom to the top, with little diminution. On this Pillar are plac'd about seventeen round brazen wheels, made with many spokes round about like stars: they are to support the

---

[1] See *ante*, p. 259, note 4.

[2] Probably laterite. See Eastwick's *Handbook of Madras*, p. 303, and Burton (*Goa and the Blue Mountains*, p. 191), who says: "Laterite is found in great quantities."

[3] This pillar is not mentioned in modern descriptions of the Temple.

lights in great Festivals, and are distant about three Palms one from another. The top terminates in a great brazen Candlestick of five branches, of which the middle-most is highest, the other four of equal height. The foot of the Pillar is square, and hath an Idol engraven on each side: the whole structure is, or at least seems to be, all of one piece.

The Temple, to wit the inner part where the Idol stands, is likewise all cover'd with brass. They told me that the walls of the whole Inclosure, which are now cover'd with leaves, were sometimes covered with large plates of brass; but that *Venk-tapà Naieka* carry'd the same away when, in the war of *Mangalòr*,[1] his Army pillag'd all these Countries: which whether it be true, or no, I know not. The walls of a less Inclosure (wherein, according to their custom, the Temple stands) are also surrounded on the outside with eleven wooden rails up to the top, distant one above the other little more than an Architectural Palm[2]; these also serve to bear Lights on Festival occasions; which must needs make a brave Show, the Temple thereby appearing as if it were all on fire. This Temple is dedicated to an Idol call'd *Moginato*.[3] Of what form it is I know not, because they would not suffer us to enter in to see it.

III.—Having view'd the Temple I ascended the Hill by the stairs, and passing a good way forward on the top thereof came to the habitations of the *Gioghi*[4] and their King; the place is a Plain, planted with many Trees, under

[1] See *ante*, p. 314.

[2] Probably the Italian measure, or *Palmo*, is here referred to, equal to about nine inches. The measure of a "Palm" may also be understood as equal to about 8½ inches (length of a hand), or 3 inches (breadth of a hand).

[3] Probably another title of Párasnáth, the idol worshipped here. (See Eastwick's *Handbook of Madras*, p. 303.)

[4] See *ante*, p. 37, note 5.

which are rais'd many very great stone pavements, a little height above the ground, for them to sit upon in the shade. There are an infinite number of little square Chappels with several Idols in them and some places cover'd over head, but open round about, for the *Gioghi* to entertain themselves in. And, lastly, there is the King's House, which is very low built. I saw nothing of it, (and believe it is nothing more) but a small Porch, with walls round about, colour'd with red[1] and painted with Elephants and other Animals,[2] besides in one place a wooden thing like a little square bed, somewhat rais'd from the ground, and cover'd with a cloth like a Tent; they told me it was the place where the King us'd to reside and perhaps also to sleep. The King was not here now, but was gone to a Shed, or Cottage, in a great plain field, to see something done, I know not what.

The soil is very good, and kept in tillage; where it is not level, by reason of the steepness of the Hill, 'tis planted with goodly Trees, most of which bear fruit; and, indeed, for a Hermitage so ill kept by people that know not how to, or cannot, make it delightful, it seem'd to me sufficiently handsome. I believe it was built by the Kings of *Banghel*[3] whilst they flourish'd, for it lies in their Territory, and that the place and the Seigniory thereof was by them given to the *Gioghi;* and, as they had no Wives,

---

[1] See *ante*, p. 235, note 1.

[2] There is a curious resemblance between the description of the temple at *Kádiri*, here given by P. della Valle, and that of the Jain temples at *Muda Biddari* (about thirty miles from Mangalúr) given by Eastwick (*Handbook of Madras*, p. 303). In this latter description, the pillar, the little chapels, and the figures of animals, mentioned by Della Valle, are all referred to, whereas these features are all absent from the description of the Temple at Kádiri. These features are not mentioned in Hunter's *Gazetteer*, or in Buchanan's *Journey through Malabar* in the description of *Kádiri*.

[3] See *ante*, p. 212.

the Dominion of this Hermitage and the adjacent Land goes not by Inheritance but by Elective Succession.[1]

I thought to find abundance of *Gioghi* here, as in our Convents, but I saw not above one, or two; and they told me they resort not together, but remain dispers'd here and there as they list, or abide in several places in the Temples where they please, nor are subject to their King in point of obedience, as ours are to their Superior, but onely do him Reverence and Honour; and at certain solemn times great numbers of them assemble here, to whom during their stay the King supplies Victuals. In the Hermitage live many Servants of his and Labourers of the Earth, who till these Lands, whereby he gets Provisions. They tell me that what he possesses within and without the Hermitage yields him about five or six thousand Pagods[2] yearly, the greatest part whereof he expends in Feasts, and the rest in diet, and in what is needful for the ordinary Service of the Temple and his Idols; and that *Venk-tapà Naieka*[3] had not yet taken tribute of him, but 'twas feared he would hereafter.

IV.—At length I went to see the King of the *Gioghi*, and found him employed in his business after a mean sort, like a Peasant, or Villager. He was an old man with a long white beard, but strong and lusty; in either ear hung two balls,[4] which seemed to be of Gold, I know not whether empty, or full, about the bigness of a Musket

---

[1] As to the Hindú monastic orders, see Elphinstone's *Hist. of India*, p. 103, who says: "The power of the heads of these sects is one of the most remarkable innovations in the Hindú system. Many of them in the South have large establishments, supported by grants of land and contributions from their flock." See also Buchanan's *Journey through Malabar*, vol. i, p. 21. The rule of Elective Succession here mentioned is a fertile ground of dispute and consequent litigation in India. See Reports of Judicial Committee of Privy Council *passim*.

[2] See *ante*, p. 209, note 1.

[3] See *ante*, p. 168.

[4] See *ante*, p. 195, note 1.

bullet; the holes in his ears were large, and the lobes much stretched by the weight; on his head he had a little red bonnet, such as our Galley Slaves wear, which caps are brought out of *Europe* to be sold in *India* with good Profit. From the girdle upwards he was naked, only he had a piece of cotton[1] wrought with Lozenges[2] of several colours across his shoulders; he was not very dark, and, for an Indian of colour, rather white than otherwise. He seemed a man of judgment, but upon trial in sundry things I found him not learned.

He told me that formerly he had Horses, Elephants, Palanchinos and a great equipage[3] and power before *Venktapà Naieka* took away all from him, so that now he had very little left. That within twenty days after there was to be a great Feast in that place, to which many *Gioghi* would repair from several parts; that it would be worth my seeing, and that I should meet one that could speak *Arabick* and *Persian*, and was very learned, who could give me satisfaction as to many things; and, extolling the qualities of this *Gioghi*, he told me that he had a very great Head, (to signifie the greatness of which he made a great circle with his arms) to wit of hair, ruffled and long, and which had neither been cut nor combed a great while.[4] I asked him to give me his Name in writing, for my Memory, since I was come to see him. He answer'd me, (as the Orientals for the most part do to such curious demands) "To what purpose was it?" and, in fine, he would not give it to me; but I perceiv'd 'twas through a vain and ignorant fear that it might be of some mischief

---

[1] In original, *bombace*. See p. 249, *note*.

[2] Or chequered. In original, *Scacchi*.

[3] See *ante*, p. 268, note 6.

[4] As to the value of a good head of hair, see Sir J. Lubbock's *Origin of Civilization*, p. 66 *et seq*. The *Brahman* ascetics shave the head.

to him.[1] Nevertheless at my going away, I was told by others that he was call'd *Batinato*[2]; and that the Hermitage and all the adjacent places is call'd *Cadirà*.[3]

V.—Having ended my discourse with the King I came away, and, at the foot of the Hill, without the first gate of the Hermitage, rested to dine till the heat were over, in the House, or Cottage, of one of the Peasants, (there being a small Village there) whose Wife set before us Rice, Caril,[4] and Fish, which themselves also eat, being of a Race allow'd so to do. When the heat was past I return'd, fair and softly as I went, to *Mangalòr;* and arriv'd at home a good while before night.

December the eighteenth. I prepar'd myself to go to *Carnate*[5] to see that Queen whose Territory and City is, as I have said elsewhere,[6] two, or three, Leagues distant from *Mangalòr*, upon the Sea-coast towards the North. The City stands upon a River which encompasses it, and over-flowes the Country round about. It was wont to be very strong both by Art and situation; but, during the war of *Mangalòr*,[7] *Venk-tapà Naieka*, coming with a great army to subdue and pillage all these Countries, sent for this Queen to come and yield Obedience to him. The Queen, who, as I have heard, is a Lady of much Virtue

---

1 As to this widespread belief see Sir J. Lubbock's *Origin of Civilization*, p. 248 *et seq.*, from which the following short extract is here made: "In one of the despatches intercepted during our war with Nepal Gouri Sah sent orders 'to find out the name of the commander of the British army, write it on a piece of paper, and burn it.'" Even in the present day, among civilised nations, a certain amount of impropriety is attached to the mention of a person's name on particular occasions. In India no married woman will willingly mention her husband's name.

2 See *ante*, p. 345, note 4.

3 Properly *Kádiri*.

4 See *ante*, p. 328, note 1.

5 See *ante*, p. 168, note 1, and p. 314. *Carnate* does not appear in modern maps. Formerly called *Carcára* and *Carnáti*. (See Yule's *Cathay*, *etc.*, vol. ii, p. 451.)

6 See *ante*, p. 300.

7 See *ante*, p. 314.

and Prudence, being unwilling to render herself to *Venk-tapà*, summoned her Captains together, told them that she was ready to spend and give them all the Money and Jewels she had, and not to be wanting on her part to exert her utmost power, if they would prepare themselves to defend the State. But these Ministers, either through Cowardice, or Treachery, would not attempt a defence. Whereupon the poor Queen, who as a Woman could do little by herself, (her Son also being very young) seeing her people disheartned, resolv'd by their advice to surrender herself to *Venk-tapà Naieka;* and accordingly prepar'd to go to him with a good Guard of Souldiers. Hearing which he sent to her to come alone without other company than her Attendants; which she did, not voluntarily but constrain'd thereto by her hard Fortune and the treachery of others. *Venk-tapà* receiv'd her honourably and took her into his Friendship and Protection; but withall he caus'd the City to be dismantled of the strong Walls it had, to prevent her rebelling against him afterwards, and left her, as before, the Government of the State, tying her onely to Obedience, the payment of a Tribute, and the profession of an honorable Vassalage to him.

When they dismantled the City the Queen (they say), unable to endure the sight, retir'd into a solitary place a little distant, cursing in those her solitudes the Pusillanimity and Infidelity of her own people, no less than the bad fortune and weakness of the *Portugals* her defenders, to whom she had been always a Faithful Friend. At this time she lives with her young Son, either in *Carnate*, or some other place there-abouts.

VI.—Being mov'd by the Fame of this Queen's Virtue I was desirous to go and do her Reverence; for which purpose I had got a *Palanchino* ready and Men to carry me thither. But on the morning of the aforesaid day there put into *Mangalòr* a Fleet of Portugal Ships, which they call "*l'armata del Canarà*", because it coasts along the Province of *Canarà*[1]; or else "*l'armata della Colletta*",[2] for that it is maintained with the Money of a new Impost, imposed and collected by the *Portugals* in their Indian Plantations. The Chief Captain of this Fleet was Sig: *Luis de Mendoza*, a principal Cavalier, or *Fidalgo*,[3] (as they speak) young but of very good parts. The Captain of one of the Ships was Sig: *Ayres de Siqueira Baraccio*, formerly my Friend at *Goa*, whom I waited for, that I might return thither in his Ship. Whereupon hearing of his arrival I went to seek him, and finding him already landed I understood from him that this Fleet was to go to *Calecut*, in order to carry thither two Men of the *Samorì*,[4] King of *Calecut* (*Samorì* is a Title given to all those Kings, like our Emperour, or *Cæsar*) which Men he had a little before sent to *Goa* in the same Fleet, in another Voyage which it had made upon those Coasts, to treat with the Vice-Roy about a Peace, (for he had been many years, if not at War, yet at enmity with the *Portugals*) saying that if the Vice-Roy inclin'd to Peace he would afterwards send Ambassadors with more solemnity and treat of Articles.

Now these Men were returning to *Calecut* with the Vice-Roy's Answer, and Sig: *Ayres* said that the Fleet would depart from *Mangalòr* the same night, yet would return shortly, because the Chief Captain had Orders not to stay at *Calecut* above four and twenty hours, onely till he had landed these Men and understood what resolution the *Samorì* gave in Answer, without giving him more time to think thereupon, and that in returning the Fleet would touch at *Mangalòr* and all the other Ports of that Coast, to take

---

1 See p. 168, note 1.

2 *I.e.*, "collection" or "subsidy".

3 Or "Hidalgo", from the Spanish *Hijo de algo*, or "son of somebody".

4 See *ante*, p. 345, note 2.

with them the Merchant Ships laden with Rice, (which were prepar'd, or preparing) and convey them according to their custom to *Goa*, where, by reason of scarcity of Provision, they were much desir'd. Hearing this News I was loath to lose the opportunity of seeing *Calecut*, (the King whereof is one of the most famous among the Gentile Princes of *India*, and is likely to be at Peace but a little while with the *Portugals*) and therefore resolved to go aboard the Ship of Sig: *Ayres* the same day, putting off my Journey to *Carnate*, whither I had hopes to go on my return. Accordingly, dismissing the *Palanchino* and the Men that were to carry me, together with the Servant I had taken at *Barselòr* (because he was not willing to go further with me) I went aboard alone without any Servant, assuring myself I could not want attendance and whatever else was needful in the Ship, wherein I found Sig: *Mansel Leyton*, Son of Sig: *Gio: Fernandez Leyton*,[1] embarqu'd as a Souldier (which course of life he was now first enter'd upon), besides many other eminent Souldiers, who were afterwards very friendly to me, and with whom I spent many days in good conversation.

VII.—*December* the nineteenth. We departed from *Mangalòr*, and were foremost of all, because our Ship was Captain of the Vantguard.[2] This day we pass'd by a high Hill, inland near the seashore, call'd *Monte Deli*[3]; and the

---

[1] See *ante*, p. 168 *et seq*. [2] From the French *avant*.

[3] A remarkable, partially isolated, mountain and promontory on the coast, in about Lat. 12° N.; the proper northern boundary of Malabar. Called also "Cavo de Eli", "Monte d'Ili", "Monte de Lin", "Monte de Li", "Mount Delly" or "Dilla", and "Rás Haili", by writers of various nationalities. Of this eminence, Barbosa (? Magellan) says (Lisbon edition): "It serves as a beacon for all the ships of the Moore and Gentiles that navigate the sea of India." See Sir H. Yule's *Cathay and the Way Thither*, vol. ii, p. 452. As to this place, Sir R. Burton (*Goa and the Blue Mountains*, p. 189) says: "Vincent acutely guesses *Ela Barake* (near *Nelisuram*) to be the spot near

next day (December the twentieth) by another, call'd *Monte Fermoso.*[1] At night we anchored under *Canandr*,[2] but enter'd not the Port, having sail'd from *Mangalòr* hither, always Southwards, eighteen Leagues.

December the one and twentieth. Once in the morning and once in the evening we met with *Paroes*,[3] which are very light Ships of the *Malabar* Rovers, of which this Coast was full[4]; for at *Mangalòr* ends the Province of *Canarà* and that of *Malabar* begins. We made ready our Arms both times to fight them, but they fled from us and regained the mouths of the Rivers, whereof that Coast is full, where, by reason that it was their own Territory and well guarded in those narrow and difficult places, we could not pursue them to take them; onely we discharg'd some Guns against them at a distance to no purpose, which were answer'd from the Land with the like. We might easily have attempted if not to take that one which we saw in the Evening, yet at least to shatter it from afar off with our Cannon, if the Chief Captain had not that regard to the Land they regained, which belong'd to the *Samorì*,[5] to whom, on account of the Peace in agitation, he was willing to have respect. At night we came to Anchor under *Calecut*,[6] which is twelve Leagues Southwards beyond *Canandr.*[7]

Cananore, called by Marco Polo *Eli*, and by us *Delhi*, the Ruddy Mountain of the Ancients. It derives its present name from a celebrated Moslem *fakir*, Mahommed of Delhi, who died there. Its Hindoo appellation is *Yeymullay*. No stress should be laid on the resemblance between Mount '*Delhi*' and the '*Ela*' *Barake* of the *Periplus*. The identity of the two places rests, however, on good local evidence." But Sir H. Yule is doubtful as to this.

[1] Probably a name given by the Portuguese to this mountain.

[2] More correctly *Kananúr*. See *infra*, note 7.

[3] See *ante*, p. 201, note 2.

[4] See *ante*, p. 201, note 1.

[5] See *ante*, p. 345, note 2.

[6] See *ante*, p. 344, note 1.

[7] Or Kananúr. At one time a large city, in 11° 52′ N. Lat., supposed to be the same as the town called "Jurfattan" by Ibn Batuta, and

December the two and twentieth. Early in the morning the *Samori's* two Men landed at *Calecut*, and with them a *Portugal* common Souldier, but well clad and attended, whom the Chief Captain sent to the King with the Vice-Roy's Answer, viz.: That the Vice-Roy was contented to treat of a Peace and would gladly conclude it; but on condition that the *Samorì* made Peace too with the King of *Cocin*,[1] the *Portugals'* confederate, whom it was not fit to leave out of the said Peace, and the rather because the greatest differences between the *Portugals* and the *Samorì* were touching the King of *Cocin*, whom the Portugals justly defended as their faithful Friend, and had alwayes, to the damage of the *Samorì*, his perpetual Adversary, much supported; that if the *Samorì* were contented to make Peace with both he should send his Ambassador to *Goa* with power to treat of the conditions, and they should be receiv'd very well. Within a short time the *Portugal* return'd to the Fleet; for the City of *Calecut* stands upon the shore and the *Samorì's* Royal Palace[2] is not far off: and together with the *Portugal* the *Samorì* sent to the Chief Captain a *Portugal* Boy, eight or ten years old, call'd *Cicco*, who in some Revolutions of *Cananòr* had been taken Prisoner and was brought up in his Court; he sent him well cloth'd, and accompany'd not onely by many

---

"Jarabattan" by Edrisi, and perhaps the "Harrypatan" (for Jaripatan) of Ferishta in Briggs, iv, 532; the residence of the King called "Kowil", one of the most powerful in Malabar. (See Yûle's *Cathay and the Way Thither*, vol. ii, p. 453.) The Portuguese had a fort here in 1505. It was taken by Haidar Ali in 1768, and by the British in 1783, and is now the military capital of Malabar and Kánara, and has a fort built according to regular rules. (See Eastwick's *Handbook of Madras*, p. 300, and Hunter's *Gazetteer*, *s. v.*)

[1] See *ante*, p. 199, note 1.

[2] This was probably the ancient palace, of which only two pillars and a portico now remain. (See Eastwick's *Handbook of Madras*, p. 297.)

persons but also with Pipes and Drums, that he might visit the Chief Captain in his Name and give him a Present of Refreshments to eat, namely Indian Figgs, *Lagne*[1] and other fruits.

His Answer to the proposal was that the Peace should be first made between himself and the *Portugals*, and afterwards the interests of the King of *Cocin* should be taken into consideration; and desiring the Chief Captain that he would vouchsafe to stay awhile till he had advis'd with his Ministers and deliberated about sending Ambassadors to *Goa* in the same Fleet; with other reasons, which were judg'd to be rather excuses to put off the time and hold the *Portugals* in a Treaty of Peace, till some very rich Ships which he expected from *Mecha*[2] were return'd, lest the *Portugals* should molest them at Sea, than real intentions for a Peace, especially with the King of *Cocin*, with whom he had long and intricate disputes not so easily to be terminated. The *Portugals* also demanded that the *Samori* would remove a Garrison which he had plac'd on certain frontiers, where they, for their own security and the defence of the King of *Cocin*, were fain to keep a Fort continually, with a great Garrison and at much expense; and because he show'd not much inclination thereunto it was, not without cause, judg'd that his Treaties were Artifices to hold the *Portugals* in suspense; wherefore the Chief Captain sent word that he had express Orders from the Vice-Roy not to stay longer at *Calecut* than twenty-four hours, and so long he would stay: and, if within that time the *Samori*

---

[1] See *ante*, p. 336, note 1.

[2] So spelt in the original, but probably a misprint for *Mucha* (see *ante*, p. 1, *note*), as Mekkah is not a seaport. *Mucha* (or *Mokha*) is almost identical with *Muza* of the *Periplus*. See Heeren's *Historical Researches*, vol. ii, p. 302, where an interesting account of the ancient commercial traffic on the W. coast of India will be found, and also in Appendix XI of same vol., and Smith's *Geog. Dict.*, *s. v.*

came to a resolution in accordance with the Vice-Roy's Proposition, he would carry his Ambassador with a good will; otherwise he intended to depart the next night, all the intermediate day being allowed his Highness for determination.

With this Reply he sent back the boy *Cicco*, honoring him with some small Presents, and the other Men that came with him, without sending any of his *Portugals* for this purpose, or going ashore to refresh himself and visit the *Samori*, as he was by him invited; the Vice-Roy having given him secret Instructions not to trust him too far, because these Kings, or *Samori*, had never been very faithful towards the *Portugals*. Nevertheless the Chief Captain forbad not any Souldiers to land that were so minded, so that many of them went ashore, some to walk up and down, some to buy things, and some to do other business; as also many people came to the Fleet in little boats, partly to sell things, and partly out of curiosity to sée the *Portugals*, who on account of their almost continual enmity with the *Samori*, seldom us'd to be seen in *Calecut*.

VIII.—The same day (December the two and twentieth), whilst we were aboard in the Port of *Calecut*, I took the Sun's Altitude with my Astrolabe and found him to decline at Noon from the Zenith 34 degrees and 50 minutes. The Sun was this day in the thirtieth degree of *Sagittary;* whence, according to my Canon of Declination, which I had from F. *Frà Paolo Maria Cittadini*, he declined from the Æquinoctial towards the South 23 degrees and 28 minutes, which, according to that Canon, is the greatest Declination; if it be not really so the little that is wanting may be set against the period of four hours, if not more, that Noon falls sooner at *Calecut* than in any Meridian of *Europe*, according to which my Canon of Declination may be calculated, so that, if from the 34 degrees 50 minutes in which I found the Sun to be you subtract the 23 degrees 28 minutes which I presuppose him to decline from the Æquinoctial towards the South, the remainder is 11 degrees 22 minutes, and so much is the elevation of the North Pole in this place; and, consequently, the City of *Calecut* lies 11 degrees 22 minutes distant from the Æquinoctial towards the North.[1]

After Dinner I landed also with the Captain of my Ship and some other Souldiers; we went to see the *Bazár* which is near the shore; the Houses, or rather Cottages, are built of Earth and thatched with Palm-leaves, being very low; the Streets also are very narrow, but sufficiently long; the Market was full of all sorts of Provisions and other things necessary to the livelihood of that people, conformably to their Custom; for as for clothing they need little, both Men and Women going quite naked, saving that they have a piece either of Cotton, or Silk, hanging down from the girdle to the knees and covering their shame[2]; the better sort are either wont to wear it all blew, or white strip'd with Azure,[3] or Azure and some other colour; a dark blew[4] being most esteem'd amongst them. Moreover both Men and Women wear their hair ong[5] and ty'd about the head; the Women with a lock hanging on one side under the Ear becomingly enough as almost all Indian Women do; the dressing of whose

---

[1] It is somewhat singular that in four modern authorities (Eastwick's *Handbook*, Black's *Atlas*, Brooke's *Gazetteer*, and the *London Encyclopædia*) the latitude of Calicut is given as 11° 15′, 10° 11′, 11° 12′, and 11° 18′, respectively.

[2] One end being tucked up between the legs. In Arrian's *Indica*, cap. xvi, the dress of the natives of India is similarly described.

[3] From the Arabic *lazurd*, "blue", of which the initial "l" was dropped by mistake. (See *Imperial Dictionary*, *sub verb.*)

[4] In original, *turchino*. See *ante*, p. 253, *note*.

[5] This is contrary to the more usual custom of shaving the head. (See Elphinstone's *Hist. of India*, p. 183, and Quintin Craufurd's *Sketches of the Hindoos.*)

head is, in my opinion, the gallantest that I have seen in any other nation.[1] The Men have a lock hanging down from the crown of the head, sometimes a little inclin'd on one side; some of them use a small colour'd head-band, but the Women use none at all. Both sexes have their Arms adorned with bracelets, their ears with pendants, and their necks with Jewels[2]; the Men commonly go with their naked Swords and Bucklers, or other Arms, in their hands, as I said of those of *Balagate*.[3]

IX.—The Inhabitants of the Kingdom of *Calecut* and the In-land parts, especially the better sort, are all Gentiles, of the Race Nairi[4] for the most part, by profession Souldiers, sufficiently swashing[5] and brave. But the Sea Coasts are full of *Malabari*, an adventitious people,[6] though of long standing; for *Marco Polo*, who writ four

---

[1] "Loveliness when unadorned is still adorned the most." The elegant simplicity of the Hindú mode of hairdressing was, no doubt, a pleasing contrast to the artificial monstrosities adopted by the ladies of Europe in those days.

[2] Mr. Elphinstone (*Hist. of India*, p. 183) says: "Both sexes wear many ornaments. Men even of the lower orders wear earrings, bracelets and necklaces. They are sometimes worn as a convenient way of keeping all the money the owner has. Children are loaded with gold ornaments, which gives frequent temptation to child-murder." It is a common sight in India to see children thus loaded who wear no clothes whatever.

[3] See *ante*, p. 226, and p. 185, *note*.

[4] Properly *Nayar*. See *ante*, p. 232, note 4.

[5] In the original, *bizarri*. As to the Nairs, or Nayars, and their ways, the following authorities may be referred to, viz.: Barbosa's *East Africa and Malabar*, Hakluyt edit., p. 101 *et seq.*; Sir R. Burton's *Goa and the Blue Mountains*, pp. 215 to 232; Wilks' *Hist. of Maisúr;* and Buchanan's *Journey through Malabar*; and the *Report of the Government Commission*, referred to *ante*, p. 218, note 2.

[6] The name is written "Malavári" in the original Italian. They were probably Arabs, who had crossed the Indian Ocean; "Moors of Mekkah," as they are called by Barbosa (? Magellan), *Coast of East Africa and Malabar*, p. 102.

hundred years since, makes mention of them[1]; they live confusedly with the Pagans, and speak the same Language, but yet are Mahommetans[2] in Religion. From them all that Country for a long tract together is call'd *Malabar*,[3] famous in *India* for the continual Robberies committed at Sea by the *Malabar* thieves[4]; whence in the *Bazar* of *Calecut*, besides the things above mention'd, we saw sold good store of the *Portugals'* commodities, as Swords, Arms, Books, Clothes of *Goa*, and the like Merchandize, taken from *Portugal* Vessels at Sea; which things, because they are stolen and in regard of the excommunication which lies upon us in that case, are not bought by our Christians. Having seen the *Bazar* and stay'd there till it was late we were minded to see the more inward and noble parts of the City and the outside of the King's Palace; for to see the King at that hour we had no intention, nor did we come prepar'd for it, but were in the same garb which we wore in the Ship.

Accordingly we walk'd a good way towards the Palace, for the City is great, and we found it to consist of plots set with abundance of high Trees, amongst the boughs whereof were a great many wild monkeys, and within these close Groves stand the Houses, for the most part at a distance from the common Wayes, or Streets; they appear but small, little of their outsides being seen; besides low walls made of a black stone[5] surround these Plots and divide them from the Streets, which are much better than those of the *Bazar*, but without any ornament of

---

[1] See M. Polo's *Travels*, vol. iii.

[2] This is not correct as to *all* the inhabitants of Malabar, many of whom (and probably the majority) are Hindús. Barbosa (? Magellan) estimates that the "Moors", or Muhammadans, formed a fifth part only of the population of Malabar.

[3] A misapprehension. See *ante*, p. 121, note 4.

[4] See *ante*, p. 201, note 1.

[5] Probably laterite.

Windows, so that he that walks through the City may think that he is rather in the midst of uninhabited Gardens than of an inhabited City. Nevertheless it is well peopled and hath many inhabitants, whose being contented with narrow Buildings is the cause that it appears but small.

As we walked in this manner we met one of those men who had been at *Goa* with the Vice-Roy; and because he saw many of us together and imagin'd there was some person of quality amongst us, or because he knew our Chief Captain, he invited us to go with him to the King's Palace, and, going before us as our Guide, conducted us thither. He also sent one before to advertise the King of our coming, and told us we must by all means go to see him, because his Highness was desirous to see us and talk with us. Wherefore, not to appear discourteous, we were constrain'd to consent to his Request, notwithstanding the unexpectedness of, and our unpreparedness for, the visit.

X.—The first and principal gate of the Palace opens upon a little Piazza, which is beset with certain very great Trees affording a delightful shade. I saw no Guard before it; it was great and open; but before it was a row of Balusters,[1] about four or five palms[2] from the ground, which serv'd to keep out not only Horses and other Animals but also Men upon occasion. In the middle was a little flight of Stairs, outside the Gate, leading into it, and another within on the other side. Yet, I believe, both the Stairs and the Balusters are movable, because 'tis likely that when the King comes forth the Gate is quite open; otherwise it would not be handsome, but this is only my

---

[1] Usually, but incorrectly, written as "banisters". The word "baluster" is derived from the Latin word *palus*, "a pole", according to Webster (see *Dictionary*, *s. v.*), or from *Balaustium*, the flower of the wild pomegranate, according to the *Imperial Dictionary*.

[2] See *ante*, p. 348, note 2.

conjecture. We enter'd this Gate, ascending the Stairs above the Rails, where we were met by the Messenger whom the above-said person had sent to the King and who again invited us into the Palace by the King's Order. Within the Gate we found a great Court, of a long form, without any just and proportionate figure of Architecture; on the sides were many lodgings in several places, and in the middle were planted divers great Trees for shade. The King's chief apartment, and (as I believe by what I shall mention hereafter) where his Women were, was at the end of the Court, opposite to the left side of the Entrance. The Edifice, in comparison of ours, was of little consideration; but, according to their mode, both for greatness and appearance capable of a Royal Family. It had a cover'd porch, as all their structures have, and within that was a door of no great largeness leading into the House.

Here we found *Cicco* the Portugal youth,[1] become an Indian in Habit and Language, but, as himself told us, and as his Portugal Name,[2] which he still retain'd among the *Gentiles*, demonstrated, no Renegade but a Christian; which I rather believe, because the Indian *Gentiles* admit not nor care to admit other strangers to their Religion, as I have elsewhere noted[3]; for, (conjoyning so inseparately, so to speak, as they do, their Religion to the Races of Men) as a Man can never be of other Race[4] than what he was born of, so they also think that he neither can, nor ought to, be of any other Religion, although in Habit, Language and Customs he accommodate himself to the people with whom he lives. With the said *Cicco* we found

[1] See *ante*, p. 357.

[2] There seems to be room for some doubt as to the name being a Portuguese name; *chikka* in the vernacular being "young" or "small". See *ante*, p. 315, note 3.

[3] See *ante*, p. 80, and note 2.

[4] Or caste. See p. 77, note 4.

many others of the King's Courtiers who waited for us, and here we convers'd with them a good while before the Gate, expecting a new message from the King, who, they told us, was now bathing himself, according to their custom, after supper. Nor was it long before an Order came from the King for us to enter, and accordingly we were introduced into that second Gate; and passing by a close room like a chamber, (in which I saw the Image of *Brahmà* on his Peacock,[1] and other Idolets) we enter'd into a little open Court, surrounded with two rows of narrow and low Cloysters, to wit one level with the ground and the other somewhat higher. The pavement of the porch was also something raised above the plane of the Court, so much as might serve for a man to sit after our manner. The King was not in this small Court, but they told us we must attend him here, and he would come presently. Whereupon we betook ourselves to sit down upon that rais'd pavement in the Porch, the Courtiers standing round about us; amongst whom, the Portugal *Cicco* and another Indian Man (who, as they said, was a Christian and, being sometime a slave to the *Portugals*, had fled hither for Liberty and was entertain'd in the King's guard) serv'd us for Interpreters, but not well, because the Man spoke not the Portugal Tongue so much as tolerably, and *Cicco*, having been taken when he was very young, remembered but little of his own Language.

XI.—No sooner were we seated in this place than two girls about twelve years old enter'd at the same Gate whereat we came in: they were all naked, (as I said above, the Women generally go) saving that they had a very small blew cloth wrap'd about their waists, and their Arms, Ears and Necks were full of ornaments of Gold and very rich Jewels. Their colour was somewhat swarthy, as all

---

[1] See *ante*, p. 235, note 4.

these Natives are, but, in comparison with others of the same Country, clear enough; and their shape no less proportionable and comely than their aspect was handsome and well favour'd. They were both the Daughters, as they told us, of the Queen, that is, not of the King but of his Sister who is styl'd, and in effect is, Queen; for as these *Gentiles* derive their descent and inheritance by the line of the Women,[1] though the Government is allowed to Men as more fit for it, and he that governs is call'd King, yet the King's Sister, and amongst them, (if there be more than one) she to whom, by reason of Age, or for other respects, the right belongs, is called, and properly is, Queen, and not any Wife, or Concubine, of the King who has many. So also when the King (who governs upon account of being Son of the Queen-Mother) happens to die his own Sons succeed him not, (because they are not the Sons of the Queen) but the Sons of his Sister; or, in defect of such, those of the nearest kinswomen by the same Female line. So that these two Girls, whom I call the Nieces of the *Samorì*, were right Princesses, or *Infantas*, of the kingdom of *Calecut*.

Upon their entrance where we were all the Courtiers present shew'd great Reverence to them; and we, understanding who they were, arose from our seats and, having saluted them, stood all the time afterwards before them bare-headed. For want of Language we spoke not to them, because the above-said Indian slave had retir'd to a distance upon their coming, giving place to other more noble Courtiers: and *Cicco* stood so demurely by us that he durst not lift up his eyes to behold them, much less speak; having already learnt the Court-fashions and good manners of the place. Nevertheless they talked much together concerning us, as they stood, and we also of them,

[1] See *ante*, p. 218, and note 2.

and all smil'd without understanding one another. One of them, being more forward, could not contain herself, but, approaching gently towards me, almost touch'd the Sleeve of my Coat with her hand, making a sign of wonder to her Sister how we could go so wrapp'd up and entangled in Clothes as we seem'd to her to be. Such is the power of Custom that their going naked seem'd no more strange to us than our being cloth'd appear'd extravagant to them.[1]

After a short space the King came in at the same door, accompany'd by many others. He was a young Man of thirty, or five and thirty, years of age, to my thinking; of a large bulk of body, sufficiently fair for an Indian and of a handsome presence. He is call'd (as a principal Courtier, whom I afterwards ask'd, told me) by the proper name of *Vikirà*.[2] His beard was somewhat long and worn equally round about his Face; he was naked, having onely a piece of fine changeable[3] cotton cloth, blew and white, hanging from the girdle to the middle of the Leg. He had divers bracelets on his Arms, pendants at his Ears, and other ornaments with many Jewels and rubies of value. In his Hand he carry'd a painted staff, (if it were not an Indian Cane) like a Shepherd's Staff, upon which, fixed in the earth, just as Shepherds are represented in our Comedies, he stood leaning for a while.

When he was saluted by us he receiv'd us smiling and with much courtesie; and whilst his two Nieces stood by him, leaning against a high bank made to sit upon, we stood in order in the Court just before the King, the whole

---

[1] This is a mistranslation. It should be, "just as their going naked seemed strange to us, so our being clothed appeared extravagant to them."

[2] See *ante*, p. 345, note 1.

[3] The term "changeable" is used to denote the quality of altering its external appearance in the manner of "shot silk". Shakespeare speaks of "a doublet of changeable taffeta".

Court and Porches being full of other Courtiers who came in, partly with the King and partly by some other little entrances. I will not omit to mention the manner how those who entered saluted the King; for I saw more than one do it, and particularly a Youth who enter'd a good while after the King by one of those little Gates; to whom in particular the King spake much, and of whom he seemed to make great account. In his salutation he advanced his joyned Hands over his Head, then, parting them a little so extended and exalted, he smote them lightly together twice, or thrice, to wit the palm of one hand with the four longest Fingers of the other joyned together; which whole action he repeated twice, or thrice. Such as had weapons lifted up their joyned Hands above their Heads, with their Swords, Ponyards, Bucklers, or other Arms, in them; and, instead of striking with their Fingers, as by reason of their Arms they could not, they bowed down their Hands so conjoyned and made the points of their Swords touch the ground.[1] No less full were the higher Cloysters round of the Women who stood there to behold us; amongst whom stood apart in the most eminent place the Queen, Sister to the King, a Woman of ripe Age, cloth'd in blew Cotton as to her lower parts and abundantly adorned with Jewels.[2]

[1] The time-worn phrase, *quot homines tot sententiæ*, might be written as *quot homines tot salutationes.* For an account of some of the many forms of salutation prevailing among different peoples, see Sir J. Lubbock's *Origin of Civilization*, p. 35 *et seq.*

[2] A similar scene is described by Captain Hamilton in his travels, and he describes the Queen and her daughters as being "all naked above the waist and barefooted". Sir R. Burton (*Goa and the Blue Mountains*, p. 179), quoting this passage, says: "Two hundred years ago the white man was allowed to look upon a black princess in the presence of her husband. How long will it be before such privilege will be extended to him again in India?"

XII.—The King, desiring to talk with us, caused the youth *Cicco* to draw near and afterwards called for the Indian Slave above mentioned; because *Cicco*, either out of excessive Reverence, or because he had forgotten the *Portugal* Tongue, durst not undertake to interpret. He asked our Captain who he was, and how called? The Captain would not confess himself to be Captain of a Ship, and so become known, but, counterfeiting another Name, said he was a private Souldier and Companion to the rest of us, which the King seemed not to believe. He enquired likewise concerning the other Souldiers present; and, above all, very particularly concerning me, pointing out the pendant which I wore in my Ear,[1] almost like their Custom of *India*, and looking upon me for it with some wonder, as a thing which he knew to be not usual among the *Portugals;* whereupon I told him who I was, to wit of what Country, and something I said briefly concerning the curiosity[2] of my Travells; that I had run through so many Countries onely to see the world, and was at length come to his Court, being no *Portugal*, but one of *Rome*, a different and remote Nation from *Portugal;* with all which he seem'd well pleas'd.

He bid us several times put on our Hats, but our Captain, whose example 'twas fit for us to follow, being resolv'd not to make himself known, not onely would not do it, but refus'd it both by gestures and words, which I liked not well; for, shaking his Head and smiling, he answer'd that he would not, that they should not cause

---

[1] See *ante*, p. 195.

[2] This word *curiosita* may refer either to the natural inquisitiveness which led to our author's travels, or to the apparent strangeness of an European coming so far without any apparent object in view except the gratification of his curiosity.

him to commit that false Latine,[1] what ever else he did; that indeed it was not a thing to be jested at, with other such gallantries: he conceiving, as I believe, that herein consisted all the punctuality[2] of this Audience on his part, so that none of the rest of us cover'd himself; but it would not have been ill done, if the favour had been shown with better Answers than by saying, as the Captain did twice, or thrice, (with greater Courtship, as he thought) that it was hot, and therefore he would not put on his Hat, which his smiling betray'd to be but an excuse; though he conceiv'd he thereby shew'd himself an excellent Courtier.[3]

Then the King began to speak to our Captain (whom he well perceiv'd to be the Chief of the company) concerning the Peace, yet saying no more than what he had signifi'd to our Chief Captain; and desiring him to perswade the Chief Captain not to depart so soon from *Calecut*, but to stay till he had consulted better with his Ministers and had time to give a better and more determinate Resolution. The Captain answer'd cunningly that these matters did not belong to him, who was a private Souldier and was come thither onely to see the City and the Palace, whither he had been unexpectedly invited by his Highness; that as to the Peace, it was to be treated of with the Chief Captain, who had already answered his Highness as

---

[1] Or "Latinism" or "Latinity". The word is used generally to express an antiquated mode of expression; and hence also to denote an impropriety of behaviour, just as the word "solecism" was originally used to denote merely an impropriety of language, but is now more generally applied to an act of social misbehaviour.

[2] This word is here used in its old sense of *punctilio*, though it now is more often used to denote accuracy in regard to *time* only.

[3] See *Hamlet* (Act v, Sc. 2):

"*Hamlet.* Your bonnet to its right use; 'tis for the head.
"*Osric.* I thank your lordship, 'tis very hot.
"*Hamlet.* No, believe me, 'tis very cold; the wind is northerly.
"*Osric.* It is indifferent cold, my lord, indeed,"

far as he could, according to the Orders given him by the Vice-Roy; nevertheless, in obedience to his Highness, he would deliver this Message to him in the Evening.

The King saw that a Souldier of ours had one of those Arquebuses[1] which the *Portugals* call *Baccamarti*,[2] which are very short, of a large bore and with a Flint-lock after the English fashion. He asked to have it brought to him to look upon; whereupon a Courtier, taking it out of the Souldier's Hand, reach'd it to the King, not giving it into his Hand (for 'tis not lawful for them to touch a thing at the same time as the King) but, because it would neither have been handsome to have lay'd it down on the ground for the King to take up, therefore he took this Course. He set the but-end of the Arquebuse upon the ground at a little distance from the King, and then, giving the muzzle a gentle cast from himself, made it fall into the Hands of the King who held them ready for that purpose. The King taking the Arquebuse in his hand, presently shook the powder out of the pan upon the ground, lest any disaster should befall him, (for he perceived it was charged) then, lifting it up to his Eye, he looked through the sight, shewing thereby that he was a good marksman, as they told us afterwards he was. He look'd much upon the Flint-lock as a thing unknown to them, for their Guns have

---

[1] From the French *arquer*, "to make crooked," and *bus* or *büchse*, a Teutonic word for a pipe, or tube (see Webster's *Dictionary*). Or (according to the *Imperial Dictionary*) from the German *haken*, a hook, or forked rest from which it was fired. The name is sometimes written "Haquebut", "Hackbut", and "Hagbut". Such arms were used up to the time of the Civil War in England, when they were superseded by a lighter weapon without any rest. (See Garrard's *Art of War*, and Meyrick's work *On Armour*.)

[2] So in original; but it should perhaps be *boccomarti*, a kind of blunderbuss, or large-mouthed firearm.

onely matches[1]; and, being[2] he seemed much taken with this piece, I told the Captain it would be handsome to present it to him, and indeed had it been mine I should willingly have given it to him. The Captain spoke to the Souldier, who, incapable of such noble thoughts, answered that he would give it to the King if he might have forty Piasters[3] for it, which was twice the value, so that the King not offering to buy it, nor the Captain offering to lay out so much money in order to present it to him, the pleasuring him therewith was waved; nor was it otherwise offered to him, as in my opinion Civility required. Nevertheless the King never let it go out of his Hand so long as we were with him. Afterwards he shewed us a little Parrot standing in an open Cage under the porch; he endeavoured to cause it to speak in our presence; and because our Interpreters were not very good he sent to call an eminent Servant of his, who spoke the *Portugal* Tongue better, to come and interpret in this conversation.

XIII.—The *Signori Portoghesi* my Companions, little accustomed to Prince's Courts, though otherwise well bred, gave me occasion to laugh within myself at two things. The first was that, it appearing to them unhandsome that the King stood all the while he discoursed with us, as he did, or, at most, leaned onely against the wall on his staff, they took upon themselves to speak to his Highness, asking him to sit down and not put himself to such trouble. I disswaded the Captain from it by all means,

---

[1] Matchlocks were used in Europe also up to the end of the sixteenth century.

[2] For "since"; see p. 28, note 1.

[3] From the Italian *piastra*, a thin plate of metal. The coin had different values in different countries. The Portuguese *piastra* was equivalent to about 4*s*. of English money.

because Kings are Kings, and sit, or stand, when they please and do what they list; 'tis their part to command; nor are we to use those Compliments with them which we do to our equals, but always leave them to their own will and pleasure, for this is the behaviour of the Court. But my counsel prevailed little, for the Captain was resolved to speak and to desire him to sit down, as he did, not once, but twice or thrice; of which nevertheless the King made little account and anſwered onely with a smile.

The second thing that made me laugh was that, when the King enter'd into the little Court, the door, whereat he and we had enter'd before, was immediately made fast with an Iron Bar, people also standing continually to guard it; and so likewise when anyone came in, or was sent out by the King, it was presently shut with diligence. The Captain and the other *Portugals* did not like this shutting of the door and began presently to mutter amongst themselves and to suspect that the King intended to detain them prisoners there, or to put some trick upon them; and asked what would the Chief Captain and others say in *Goa* for their coming to put themselves in a cage thus, without the order and leave of their Chief Captain, onely upon meer curiosity? I advis'd them to be quiet, telling them that it was not befitting a King to do such an act, nor was there any occasion why the King should be so treacherous; that we were not so many, nor so considerable, that the doing thereof would be of any profit to him, or damage to the *Portugal* Nation. That it was fit the doors should be shut whilst the King was there in that manner, giving Audience to so many strangers together, arm'd and so little trusted by him as we were. That, on the contrary, he had done us much Honour in inviting and admitting us to his presence with all our weapons, there being no Ambassador, nor publick person, or anyone so much as known amongst us. This partly quieted them, although they very ill endur'd to see themselves shut up.

I told them further that it belong'd to the King to dismiss us when he pleas'd, and that, should we be late, the Chief Captain would excuse us for our delay at least, if not for our too great Curiosity, which yet was no high crime as the case stood, almost all the Souldiers being come ashore this day. Nevertheless they twice, or thrice, demanded of the King that he would let them go, alledging that it was already late to return aboard, as indeed it was; but the King alwayes made excuses, and would not dismiss them, saying that we must stay till the Man he had sent for was come, because he was desirous to talk a little better with us, and that he would send us aboard in his own Boats at any time when it should be needful; for, there being no form'd Harbour at *Calecut* but an open shore, the Ships rode at a good distance from the Land.[1]

XIV.—At length came the expected Interpreter, who was a principal *Brachman* and a Man of great Authority with the King; for I observed that he alone of all that were present leaned upon his staff as the King did, and he himself said that he had sometimes treated of weighty affairs on his King's behalf with the *Portugals* in the enterprize of *Cognale*,[2] perhaps not in the days of this *Samorì*,[3] but of his predecessor. So that he said he was very well

---

[1] The western coast of India south of Goa being almost wholly devoid of bays, or harbours, is naturally dangerous for ships, especially in a south-westerly gale of wind. In 1781 H.M. ship *Superb* of 74 guns was lost on this coast (at Telicheri). (See Eastwick's *Handbook of Madras*, p. 299.)

[2] It is uncertain what enterprise is here referred to. But the name "Cognale" is probably meant for *Koilandi*, a place on the coast, not far from Kálíkot. (See *Handbook of Madras*, p. 298.) The name is written also as "Coilandy", "Coulandi", and "Coulete". (See Yule's *Cathay, etc.*; vol. ii, p. 454.)

[3] See *ante*, p. 345, note 2.

known to the Vice-Roy and the Chief Captains of *Goa* acquainted with those parts.

Upon the entrance of this Man the King call'd our Captain to come up to him upon the rais'd pavement of the Porch; he refused at first twice or thrice, but at length was prevailed with, by the instances both of the King himself and of this *Brachman*. Here the King fell largely to discourse with him and with us about the Peace, about his desire to have the Fleet stay awhile longer for establishing a firm Friendship with the *Portugals* and about divers other things; many of which were the same that he had spoken of before. In short, the Audience lasted till night, the two little Ladies, his Nieces, being present almost all the time, (for they went and came now and then) and the Queen in the Upper Cloyster; in beholding of whom, to speak truth, I was more attentive than in hearing all these discourses, which I well saw were of little importance, and therefore I cannot relate them more punctually.[1]

At length, it growing dark, upon our Captain's importunity the King dismiss'd us, and, the door being open'd, we were suffer'd to go forth; but first he caused many bunches of Indian Figs[2] and *Lagne*[3] to be brought and presented to us; the Courtiers giving them to our Captain and the other Souldiers, not by stretching forth the Hand, but by tossing them in the Air, as their Custom is, I believe, to avoid being contaminated by our contact. The King did the like when, at our departure, he restored the Arquebuse to its owner; for he cast it after the same manner into the hands of one of his Courtiers as it was cast to him, bowing himself almost to the ground for that purpose, as it was necessary to do by reason of the short-

---

[1] See *ante*, p. 370, note 2.

[2] See *ante*, p. 327, note 1, and p. 337.

[3] See *ante*, p. 336, note 1.

ness of the piece. These Ceremonies of not being touch'd and the like, of which in publick demonstration they are so rigorous, yet in secret, and when they please, they do not exactly observe; and 'twas told us of this King that he is a great drinker of Wine, though rigorously prohibited by his Religion, and that he hath sometimes eaten and drunk at the same Table with *Portugals* very familiarly; and that he is a Man of very affable humour and a great friend to a jovial life, which also his carriage towards us demonstrated.

Besides the *Lagne* and the Figs, which he appointed some of his Servants to carry for us even to the Boats, he gave our Captain a wild Pig alive, which he caus'd to be brought from some inner rooms of the Court, and, being ty'd with a Rope, to be carried likewise to the Sea-side, whither he also sent many and some of the principal of his Courtiers to accompany us. A little after us he sent again to the Chief Captain one of those two Men who had been at *Goa*, (to wit he who conducted us to the Palace and was present at the whole Audience) to visit the Chief Captain in his Name, carry him new refreshments of Fruit, and desire him not to depart so soon.

But before I proceed further, for the better understanding of what I have already written, I will here present to your view a rough and unmeasur'd ground-plan of the *Samori's* Palace and the place where he gave us Audience.[1]

---

[1] In connection with this potentate the following extract from the *London Gazette* of May 25th, 1892, may be found to be of some interest:—"To be Knight Commander of the Most Exalted Order of the Star of India—Maharaja Mana Vikrama Bahadur, Zamorin of Calicut." *Stat nominis umbra!*

The *Zamorins* of Kalikot have been since 1792 the stipendiaries of the English Government. The Palace here referred to was probably the same building as that in which V. da Gama was received in 1498.

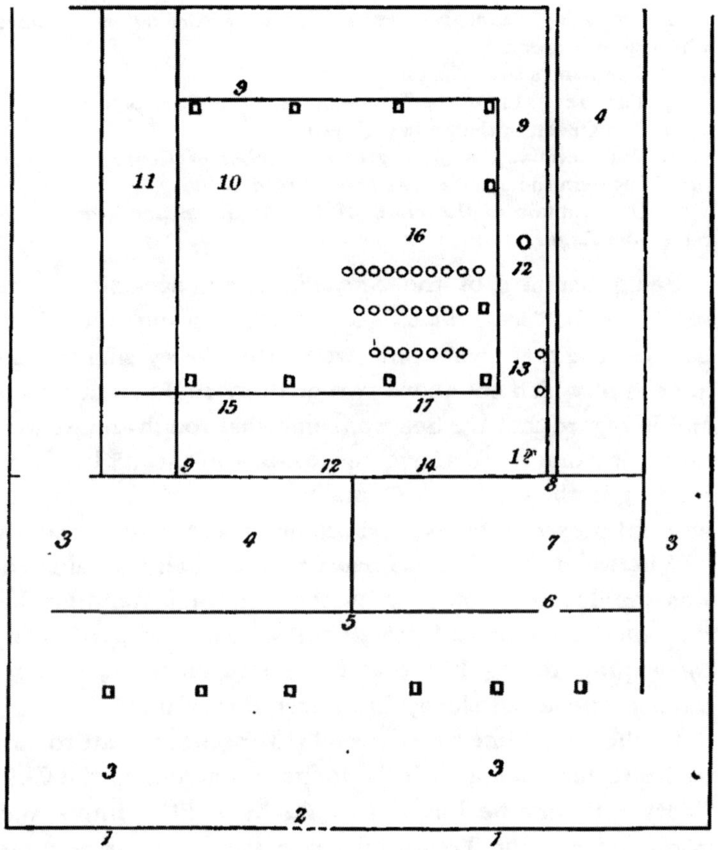

1. The little Piazza without the first Gate of the Palace.
2. The first Gate guarded with Balusters.
3. A great Court within the first Gate, which should be longer in proportion to the breadth, but is drawn thus in regard of the scantness of the paper; it hath lodgings about it in several places.
4. The King's House and the Apartment of his Women.
5. The Porch of the said House.
6. The second Gate.
7. Entrance with iron bar, kept shut.
8. A Door leading into the little Court.
9. Several Lodgings.
10. The little Court.
11. The place whence the wild Pig was brought.

12. The King, denoted in several places, according as he moved whilst he was speaking.

13. The King's two Nieces.

14. The great Man of the King who serv'd for Interpreter.

15. The Queen in the higher Cloyster.

16. Our Company, with a greater number of Courtiers on each side of us than the place allows here to be denoted.

17. Our Captain at the close of the Audience and when he received the *Lagne*.[1].

Being dismiss'd by the *Samori*, as is above-said, we return'd to the Sea-side to go aboard, it being now night; but because there were but two or three very small boats, in each of which not above two or three could go at a time, and in regard that the Sea was somewhat rough and we were many, it came to be above one o'clock in the night before we all got aboard. Our Captain was one of the first, and he went presently to give an account of what had pass'd this day between us and the *Samori* to the Chief Captain, who was minded to depart forthwith; but, understanding that the Souldiers were not yet all embarqued, and particularly the Captain telling him that I was still on shore, he gave order to move but slowly in expectation of me.

In the meantime the *Samori's* Messenger went to him to desire him to stay a little longer; whereupon the Chief Captain, though he knew it would be of little importance in reference to the Treaty of Peace, yet not to appear discourteous, and perhaps also on account of some expediency in regard to our Navigation, determined to stay all this night in the Port of *Calecut*. The Messenger, returning ashore with this answer, found me, alone of all the Fleet, still there, where some of the principal *Nairi*[2] kept me company all the while, and left me not till they saw me in the Boat, using much diligence to dispatch all others as soon as possible, and in the meantime, while we waited, which

---

[1] See *ante*, p. 336, note 1.

[2] See *ante*, p. 232, note 4.

was above an hour, holding me by the hand and expressing many other caresses and demonstrations of kindness to me.

XV.—Before I leave *Calecut* I shall here observe one strange custom[1] of the people of these parts. The Gentile *Nairi* have no peculiar Wives; but all Women are common amongst them; and when any man repairs to visit one of them he leaves his weapon at the door, which sign sufficiently debars all others from entering in to disturb him; nor does this course beget any difficulty, or jealousie. The Women are maintained by those men that have to do with them. The children neither seek to know, nor many times do know, who their Father is, but their descent by the Mother is alone considered, and according to that all inheritances are transferred. The same rule is observed among Princes and their Wives, the Queens, who are the King's Sisters, being used to marry other neighbouring Kings, and to go into their States to have children, who are to succeed in the Kingdoms of their Uncles, and by this means are of Royal blood both by Father and Mother. These Princesses are held in great esteem by the Kings, their Husbands; yet if they are minded to try other Men they are not prohibited, but may and often times do so, making use of whom they fancy for their pleasure, but especially of some *Brachman*, or other of their Husbands' principal Courtiers, who with their privity and consent are wont to converse and practise with them most intrinsecally[2] in the Palace.

The King and all others, as I have said, commonly go naked; onely they have a cloth wherewith they are girded, reaching to the mid-leg. Yet, when upon any occasion the

---

[1] As to the Nairs and their customs, see *ante*, p. 218, note 2.

[2] This is the old way of spelling the word, which is here used in its obsolete sense of intimately", or "familiarly"

King is minded to appear much in Majesty, he puts on onely a white vestment of very fine cotton, never using either Cloth of Gold, or Silk. Others also when they please may wear the like garment, but not in the King's presence, in which 'tis not lawful for anyone to appear otherwise than naked, saving the cloth above-mentioned. The Arms which everyone wears must not be laid aside at any time, especially not before the King; and, as I have elsewhere noted, everyone keeps to one sort of Arms which he first takes to, without ever changing.

When two Kings happen to war together each Army takes great heed not to kill the opposing King, nor so much as to strike his Umbrella wherever it goes, which is amongst them the Ensign of Royalty,[1] because, besides that it would be a great sin to have a hand in shedding Royal blood, the party, or side, which should kill, or wound, him would expose themselves to great and irreparable mischiefs, in regard of the obligation that the whole Kingdom of the wounded, or slain, King hath to revenge him with the greatest destruction of their enemies, even with the certain loss of their own lives if it be needful. By how much such Kings are of greater dignity among them so much longer this obligation of furious revenge endureth. So that if the *Samorì*[2] should be killed, or wounded, by the Army of the King of *Cocin*,[3] who is his enemy, but of greater dignity, the people of the *Samorì* stand obliged to one day of revenge, (others say three days) during which everyone is obliged to act his utmost to the utter destruction of those of *Cocin*, even with the manifest hazard of his own life. But if the King of *Cocin*, who hath a greater repute, for honour at least, if not for power, should happen to be slain, or wounded, by the people of the *Samorì*, the fury of

---

[1] See *ante*, p. 268, note 6.

[2] See *ante*, p. 345.

[3] See *ante*, p. 199, note 1.

revenge is to last in those of *Cocin* all the time of their lives (others say once a year), which would cause a great destruction of both sides. They call this term of time, or manner of revenge, *Amocò*[1]; so that they say the *Amocò* of the *Samorì* lasts one day; the *Amocò* of the King of *Cocin* lasts all the life, and so of others.[2]

XVI.—On *December* the twenty-third, a good while after Sun-rise, we departed from *Calecut*, but had the wind all day against us and made but little way. At night we cast Anchor, because there is seldom wind enough for sailing in the night time; and being[3] we coasted along the shore we might cast Anchor at any time we pleased.

December the twenty-fourth. We had the Wind contrary again, making very little way; so that we cast Anchor many times, and in the Evening, because it was Christmas-Eve, the Litanies were sung in all the Ships; and afterwards we had Collations[4] of Sweetmeats and celebrated the Feast as well as the place afforded. In our Ship some Souldiers, who were employ'd to make a sort of sweet fritters of Sugar, for sport put into many of them certain powders which caused giddiness; so that almost all the Souldiers that ate of them seem'd drunk after the Collation, and were constrain'd to betake them-

---

[1] The derivation of this word is uncertain. (See Sir H. Yule's *Hobson-Jobson.*) Our English word "amuck" is no doubt the same. For an early mention of the custom referred to see Barbosa's (?Magellan's) *Coast of East Africa and Malabar*, p. 194 (Hakluyt edition).

[2] Here follows a passage, for which the curious reader is referred to the original Italian.

[3] For "since"; see *ante*, p. 28, note 1.

[4] The use of this word *Collatione* here is interesting, showing, as it does, the early use of the word in its modern sense of a "repast" or "meal". The word was originally applied to the meetings, or "collections" of monks, for the purpose of reading together, and as they ate food at the same time, the word afterwards came to denote any light repast. (See *New English Dictionary*, *sub verb.*)

selves to sleep, which they did all night much more than that time and place requir'd; for had Enemies come, the greatest part of the Souldiers being in this manner, I know not how we should have done.

On *December* the twenty-fifth by break of day we arriv'd at *Canandr*,[1] where we presently landed to hear the divine Offices. *Canandr* is a little place upon the shore, but near a Promontory which makes a kind of Haven. The City is surrounded with walls, not very strong, or well made, and in some places, I know not by what negligence, decay'd. It hath four Churches,[2] to wit *La Sede*,[3] or the Cathedral; *La Misericordia*,[4] which is a Confraternity, and pious institution. There are some of them in all the settlements of the *Portugals*. They correspond with one another, and do many good works, much like our *Monte della Pieta*, *Santo Spirito*,[5] and other such; for almost all the pious works, which amongst us are done by divers Houses and Societies, this Institution of *La Misericordia* does amongst the *Portugals;* as keeping things deposited; transmitting Bills of Exchange safely; relieving the poor, the sick and imprisoned; maintaining exposed children; marrying young maids; keeping Women of ill Lives when converted; redeeming Slaves; and, in short, all works of Mercy whereof a City, or Country, can have need. A pious thing, indeed, and of infinite benefit to the Publick; the rather

---

[1] See *ante*, p. 356, *note*.

[2] One at least still remains. (See *Handbook of Madras*, p. 300.)

[3] See *ante*, p. 133, note 4.

[4] The well-known Society of Misericordia was founded on the remains of the "Irmandade de Piedade", in the days when pestilence was raging so fiercely that the dead lay uncared for in the streets, because no one dared to bury, or even to touch, them. The Society still exists and performs many charitable duties. Its members are drawn from all classes of Society, and when rendering their services are disguised completely by a cowl covering the head and face, with two holes in it for the eyes to see through. (See *Fonseca*, p. 244.)

[5] These are well-known charitable institutions.

because they are in all Territories of the *Portugals*, and hold correspondence together, even those of *India* with those of *Portugal;* so that they all seem but one body, extending itself to several Countries and becoming incredibly useful to all. This pious institution is govern'd by secular Confriers,[1] to which Confraternity none are admitted but worthy Persons, upon certain decent conditions and to a set number. So that the good works which they do and the great sums expended therein every year, accrue to the benefit, not only of the Confriers, but of the Publick in general, together with much Charity; hence I do not account my time lost in making this little Digression.

The third Church of *Cananòr* is that of *San Francesco*, where the Fryers of that Order[2] reside; and the fourth, if I remember right, is that of *Santa Maria della Vittoria.* Without *Cananòr* is an entrench'd Fort, contiguous to the walls of the City, and under the *Portugals'* jurisdiction. But about a musket shot distant, or more, is a great open space, which they call the *Bazàr*, where all sorts of Provisions and other Merchandize are sold; it is like that of *Calecut*, and perhaps better; yet this territory is under the jurisdiction of the *Gentiles* (though the Inhabitants are in a great part *Malabar Moors*), and by authority from a King of this Country, whom they call the King of *Cananòr*, and who resides far from the Sea, 'tis governed by a famous *Malabar Moor*, nam'd *Agà Begel*,[3] whose House I saw, but not himself, having spent this whole day in walking up and down *Cananòr* and the *Bazàr* of the *Gentiles*, for I dined with our Captain on shore in the House of a *Portugal* married there. At night having viewed all, and bought abundance of dried Indian Figgs and many Vessels of Conserves of the Pulp of young Indian Cane, or

---

1 Or "confriar", one of the same Order.

2 See *ante*, p. 156, note 3.

3 Probably *Aga Beg* (or *Bey*). See *ante*, p. 225, note 4.

Bambù,[1] (which is very good to eat after this manner) and of green Pepper, Cucumbers and other Fruits wont to be pickled by them in Vinegar,[2] and vendible here, very good and in great plenty, at length we returned on Ship-board.

XVII.—On *December* the twenty-sixth we set sail from *Cananòr*, but for three dayes together sailed but little by reason of the accustom'd contrary wind and our casting Anchor frequently, as well in the day-time as at night.

December the twenty-ninth. We passed before *Cagnarotto*,[3] whence some Men came in a Boat from the King of *Banghel*,[4] (who lives there in Sanctuary with the King of that place, his Friend and Kinsman) to visit and make presents to our Chief Captain in the Name of their Lord.

On *December* the thirtieth, about noon, we entred the Port of *Mangalòr*.[5] I had a desire to go to *Carnate*[6] to see that Queen,[7] and had already given Money for a Boat to carry me thither, being[8] I might sooner and better go so than with a *Palanchino;* but this journey was prevented as well as my former one, I know not by what unhappy destiny; for I understood that the Fleet was by all means to depart from *Mangalòr* the next day, so that I could not have time to go and return; and if I lost the opportunity of this Fleet, God knows when I should have another of passing to *Goa*, whither other considerations of my business required me to repair as soon as might be. So I deferr'd my going to *Carnate*, but with no small regret at being deprived of the knowledge of that Queen, who was reported to me as a Lady of great worth and valour.

---

[1] See p. 220, note 3.

[2] See *ante*, p. 327, note 4.

[3] See *ante*, p. 286, note 1. But this may be the modern *Chandragadi* (see Eastwick's *Handbook of Madras*, p. 301), identical with the ancient *Cangerecora*. (See Yule's *Cathay, etc.*, vol. ii, p. 451.)

[4] See *ante*, p. 286.

[5] See *ante*, p. 212, note 2.

[6] See *ante*, pp. 168, 314, and 352, note 5.

[7] See *ante*, p. 353.

[8] For "since"; see *ante*, p. 28, note 1.

Whilst we stay'd ashore I went to the Church of *San Francesco* to visit those Fathers, where I found the Chief Captain of our Fleet, Sig: *Luis di Mendoça*, whom I had never seen before. We conversed together for some time, as he wished to know more of me, and I found him a very compleat and gallant Cavalier, and, having been bred in the Court of *Spain* as the Queen's Page, a much better Courtier than other *Portugal* Cavaliers of *India*, who have not seen other Countries, are wont to be.

On *December* the one and thirtieth I heard Mass in the fore-noon and dined ashore with the Brother of Signor *Tomè de Barrios*, my Friend in *Goa*, at the House of the *Padre Vicario* of *Mangalòr*, nam'd . . . . . .[1] and known to me likewise at *Goa*. In the evening I went aboard, and when it was dark we went out of the mouth of the Port to put ourselves before the whole *Cafila*,[2] which here began to joyne with our Fleet, very numerous indeed, consisting of above a hundred and fifty Ships, laden with Rice, which were going to *Goa*, from whence all that Provision is dispersed abroad; of which *Cafila* our Ship being Captain of the Vant-guard[3] it behoved us to go first; but, being[4] the *Cafila* was so great, we cast Anchor just without the mouth of the Port, there expecting the day and a sign to be given us by the Chief Captain with his Cannon. For it was requisite for all to keep as close together as possible, to the end that so many ships of Merchandize, (disarmed and without Souldiers, saving the Convoy[5] consisting of the few Ships of our Fleet, some of which went before, some in the middle and some alwayes behind) might go secure from the assaults and surprizes

---

[1] This hiatus occurs in the original. [2] See *ante*, p. 121, note 3.

[3] Old form of spelling, from the French *avant*.

[4] For "since"; see p. 28, note 1.

[5] The word "Convoy" is used correctly to denote either the protecting, or protected, fleet.

of Pirates; and, indeed, to guard so many disarmed and laden Ships that took up so much room at Sea with so few armed Vessels was no easie matter. But so it was arranged that we, above all the rest, were to take particular care that no Ship got before us, or separated from the Company, lest some disaster might befall them.

XVIII.—On the first of January 1624 we set sail from *Mangalòr*[1] towards *Goa*, with the whole *Cafila*, which encreased hourly; other Merchant Ships joyning with us at all the Ports by which we passed, we giving them a sign with our Cannon, and many times waiting for them till they came out. This first day we sailed not above three Leagues, and anchored under *Carnate*,[2] but not in such a place and time that I could go to see the Queen as I desired.

On *January* the second we set forth again very early, but a contrary North-West Wind arising caus'd us to anchor among the Rocks, which they call *Scogli di Santa Maria*[3]; whence some Men that went on shore brought me some Jasmen,[4] of a very goodly Scarlet[5] Colour,[6] of which sort I had never seen any Jasmen before, in any

[1] As this is the last mention of *Mangalúr*, a few details regarding the place may here be added to those given at p. 212. The name of the town is probably derived from the goddess *Mangala Devi*, who has a temple there. It is the principal civil and military station of S. Kanara, and was the scene of a gallant defence by the English and native troops in 1782 against Tipu Sahib's whole army. (See Wilks, ii, p. 466.)

[2] See *ante*, pp. 168, 314, and 352, note 5.

[3] See *ante*, p. 300, note 3.

[4] Spelt *Gesmini* in the original Italian. The name is a corruption of the Arabic *Yasimon*.

[5] In the original, *cinabro*, or vermilion.

[6] Probably one of the *Bignonia* tribe, noted for the gay colours of their flowers, which somewhat resemble thôse of the jasmin in shape, but are deficient in scent, which is one of the chief attractions of the latter species (see Lindley's *Vegetable Kingdom, sub verb.*). It may, possibly, have been the *Bignonia Venusta*, which somewhat resembles a jasmin, and bears flowers of a vermilion or orange colour.

other place of the world; but for smell it had little, or none at all.[1]

On *January* the third we set forth again at our usual hour, and the wind began to blow from the land, which in that place is on the East. We pass'd by *Barselòr*,[2] and, a League beyond, anchored at the Rock of *Camboli*,[3] where we waited for the *Cafila* of *Barselòr;* we not entering there ourselves that it might dispatch the sooner.

January the fifth. Whilst we stay'd at *Camboli*, expecting the coming forth of all the *Cafila* of *Barselòr*, in the Morning we discover'd twelve Ships coming towards us from the South; and knowing that they were not Merchant ships but Men of War, and having no news of any *Armado* that was to come from *Goa* at this time, we judged them to be *Paroes*[4] of *Malabar* Pirates, as indeed they appear'd; for the said *Paroes* are almost like the Ships of the *Portugals*, but somewhat lighter. And because we saw them make directly up to us we prepar'd for fight and sailed forward to meet them; assuring ourselves that if they were *Paroes* they came to assault us; since they could not but know that the Ships of our *Armado*, which alone were fit for fight, were fewer than theirs, and that the other Merchants' Ships of the *Cafila* whom we convoy'd could serve for nothing else but either to fly away, if they were able, or to increase their booty in case the few arm'd Vessels should be beaten.

---

[1] Indian flowers, with some notable exceptions, are generally somewhat disappointing in regard to scent. Hence arose the remark, attributed to a late Financial Member of Council, that "India is a place where everything smells except the flowers".

[2] See *ante*, p. 250, note 2.

[3] It seems probable that *Camboli* is identical with *Cumbala* or *Cambulla* (mentioned in Yule's *Cathay*, *etc.*, vol. ii, p. 451), the modern *Kumblah* (see Eastwick's *Handbook of Madras*, p. 301). But this place is *south* (not north, as here stated) of *Mangalúr*.

[4] See *ante*, p. 201, note 2.

The Ship wherein I was, being the Captain of the Vantguard,[1] was far before the rest and alone, towards that part whence the abovesaid Ships were coming. Having betaken ourselves to our Arms, (which yet was not done without some confusion, because the things in the Ship were out of order, and the Souldiers unprovided with Powder, which was to be fetch'd out of the place where it was kept, and distributed thus hastily in small quantities, being[2] our store was but small) we consulted a while what to do, whether to wait for our other Ships, which were behind, and so joyn all together in encountering the Enemy; or else to begin the fight alone, as we were, till the rest came up to us.

The first Course seem'd safest and most judicious, the latter was more magnanimous, but withal temerarious,[3] because we were so distant from our Company that, before they could come to succour us, our Ship might be wholly destroy'd; as, being but one, it might very easily be by so many, especially in that extreme, furious, way of fighting practis'd here, wherein there is great use of fireworks.[4] Yet our Captain and the rest of us thought it was no time to demur longer and consult together, because the Enemy was so near that to wait for our Company would have little advantag'd, but might much have prejudic'd, us, giving them thereby presumptions of our weakness and fear. Wherefore we all cried out to go on; that, since we were come to this pinch, 'twas better to incur our loss alone with a valorous temerity by doing our duty than to hazard the loss of the whole *Armado* and its Reputation, if

---

[1] See *ante*, p. 385, note 3.

[2] For "since"; see *ante*, p. 28, *note*.

[3] An obsolete word, used by Bishop Latimer and other writers.

[4] In original, *artificii di fuoco*, which words probably refer to some contrivances for setting fire to the enemy's ship. As to the use of fire in Indian warfare, see Wilks' *Southern India*, vol. ii, p. 471.

the Enemy, perceiving us timorous and weak, should take heart against us from our imprudent fear; that as it was our duty to go forward, so it was the duty of our Companions to follow us and succour us, and not let us perish alone; that this care belong'd to them: that if they did otherwise the fault would lie upon them, not upon us; (in fine) let us give the onset and leave Heaven to take care of the rest.

Thus resolv'd we desperately sail'd forward. Our Companions who were nearest would have done the like; but the Chief Captain, who was far behind in another place of the *Cafila*, shot off a Piece to command all to stay for him, reasonably conceiving it the best way to attack the enemy all together; whereupon all the other Ships of the Fleet which were behind us stood still awhile; but we alone, seeing ourselves so far engag'd and so near the Enemy, whatever the others did, would by no means stay but continu'd our course. Which Sig: *Francesco Pesciotto*, Captain of one of the nearest Ships, beholding, and misliking that we should charge thus alone and he quietly look on at a little distance, lost all patience and began again to make up after us, though afar off; the same did all the rest soon after, conceiving it the best way. We were now within Falcon-shot (for greater Pieces than Falcons[1] these Ships carry not) but forbore to fire till a nearer approach might make the shot more certain; which seem'd also to be the Enemies' design; when, being come so near as to speak and be heard, and standing ready to give fire both by the Ordnance and Musket, by the voices

---

[1] The name "Falcon" was applied to cannon whose diameter at the bore was 5¼ in., and weight 750 lb.; its length 7 ft., and weight of shot 2½ lb. The derivation of the name is uncertain, but it was originally applied to an instrument used for making holes in walls (from *falx*, "a hook"), and hence probably was applied to small cannon used for the same purpose.

and cries on either side we found each other to be friends, for these Ships were an unexpected and extraordinary Fleet of *Portugals*, sent to *Cocin*[1] to convey securely from thence to *Goa* certain moneys of the Confraternity *della Misericordia*[2] and other Provisions. Hereupon, the feud ceasing, the deadly firing was turn'd into joyful Salutations, with cheerful noise of Drums and Trumpets; at the sound whereof the Dawn, beginning to break, seem'd also to hasten to rejoyce with us and to part our erroneous fray.

I have mention'd this occurrence at large to the end that the successes,[3] and inconveniences, and the counsels and resolutions ensuing suddenly thereupon may be known; from all which prudent advice for other occasions may be deduced, and also to make known to all the world the demeanour of the noble *Portugal* Nation in these parts; who indeed, had they but as much order, discipline and good government as they have valour, *Ormùz* and other sad losses[4] would not be now lamented, but they would most certainly be capable of achieving great matters. But God gives not all things to all.

XIX.—It being now broad day we set sail with the whole *Cafila;* but, by reason of contrary wind, sail'd no more than three leagues, and late in the evening came to anchor, in the place where we happened to be; the contrary Northwest wind beginning to grow more boisterous.

January the sixth. We had the Wind still contrary, and, having sail'd three other leagues, at the usual hour we cast anchor near the Rocks of *Baticala*.[5]

---

[1] See *ante*, p. 199, note 1.
[2] See *ante*, p. 382.
[3] Or, rather, "adventures".
[4] See *ante*, p. 171, note 5.
[5] Marked *Batcull* and *Batkal* in modern maps, in 14° N. Lat. Identical with the *Batigala* of Jordanus. It was a great place, with many merchants, where ships of Ormuz and Aden came to load sugar and rice, but was destroyed by the rise of Goa. There was an English

On the seventh, the said wind blowing somewhat favourably, about noon we pass'd by *Onòr*,[1] and, without staying, discharg'd only one Gun to give notice for the Ships to come out of the port, if any were there that would accompany us; for greater diligence was not needful, because few come from thence. In the Evening, the usual contrary North-West wind arising, we came to an Anchor, a little distant from *Mirizeo*.[2] At the second watch of the night a good stiff South wind arose; and in the forenoon next day we pass'd by the Rocks, call'd *Angediva*,[3] and at night came to an anchor somewhat Southwards of *Capo falso*.[4]

On *January* the ninth the wind was contrary and our way short; and because we could not proceed forwards we cast anchor near *Rio del Sale*[5]; also the next day, for the same reason, we could get no further than an *Enceada*

---

factory here in the 17th century. It is mentioned by Barbosa and De Barros. (See Yule's *Cathay*, vol. ii, p. 451.) Barbosa (?Magellan) mentions iron and *myrobolans* (see *ante*, p. 233) also among the exports, and also "spices and drugs"; and, among the imports, horses, pearls, coco-nuts, palm sugar, coco-nut oil, and palm wine. For these and other details, see *East Coast of Africa and Malabar* (Hakluyt edition), pp. 80 and 81. It is frequently mentioned also in the *Commentaries of Dalboquerque, quod vide.* Not to be confused with *Bathecala*, further north, the modern *Beitkul*. (See Yule's *Cathay, etc.*, vol. ii, p. 450.)

[1] See *ante*, p. 190, note 3.

[2] Marked *Marjel*, and *Mirjau*, in modern maps. So called from the river *Mergeo*, or *Mergeu*, north of *Kumtah*, from which much rice was exported. There is still a place here called *Mirjau*, the *Meerjee*, or *Meerzah*, of Rennell. *Mergeo* is described by Barbosa (*East Coast of Africa, etc.*, p. 79). (See Yule's *Cathay*, vol. ii, p. 450.)

[3] See *ante*, p. 201, note 4.

[4] Marked as Cape *Ruma*, or *Ramas*, in modern maps. Probably called *Falso* from being sometimes mistaken for Cape *Marmagaon*, further north.

[5] A small estuary, as its name imports.

(as they speak) or Bay, call'd *Mormogòn*,[1] in the Island of *Salsette*,[2] contiguous to that of *Goa* on the South, but greater, and divided from the same only by a River.[3] This Island of *Salsette* is full of very fair Towns[4] and abundance of Houses. Above all the *Jesuits* have the goodliest places, and 'tis counted that perhaps a third part of the Island is theirs; for, besides three good Towns which belong wholly to them, they have also dominion and government in all the other Towns too which are not theirs; they have Churches everywhere, Lands and store of goods, and, I believe, all the Parishes are govern'd by them in Spirituals with Supreme Authority; whence this people acknowledge more Vassallage to the *Jesuits* than to the King himself. The case is the same in another Island call'd *Bardeos*,[5] adjacent also to that of *Goa*, but more Northward, which is under the government of the *Franciscans*. Nor is it otherwise in almost all the other Territories of the *Portugals;* so that it may justly be said that the best, and perhaps too the greatest part of this State is in the hands of Religious Orders.[6]

XX.—Having anchor'd in the Bay of *Mormogòn* in good time and knowing that we were not to depart the

---

[1] More correctly, *Mármagaon;* see *ante*, p. 154, note 2. It is described by a recent visitor as "a miserable shelf of a place, all quay and sandy cliff, and railway goods terminus". (See *Murray's Magazine* of November 1890, p. 652.)

[2] This was one of the three original provinces forming the old conquered territory of Goa, the other two being *Ilhão* and *Badez* (sometimes written as *Bardes*). (See Eastwick's *Handbook of Bombay*, p. 229.)

[3] The *Tuari* river. See *ante*, p. 175, note 1.

[4] In original, *Ville*, which may mean towns, but here probably should be rendered as "country residences".

[5] Or *Badez*.

[6] On this subject, see *ante*, pp. xv, 156 (note 7), and 162 (note 4).

night following, our Captain, with some others of us, went ashore to see a Place and Church of the Jesuits call'd *S. Andrea*,[1] which they told us was hard by; yet we found it not so near, but that we walk't about a league to get to it, because we knew not the right way, but mistook it and were fain to leap over very broad and deep ditches of water, into one whereof one of our Company happened to fall, to the great laughter of the rest, besides many other inconveniences. We found the Church large, neat and well built, with a fair square Court, or Yard, before it, surrounded with handsome stone walls, and within it some great Trees, under which were Banks rais'd to sit upon in the shadow. On one side of the Church was a very fair and well-built House for the *Padre Rettore*, who hath the present superintendence thereof; which Church and Building would be very magnificent, not only for this place but even for the City of Rome itself.

We stay'd a good while, discoursing with the Rector, who told us sundry news from *Goa* and invited us to Supper; but, fearing to arrive too late at the Fleet if we stay'd to sup here, we wav'd the Courtesie and, taking leave of him at Sun-set, return'd to the place where we had left our Ships; and, though we had a Guide to conduct us by the best and nearest way, yet we got not thither to imbarque before two hours of the night.

January the eleventh. At our departing from the Port of *Mormogòn* this day, on which we were to arrive at *Goa*, the Chief Captain, who was wont to go in the Rear-guard, being now minded to go in the middle of the *Armada* commanded our Ship (hitherto Captain of the Vant-guard) to remain behind all the rest for guarding the Rear-guard, where great diligence was to be used, both that no straggling Ship might be in danger of being surpriz'd by

---

[1] This church is apparently not standing in the present day.

Rovers, or any of the Merchants' Vessels slip aside to avoid paying Custom at *Goa*, and go to unlade in other places of Counterband.[1] Wherefore, having sail'd the little remainder of the way and caus'd all the other Ships to enter, which were in number more than two hundred and fifty, we at length enter'd the Bar, or Mouth, of the *Rio* of *Goa*,[2] where we anchor'd under a Fort hard by, without going further towards the City; it being the custom for no Fleets to arrive at the City without giving notice and obtaining the Licence of the Viceroy.

Here we found the Ship, which alone was to go this year to *Portugal*, already laden and ready to sail; as also some Galeons in readiness likewise, whether to be sent to *Ormùz*, or elsewhere, I know not. Sig: *Ayres de Siqueira*, Captain of our Ship, having got leave of the Chief Captain, went to *Goa* with a *Manciva*,[3] or Boat, which came to him for that purpose; and I, with Sig: *Francesco Pesciotto*, Captain of another Ship, Sig: *Manoel Leyera*, and some few Souldiers, accompanied him. We arriv'd at *Goa* when it was dark night, because 'tis three leagues from the mouth of the Bar to the City, almost directly from South to North; so that there is a considerable difference between the altitude of the Pole at *Goa* and at the Bar. Having landed, everyone went to his own home; and I, who had no house ready for me, nor yet any servant, went, alone as I was, to lodge in the House of Sig: *Antionio Baraccio*, my friend, according as himself and Sig: *Ruy Gomes*, his Brother, had promis'd I should when I departed from *Goa*. As I was going thither I was unexpectedly met by the said two Brothers, who receiv'd me with their wonted courtesie. My Bed and Goods which

---

[1] An obsolete word for "contraband".

[2] *I.e.*, the river *Mandavi*. See *ante*, p. 175, note 1.

[3] See *ante*, p. 211. Sometimes written *Manchua*.

I had in the Ship were soon after brought to the same place by the procurement of Sig: *Ayres.*

I understood here that my quondam servant, the honest *Cacciatùr*, coming hither from *Ikkerì* to *Goa* after his false dealing with me,[1] had attempted to put a trick upon Signora *Maria*[2] also, but it did not succeed. He feign'd that I had sent him beforehand to take orders for a house against my return, and was importunate for money to prepare and provide things necessary. My letter he ventur'd not to present, but pretended a misfortune at Sea, whereby it was lost, with other such inventions. Hereupon Signora *Maria* suspected him, and, without my Letters, gave no credit to him, as neither did Signora *Maria da Cugna.*[3] So that, finding his devices to get money from them prov'd ineffectual, he came no more in sight; and we believe he is gone into the territories of the Moors amongst the Mahometans, having heard no more news of him.

XXI.—On *January* the twentieth a Proclamation was put forth by the Vice-Roy for all *Portugal* Souldiers (they call all such as have not wives *Soldati*) and also all *Dispacciati*,[4] though married,[5] to prepare to go to *Ormùz;* it being given out that the Vice-Roy intended to pass thither in person with a great *Armada* and Galeons. Amongst the *Portugals* those are call'd *Dispacciati* who having ended their Service, (which everyone is oblig'd to perform for eight years, only with that small pay and maintenance which is given to servants, which indeed is very slender)

---

[1] See *ante*, p. 292.

[2] See *ante*, p. 24, note 1.

[3] See *ante*, p. 160. This lady's husband was probably a descendant of the celebrated Tristão da Cunha, who discovered the island (in 37° 6′ S., and 12° 2′ W.), as described in *Commentaries of A. Dalboquerque* (Hakluyt edit., vol. i, p. 24), which is named after him.

[4] Or "time-expired" men.

[5] In original, *accasati*, or "settled in houses", which, no doubt, would generally imply the married state.

upon petition to the King in *Spain* and representation of the faithfulness of their services, according as the same are greater or less, are dismiss'd by the King with some honourable and profitable Charge, as Captain of a Fort, and the like, to enjoy the same for three years, or some other determinate time. Which charges they enter not upon as soon as the same are granted, but when it falls to them in due course, according to the time of their dismission; whereby it comes to pass that some never enjoy them as long as they live, nor yet their Sons sometimes, unless very late, (in case the favour extend to their sons too) because all the said charges, or offices, go by seniority; every man's time beginning from the day of his dismission; and oftentimes it happens that forty, or fifty, are dismissed at the same time with him, all of whom must first enjoy the same Office, or else die to make way for him.

In brief, 'tis an invention of the Kings of *Portugal* much for their own interest; for, not having much to give in recompense of services, they by this means pay the greatest part of those that serve them with hopes alone; which also prove very well for them; the men of this nation being of such an humour that they not only are contented with these bare hopes, and hold themselves well requited for many great and toilsome services, but make great account thereof; for the value of these Reversions, which are to fall God knows when, forms the estate and support of many Daughters, and, in brief, in respect of the little other estates they have in *India,* is one of the best and most considerable advantages that they possess, besides their being of much reputation and honour.

Now to all such as were in this manner dismissed was this Proclamation directed, obliging them to go to *Ormùz* with the Viceroy, under penalty of losing all their Reversions. But, for all this, intelligent men did not believe that the Vice-Roy would undertake this Expedition, both because they did not hold him to be a man likely to take up such a resolution, and because there were not such preparations made in *Goa* for his voyage as were requisite.

XXII.—On *January* the two and twentieth a Galeot, under the command of Sig: *Manoel de Paiva*, our friend, arriv'd at *Goa* from *Sindi*,[1] in which were many persons who had come to *Sindi* in other Ships from *Mascàt*[2]; amongst the rest there was a considerable[3] Souldier belonging to *Ruy Freira*,[4] who brought certain news of his own knowledge how the said *Ruy Freira*, having held *Ormùz*[5] closely besieg'd for a long time, and brought the Defenders to great distress for want of all things, at length, no relief coming to him, and having no provisions wherewith to continue the siege, (his victuals failing him) was constrain'd to raise the Siege and return to *Mascàt* with all his Army; yet with intention to make new provisions, and get new succour and ammunition, and then to return again to besiege the place, which, in the meantime, the Moors omitted not to supply with all sorts of necessaries for a long time, to repair the Fortifications, and reinforce it with fresh Soldiers.

All which consider'd, I hold the retaking of *Ormùz* to be very difficult, both in regard of the courage the enemy hath recovered by this Action, and because the same scarcity of Victuals will happen frequently, and, in a short

---

[1] Probably meant for *Sindu*, the old name for *Diul* or *Daibul*, a port at the mouth of the *Indus*. (See Yule's *Cathay*, *etc.*, vol. i, p. clxxviii, and *ante*, p. 136, note 4.)

[2] See *ante*, p. 158, note 7.

[3] In the original, *grave*, *i.e.*, of rank, or importance.

[4] See *ante*, p. 187.

[5] See *ante*, p. 2, note 1. A full description of *Ormùz* will be found in P. della Valle's Letter No. XVIII from Persia. See also Arrian's *Indica*, cap. 37, where the island is described under the name of *Organa*.

time, to the besiegers no less than to the besieged, being[1] the Island affords nothing of itself, and our provisions must be fetched from greater distance than those of the enemies; wherein if much diligence be not us'd on our part, I doubt not but it will be very difficult for them to hold the Siege for long; and whenever they intermit the same never so little, as they have done now, that short time is sufficient to secure the place from famine; because, having the Continent so near at hand and provisions there in much plenty, it may be in one day alone supply'd for many months. As for taking it by battery, or otherwise, the Portugals being so few and little skill'd in such Arts, and on the other side the enemy being so numerous and indefatigable in undergoing toil and pains, I hold it to be very difficult.

The Viceroy of *Goa*, who had been so cold in sending succours to *Ruy Freira* because he would not that he should take *Ormùz*, but only hold it streightened till he himself went in person to reap the fruit of others' labours, (that so he might with the glory of this victory cover the previous neglect he had committed in the shameful loss of the Ships on the Voyage when he came to *India*), now, hearing this news, and how *Ormùz*, which he thought he had in his clutches, was by the retreat of *Ruy Freira* (who would infallibly write into *Spain* of the wrong done him in not sending him any forces, or succour, during a year's time that he had been upon the attempt, and would heinously charge the Viceroy for it) escap'd out of his hands and become very difficult to be taken, was infinitely troubled thereat; and, indeed, I do not know how he can excuse himself to his Master for so great negligences; and some have heard him lament much, and say that it was his own fault. However it be, the talk of his going to *Ormùz*

[1] For "since"; see *ante*, p. 28, note 1.

became very cold upon this news; and, if it was not believ'd at first, after this it was held to be entirely given up; although, to encourage others to the expedition, he still kept up the report.

The same Ship brought news how *Ruy Freira*, whilst he was at the Siege of *Ormùz* with his few Ships, sent two to the Streight of *Mecca*,[1] to see whether they could get any booty which might serve to support his forces; another to *Sindi*[2] to fetch provisions, and to advertise the *Mogul's* Ministers there not to send any Ships into *Persia*,[3] otherwise he should take them; yet neither those of *Mecca* nor this of *Sindi* ever return'd to him, neither did his Captains send him anything from *Mascàt:* so that he was constrain'd to remove his quarters. Besides, during his stay before *Ormùz*, he had sent some other Ships to fall upon the Country of those *Arabians*[4] living upon the coast of Persia in the gulf above *Mogostàn*,[5] who are called *Nachilu*,[6] and this enterprise succeeded well enough, they

---

[1] A name applied to the entrance of the Red Sea. (See *Comm. of A. Dalboquerque*, vol. iii, p. 55 (Hakluyt edit.).

[2] See *ante*, p. 397, note 1.

[3] *I.e.*, to the relief of *Ormùz*.

[4] It may be open to doubt whether these people were true Arabians, or whether they were *Arabitæ*, an Indian race, mentioned by Arrian, who lived on this coast, so called from the river *Arabius*. See Heeren's *Historical Researches*, vol. i, p. 191, and Arrian's *Indica*, chap. xxi, where he says: "Near this place (*Crocala*) dwells an Indian tribe called the *Arabii*, who derive their name from the river *Arabis* (the modern *Púrali* or *Al-Mend*), which flows through their country to the sea, parting them from the *Oritæ*." And in chap. xxv he says: "The length of the voyage along the coast of the *Arabii* was 1,000 *stadia*."

[5] At the southern end of the Persian Gulf, between *Kohistan* and *Laristan* (see *ante*, p. 45, note 3). These three districts formed the ancient province of *Karmania* described in Arrian's *Indica*, chap. xxxii.

[6] In modern maps *Nackiloo*. On the coast of *Laristan*, in Persia, in Lat. 26° 57′ N., and Long. 53° 40′ E.

having made great destruction and taken much spoil; but afterwards the Captains of the same Ships, being greedy of prey, contrary to the order of *Ruy Freira* and against the judgment of one of them who was the head of all the rest (little obedience is an ordinary thing among the *Portugals* and causes infinite disorders) design'd to set upon another place, whose Governour, who was an Arabian *Sceich*,[1] at first attempted to make them forbear with good words, saying that he was their Vassal, etc., but, when he saw that Courtesie prevailed not against their rapacity, he got his men together and made head against them; so that, assaulting them in a convenient place as they were out of order, he defeated them, killing many, and, amongst those, divers captains and Soldiers of valour; which was no small loss.

It was further related that during the Siege of *Ormùz*, the besieg'd being in great streights for all other things, and, which was most important, of water also, which within the Fort[2] fail'd them and was corrupted, yet *Ruy Freira* could not hinder them from fetching plenty of very good water as often as they pleas'd at a place in the Island, without the Fort, which they call *Trumbàk*[3]; where, not through want of Soldiers, (for he might have had *Arabians* enough and others of those Countries) but for want of money to pay and support them, he could never

---

[1] For *Sheikh*, or chief. Literally "old man", a title of dignity properly belonging to the chiefs of the Arab tribes, or clans. It is also the title of the higher order of religious preachers. But it is widely used among Muhammadans as a title of respect.

[2] A full description of this Fort will be found in P. della Valle's Letter No. XVIII from Persia.

[3] Or *Turumbaque* (see *Commentaries of A. Dalboquerque*, vol. i, pp. 175-77, Hakluyt edition), where were the pools, or cisterns, from which the garrison was usually supplied with water. An old plan of the Fort at Ormùz will be found at p. 112 of vol. i of the work referred to.

place a guard to prevent the enemies from fetching as much water as they pleas'd. They said lastly that *Ruy Freira* was at *Mascàt*, soliciting for aid and preparing to return to *Ormùz* as soon as he should be provided with what was needful.

XXIII.—By the same Ship a Jew came from *Sindi*[1] who had lately dwelt in *Ormùz*, and came to *Sindi* by sea from *Guadèl*,[2] which is a Port of the Kingdom of *Kic*[3] and *Macran*,[4] and was come to *Guadel* by land from *Sphahán*. He was a sagacious person, and affirmed to me for certain that the Prince of *Kic* and *Macran* was a friend of, and obedient to, the *Persians*, and that there passed through his Country infinite *Cafilas*[5] of Merchandise which came from *India* upon Camels; and that this way was not onely frequented since the taking of *Ormùz*, which was declined through the War,[6] but was also very secure, and afforded much profit to the said Prince of *Macran*, because at *Guadèl* he received divers Customs of the abovesaid Merchandise; and before this pass was open he had no profit at all. Yet this Jew could not tell me whether this friendship and obedience of the *Macranite* to the *Persian* was because the Prince, who reigned there, was dead, and was succeeded by his younger Brother, who many years

---

[1] See *ante*, p. 397, note 1.

In Lat. 25° 11′ N., and Long. 62° 15′ E., sometimes written as *Gwadel*, and *Goadel* in the ancient chart (from the Sloane MS.), to be found at p. 80 of vol. i of the *Comm. of A. Dalboquerque* (Hakluyt edition), in which the name is also applied to the province in which the port is situated.

[3] This name is probably meant for *Kej*, the chief town in this province, in Lat. 26° 25′ N., and Long. 62° 58′ E., not far from Guadel; perhaps identical with *Kissa*, mentioned by Arrian (cap. xxxvi).

[4] See *ante*, p. 7, note 2, and Heeren's *Historical Researches*, vol. i, p. 173.

[5] See *ante*, p. 121, note 3.

[6] On the effects produced on commerce in Asia by wars and revolutions, see Heeren's *Historical Researches*, vol. i, p. 21 *et seq.*

ago had fled into *Persia* to the *Sciàh*,[1] as I have elsewhere mentioned in this Diary,[2] or else because the two Brothers never agreed together, and that he who reign'd still, either for his own interest on account of the said passage of the *Cafilas*, or through fear since the taking of *Ormùz*, or perhaps forced by War, or other like Accidents, had dispos'd himself to be friendly and obedient to the *Persians*.

XXIV.—On *January* the twenty-fifth the *Jesuits* of the Colledge of Saint *Paul*,[3] (this day being the feast of their Colledge) began to make part of their Solemnities, which were to be made for joy at the Canonization of their Saints *Ignatio* and *Sciavier*[4]; the Celebration of which was deferred till now, that more time might be allotted for preparation. They came forth with a Cavalcade of all their Collegians, divided into three Squadrons under three Banners, one of which represented the *Asiaticks*, one the *Africans*, and another the *Europeans;* those of each Squadron being clothed after the manner of their respective Countries. Before the Cavalcade went a Chariot of Clouds with *Fame* on the top, who, sounding her Trumpet with the adjunction of Musick, published the news of the said Canonization. Two other Chariots accompany'd the Cavalcade, the hindermost of which represented *Faith*, or the *Church;* the other in the middle was a Mount *Parnassus*, with *Apollo* and the Muses, representing the Sciences professed in the said Colledge; both which Chariots were also full of very good Musick and many

---

1 *I.e.*, Shah Abbas, as to whom much interesting information will be found in P. della Valle's Letters, Nos. IV and V, from Persia.

2 In one of the Letters from Persia.

3 See *ante*, p. 142, and p. 185, note 3.

4 For Xavier. See *ante*, p. 170, notes 2, 3, and 4. See also *F. Pyrard's Voyage*, vol. ii, p. 62, Part I (Hakluyt edition), where an engraving of the silver shrine of this latter Saint will be found.

people. Moreover they remov'd from place to place amongst the Cavalcade five great Pyramids upon wheels, drawn by Men on foot, well cloth'd after the Indian fashion. Upon the first were painted all the Martyrs of the Order of *Jesuits;* upon another all the Doctors and Writers of Books; upon another figures of Men of all such Nations in their proper habits, where the said order hath foundations, to represent the Languages in which the Fathers of it preach. Another had abundance of Devices relating to all the Provinces of the said Religion; and, lastly, another had all the Miracles both of *Sant Ignatio* and *San Francesco Sciavier.*

All of these Pyramids had Epitaphs, Statues and other Ornaments both on the Pedestal and at the top; and passing in this manner through the principal streets of the City, they planted and left the said Pyramids in several places, one before the See,[1] or Archiepiscopal Church[2]; one before the profess'd House of *Giesu*[3]; one before the Church of *San Paolo*,[4] where at first they kept the Colledge, but by reason of the badness of the air, remov'd it from thence,[5] yet the Church remains to them, which was sometimes much frequented and magnificent, but at this day is but meanly provided for, so that they are still in contest about it with the City which unwillingly consents to this changing of the Colledge. The last they left before the new Colledge, the Church whereof they are wont to call *San Rocco*,[6] and by the other name also; for the *Jesuits*, resolute to keep their Colledge by reason of the fairness of the place, notwithstanding the opposition of the

---

[1] See *ante*, p. 133, note 4.

[2] See *ante*, p. 156, note 9, and Eastwick's *Handbook of Bombay*, p. 224.

[3] See *ante*, p. 162, note 3.

[4] See *ante*, p. 178, note 2.

[5] See *ante*, p. 186, *note*.

[6] See *ante*, p. 185, note 3.

Augustine Fryers,[1] who by long and intricate suits use their utmost endeavour to hinder them from it, onely to the end not to have them as neighbours, under pretext that they deprive them of fresh air and the prospect of the Sea, the *Jesuits*, I say, resolute to abide there, prevailing hitherto both against the City (which recalls them back to *San Paolo Vecchio*, for greater convenience of the Students) and against the *Augustines*, and against the King himself, who hath many times ordained their removal and the destruction of their new Colledge, nevertheless maintain themselves in possession of their new and sumptuous Fabrick, which also they daily inlarge, and nominate *San Paolo Nuovo*, for in *India* they will have all their Colledges dedicated to Saint *Paul*, the Doctor of the *Gentiles*.[2]

XXV.—On *January* the nine and twentieth I went, together with the *Signori Baracci*, my entertainers, and other friends, to see and spend a day at *Guadalupe*,[3] which is a place of Recreation in the Island of *Goa*, distant from the City about two leagues, populous and full of Houses and Gardens of several *Portugal Signori*, who for pleasure go to dwell there some time of the year, as you at Rome do to *Frascati* which is the ancient *Tusculanum*. *Guadalupe* lies at the foot of a certain Precipice, in a plain upon a spacious Lake, which at one time of the year is quite dry'd up and sown with Rice,[4] so that the prospect is always very lovely; because the Lake is either full of water, in which grow abundance of pretty flowers and aquatick Plants; or else 'tis all green with Rice, which is sown before the Lake is totally dry and grows up to

---

[1] See *ante*, p. 156, note 1. [2] See *ante*, p. 142.

[3] This is probably the "place oı pleasure" referred to at p. 182. The first part of the name is a contraction of *Aguado*, a watering-place.

[4] See *ante*, p. 175, note 4.

maturity before the Water returns; so that it makes a very pretty Show, and the more because this Water, being collected in time of great rain, is fed also by a small but constantly running River; and, though so kept there for many months, yet causes not any bad affection of the Air; but through the goodness of the Climate the Air is always better here than anywhere else.

Nor is the Sea far distant, to wit the shore of the other more Southern River,[1] which forms the Island of *Goa*, on the other side, opposite to the City; the mouth of which River makes a secure and spacious Harbour, where sometimes even the greatest *Portugal* ships ride, and in old time the City stood there, so that they call the place *Goa Vecchia*, or old *Goa*.[2] As we return'd we saw abundance of Villages and Palmetos[3] full of all sorts of fruits,[4] and many fair and well-kept Churches, as *San Lorenzo*,[5] and others within a small distance; so that I had reason to judge this place to be held the most delicious of *Goa*.

On *January* the thirtieth being in *Guadalupe*, in the Garden of the House where we were, which belong'd to *Signor Simon Gomes* our Friend, and Kinsman to the *Sig: Baracci*, I saw a *Cannella*,[6] or Cinamon Tree, of which some

---

[1] The river *Tuari*. See *ante*, p. 175, note 1.

[2] What is now called "New Goa", or Panjim, occupies the site of the town here called "Old Goa", while the present "Old Goa stands where "New Goa" was in 1624.

[3] See *ante*, p. 182, note 3. But the word *Palmeto* should probably be translated as "Palm groves". As to the Spanish, or Portuguese, word *palmito*, see *Comm. of A. Dalboquerque*, vol. ii, p. 195 (Hakluyt edition).

[4] As to the various fruits of palm-trees, see Bates' *Naturalist on the Amazons*, pp. 59, 63, 184, 246, and 267.

[5] This church does not appear to be standing at the present day (See "A Recent Visit to Goa", in *Murray's Magazine* of November 1890.)

[6] That is, probably, *Canella alba*, called *Canella* (pipe) from the appearance of the bark when rolled up for export in the form of

are found in *Goa*, but strangers.[1] 'Tis as big a Tree as any, not a shrub, as I imagin'd; some of the leaves, which have a taste of Cinnamon and are pleasant to be masticated, I keep among my baggage to shew the same in *Italy*, as also some of the Tree *Trifoe*,[2] with its odoriferous

---

what are technically called "quills". The *Canella alba* is not a true cinnamon. Of the spices used by the ancients, cinnamon is said to have been the most esteemed. It is mentioned by Herodotus. (See Heeren's *Historical Researches*, vol. i, p. 43.)

[1] Or "exotics". In the original, *pellegrini*, a word not usually applied to trees, or plants. The words, "or Cinamon Tree", are inserted by the translator, and need not necessarily mean the true cinnamon, for the *Canella alba* is often called "wild cinnamon". It is a native of the Bahamas and the West Indies (see Lindley's *Vegetable Kingdom*, p. 442), and is a tree of about 20 feet in height, as here stated, whereas the true cinnamon is a shrub, or low tree, and is a native of Ceylon.

[2] In original; *Arbor Trisoe*, a misprint for *Tristo*, the *Nyctanthes Arbor tristis*, one of the Jasminworts. It is thus described in Lindley's *Vegetable Kingdom*, p. 651: "This plant, the *Hursinghar* of India, scents the garden with its delicious perfume only during the night, covering the ground in the morning with its short-lived flowers." Compare also the following passage from Mandelslo: "There is in Sumatra a tree, in the Malayan language called *Singadi*, in Arabia *Gurae;* the Canarians call it *Parizaticco*, Persians and Turks *Gul*, the *Decanins* (*i.e.*, inhabitants of the Indian Dakhan) *Pul*, and the Portuguese *Arbor triste de dia*. . . . . The flowers are white as snow, and a little bigger than the orange flower; they blow immediately as the sun is set; so suddenly that they are produced as it were in the cast of an eye. This fecundity lasts all night, till the return of the sun makes both the flowers and leaves drop off, and so strips the tree that the least greenness is not to be found on it, nor anything of that admirable odour which perfumed the air, and comprehended all that Asia affords of sweetness. The tree keeps in this condition till the sun hath left the horizon, and then it begins to open its womb again, and deck itself with fresh flowers, as if in the shades of night it would recover itself out of the affliction which it is put into by that planet whose return enlivens the rest of the universe." Sir W. Jones (*Asiatic Researches*) also writes: "This *gay* tree (Sorrowful Nyctanthes), for nothing *sorrowful* appears in its nature, spreads its rich odour to a considerable distance every evening; but at sunrise it sheds most of

Flowers, which blow every day and night and fall at the approach of day, as I myself saw and observ'd of one that was planted before the Gate of our House. This Flower is very like the *Jasmin* of *Catalonia*,[1] but the *Cannella* hath a yellow one, which is us'd by the Country-people instead of Saffron[2] with their meats and upon other occasions.

Moreover, I saw and observ'd in the Lake two sorts of Flowers,[3] one great, the other very small, both white, with something of yellow in the midst; the lesser hath no green leaves on the stalk to be seen and the inner part of the white leaves is full of thick and long Down. The greater Flower hath smooth, long and strait petals, and grows on a Plant whose leaves are large and almost perfectly round, floating on the surface of the water, totally expanded, almost like those of a Gourd. Both these Flowers have a strange property: in the night they

---

its *night flowers*, which are collected with care for the use of perfumers and dyers." See also Moore's *Lalla Rookh*—

> "Sat in her sorrow like the sweet night-flow'r,
> When darkness brings its weeping glories out,
> And spreads its sighs, like frankincense, about."

[1] *Jasminum grandiflorum*, or great-flowered Catalonian jasmin.

[2] See *ante*, p. 334, note 3.

[3] Evidently two kinds of lotus (*Nelumbium speciosum*), of which there are three varieties known in India. It is called *Padma* by Hindús. The flower is frequently represented on Indian (and Chinese) monuments. The fruit is edible and wholesome, and the root, or stem, is also used as food in China and India. The tubers of one species (*Nelumbium luteum*), resembling sweet potato, are also eaten. The juice of the stalk and flowers is used as medicine, and the spiral vessels of the leaf and flower-stalk as wicks for lamps in Hindoo temples. The so-called lotus of Egypt (see Herodotus, Bk. ii, ch. 92) is a *Nymphæa.* With reference to the lotus the following Japanese maxim is worthy of quotation: "If thou be born in the poor man's hovel, but have wisdom, then shalt thou be like the lotus flower growing out of the mud." (See *Things Japanese*, by B. H. Chamberlain.)

are always closed, in the day always open, displaying themselves at the rising, and closing at the setting, of the Sun; besides that, they are of a very excellent fragrant smell. I could not keep any to shew, because they are so tender and full of moisture, especially the lesser sort which is the fairest, that they fade presently upon being kept in papers, as the Custom is. The Indians call them[1]. . . . . . and tell a Fable of *Brahma's*[2] being born of one of these Flowers, and afterwards re-entring into one again, wherein he hath spent ten thousand years. You see what fine Stories we have here; I leave them with you, and kiss your Hands.

---

[1] A hiatus occurs here in the original text. The word *Padma* should probably be inserted, that being the vernacular (Sanskrit) name of the lotus.

[2] See *ante*, p. 73, note 1, and p. 235, notes 3 and 4. *Brahma* is the "one self-existent spirit". (See Sir Monier Williams' *Modern India*, p. 254; and Ward *On the Hindoos*, vol. iii, p. 26.) As to the "fable' here referred to, see Dubois' *Mœurs des Peuples de l'Inde*, vol. ii, p. 396; and Wilford (*Asiatic Researches*, vol. viii), who says, speaking of the lotus, "the stalk originates from the navel of Vishnu, sleeping at the bottom of the ocean; and the flower is the cradle of Brama, or mankind." The references to the lotus in the religious books of the Hindús are innumerable, abounding, as they do, with mystical allusions to this celebrated flower, which is also referred to in the mystical Bùddhist invocation, "Om manè padme om!"

LETTER VIII.

From Goa, November 4, 1624.

MY last I writ to you by the Ship which departed from *Goa* to *Portugal* on the first of *February* and was the only Ship of that Kingdom that was sent hither this year. On which Day the Bells rung at *Goa*, and many rejoycings were made, particularly in the Churches of the *Jesuits*,[1] the *Augustines*,[2] and the *Dominicans*,[3] upon News brought of many Martyrs lately Martyred in *Japan*, amongst which were many Religious of the abovesaid Orders[4]; and particularly of *Jesuits* were Martyred three *Italians*, to wit F. *Carlo Spinola*, a *Genovese* of principal quality: F. *Camillo Costanzo*, a *Calabrese*, or rather a *Neapolitan*, of a Family whose Estate lyes in *Calabria:* and F. *Pietro Paolo*, a *Neapolitan* likewise, if I mistake not.

On *February* the eighth a Council of State was held concerning the Vice-Roy's going to *Ormuz*[5]; in which, I

---

[1] See *ante*, p. 162, note 4. [2] See *ante*, p. 156, note 1.

[3] See *ante*, p. 156, note 2.

[4] It may be useful to mention here that a work recently published, *Christian Monasticism*, by I. Gregory Smith, is a valuable text-book on the subject of these religious bodies.

[5] See *ante*, p. 395.

know not what was resolved, because some talked one thing and some another; but as for the Souldiers, it was determined that all should go and that he that refused should be imprisoned, as some were to my knowledge.

On *February* the tenth, as a beginning of the solemnities for the Canonization, the *Jesuits* sung Vespers in the Church of the Professed-house of *Giesù*.[1] The night following they caused a numerous *Maskerade*[2] of young Students, not Collegians, but Outliers, to pass through the streets on Horse-back, clothed in several rich habits and following a Standard whereon were pourtrayed the Effigies of the Saints. The next day there was a solemn Mass in the same Church, and a Sermon made by the Visitor, F. *Andrea Palmuro*,[3] at which the Vice-Roy was present. In the Evening upon a very great Theatre, erected without the Church in the Piazza, for representing many dayes together the Life of *San Francesco Sciavier*,[4] they caused a Squadron of young men mask'd in the habits of Peasants to dance many gallant Ballets with Musick.

On the twelfth of *February*, in the presence of the Vice-Roy and of all the Nobility and People of the City, (for whose conveniency scaffolds and seats were erected in the Piazza round about the Theatre, both for Men and Women) the first Act of the above-said Comedy,[5] or Tragedy, (as they said) of the Life of *Santo Sciavier* was represented. Of which Tragedy, which was a composition represented by about thirty persons, all very richly clothed and decked with Jewels, no less extravagant than grand, whereunto

---

[1] See *ante*, p. 162, note 3. [2] See *ante*, p. 177, note 5.

[3] So in original, but should be *Palmeiro*. See *ante*, p. 160.

[4] For Xavier; see *ante*, p. 170, note 4.

[5] The word "comedy" is here, of course, used in its original sense, meaning a representation of a story (real, or fictitious) not necessarily of a facetious character, as in the present day—*e.g.*, the *Divina Comedia* of Dante.

they entered to act the rare Musick, gallant dances, and various contrivances of Charriots, Ships, Galleys, Pageants, Heavens, Hells, Mountains and Clouds, I forbear to speak, because I have the printed Relations by me.

Cn the eighteenth of *February*, the Vice-Roy being indispos'd, the proceedings were suspended and nothing was done. But on the three following dayes, by two Acts a day, the whole Tragedy was rehearsed. It comprehended not onely the whole Life, but also the Death[1] of *San Francesco Sciavier*, the transportation of his Body[2] to *Goa*, his ascension into Heaven, and, lastly, his Canonization.[3]

On the seventh of the same moneth Mass was sung in the College of *San Paolo Nouvo*,[4] and a predication made by F. *Flaminio Calò*, an *Italian*, upon the Beatification[5] of the Blessed *Luigi Gonzaga*, who was also a Father of the Society. In the Evening the *Portugals* of quality passed about the streets in a *Maskerade*, accompanyed with Chariots and Musick ; about twelve of us went out of the House of Sig: *Antonio Baraccio*, all clothed in the same

---

[1] See *ante*, p. 170, note 4.

[2] The body was buried at Malacca in 1552, and transported to Goa in 1553.

[3] See *ante*, p. 170, note 2. Some further details may be here noted. The process of canonization (which is probably derived from the ancient Roman rite of deification) is preceded by a panegyric of the deceased person by one of the Consistorial advocates. The decree of canonization is then pronounced by the Pope, who appoints a day for the ceremony, at which the Pope and Cardinals are all dressed in white, and the Church of St. Peter is hung with gorgeous tapestry.

[4] See *ante*, p. 185, note 3.

[5] See *ante*, p. 170, note 2. Beatification is the act by which the Pope declares a person beatified, or blessed, after his (or her) death. The corpse and relics of the future saint are thenceforth exposed to the veneration of all good Christians, but his body and relics are not carried in procession until after canonization. In the former ceremony the Pope merely grants the privilege of worshipping, but in the latter decrees, *ex cathedrâ*, the sanctity of the deceased person.

Livery, which I took care to get made according to my Phansie,[1] and I ordered it after the fashion of the ancient Roman Warriors, just as the ancient Emperors use to be pictured; the colours were Carnation and White, with several Impresses on the breast, every one after his own Phansie; it appear'd very well by night, and was the best and greatest Body of the whole Maskerade. I bore for my Impress a Blaze of Flames, with this Italian verse of *Tasso:*

"*Men dolci sì, ma non men calde al core,*"[2]

which Impress I have been wont to use since the death of my Wife *Sitti Maani.*[3] The embroidery Work of my clothes was wholly Flames, onely distinguished here and there with Tears which shewed my grief.

On *February* the eighteenth, in the Morning, solemn Mass was sung and a Sermon made upon the Canonization of the Saints in *San Paolo Vecchio.*[4] In the afternoon Lists and a Quintain and a Ring[5] being prepared before the Church of *Giesù,*[6] many great *Portugal* Gentlemen, richly clothed, came to run Carreers[7] both at the one and the other, giving Divertisement to the ladies who stood be-

---

[1] An obsolete (but more correct) mode of spelling "fancy", contracted from "phantasy".

[2] See *La Gerusalemme Liberata*, Canto xii, 97: "Less pleasing in form, but of heart as warm."

[3] See *ante*, pp. iii, and 45, note 2, and 122, note 3.

[4] See *ante*, p. 186, *note*.

[5] "Lists" strictly means a place enclosed within bounds, the word "list" formerly being used for "boundary", or "limit". The word "quintain" is of uncertain derivation, but is supposed to have originally meant an open space, or fifth part of a camp (see *Imperial Dict.*). Tilting at a ring is a well-known form of equestrian sport, much practised at the present day by men and ladies (English) in India.

[6] See *ante*, p. 164, note 2.

[7] The word "career" originally meant the act of running, but is now more generally used to denote the progress of anyone in some definite course of life.

holding them on Balconies[1] and Scaffolds.[2] The like they did afterwards in the street of *San Paolo Vecchio*.

On *February* the nineteenth a very solemn Procession was made from *San Paolo Vecchio* to *Giesù*, through the principal streets of the City: which Procession exceeded all the rest in number of Pageants, Chariots and Ships, and other Erections, filled with people who represented several things, and good Musick, accompanyed with several Dances on Foot, and many other brave devices: of all which things I speak not, because I have a printed Relation thereof by me. In the rear of the Procession was carried by many of the Fathers, dressed in their Copes, the Body of *San Francesco Sciavier*, inclos'd in a fair and rich Silver Coffin,[3] with a Silver Canopie over it, made very gallant, and the Effigy[4] of the Saint behind. Then came, a great Standard with the pourtraytures of the Saints, carry'd likewise by some of the Fathers; and after that, all the Crosses of their Parishes of *Salsette*,[5] and onely one Company of the Fryers of Saint *Francis*.[6] Of the other Religious Orders in *Goa* none appeared here; because they said they would not go in the Processions of the

---

1 From the Persian *Bálkhánah*, an open window.

2 According to the *Imperial Dict.*, "scaffold" is really a perverted form of *catafalco*, which is derived from *falco*, "a beam", with the stem *cata* (view) prefixed.

3 This silver coffin is still to be seen, with its contents, at Goa, and is described in "A Recent Visit to Goa" (*Murray's Magazine* of November 1890) as "crowned by figures of angels wrought in silver, with incidents in Xavier's life portrayed in embossed work". It is said to be an "artistic gem", and the quantity of silver used in its construction is estimated to have been 300 lb. It was formerly studded with jewels. (See also Fonseca's *Sketch of Goa*, Hunter's *Gazetteer*, and Eastwick's *Handbook of Bombay*.)

4 This is not the present silver image of the Saint, which was erected in 1670, as the gift of Doña Maria of Portugal. (See Eastwick's *Handbook of Bombay*, p. 222, and Fonseca's *Sketch of Goa*.)

5 See *ante*, p. 392, note 2.

6 See *ante*, p. 156, note 3.

Jesuits, since the *Jesuits* went not in those of others. With this Procession, which ended about noon, ended also the solemnities for the abovesaid Canonizations.

II.—On *February* the twenty-fifth, this day being the first Sunday of Lent this year, the *Augustine* Fathers, according to custom, made a solemn Procession, which they call "*dei Passi*", in reference to the steps which our Lord made in his Passion, conducted to several places. They carried in Procession a Christ, with the Cross on his shoulders, and many went along disciplining and whipping themselves, being cloth'd with white sack-cloth, gallant and handsome, very gravely according to the humor of the Nation. In several places of the City certain Altars were plac'd, where the Procession stood still; and, after some time spent in singing, the Christ turn'd backwards, representing that passage[1] "*Conversus ad Filias Jerusalem, dixit illis, Nolite flere super me*", etc. At which turning of the sacred Image the people, who were very numerous and fill'd the whole streets, lamented and utter'd very great cries of Devotion. At length the Procession, being come to the Church *Della Gratia*,[2] where it ended, after the *Augustine* Nunns (whose Convent[3] stands near that of the Fryers in the same Piazza) had sung a while, an Image, "*del volto Santo*" (of our Lord's Countenance), like that at *Rome*,[4] was shown to the people, gather'd together in the said Piazza, from a window of one of the Bell-turrets which are on either side of the front of the said Church; and

---

[1] Gospel of St. Luke, ch. xxiii, v. 28.

[2] This church is not mentioned (by this name) in the authorities referred to.

[3] The convent of *St. Monica*, marked No. 20 in the Plan of Goa, *ante*, p. 154. It was closed in 1889, but is still in good repair. It is a vast building, but of no architectural merit. (See Eastwick's *Handbook of Bombay*, p. 227.)

[4] For a history of this portrait, see Mrs. Jameson's *History of Our Lord in Art*, vol. i, p. 38.

so the Solemnity ended. But the above-mention'd Altars in the streets are every Fryday during Lent adorn'd in the same manner, and visited by the people every day and also at many hours of the night; just as the Church of Saint *Peter* at *Rome* is visited every Fryday of March; and they call this visiting, "*Correr os Passos*", that is going about and visiting the steps of our Lord; which serves the people during this time of Lent no less for devotion than for pastime.

On *March* the first there was also another Procession in *Goa* of the *Disciplinanti*,[1] which I went not to see; the like is made every Fryday during all Lent, and therefore I shall not stay to describe it. I believe there is no City in the world where there are more Processions than in *Goa* all the year long; and the reason is because the Religious Orders are numerous, and much more than the City needs[2]; they are also of great authority and very rich, and the People, being naturally idle and addicted to Shews,[3] neglecting other Cares of more weight and perhaps more profitable to the Publick, readily employ themselves in these matters; which, however good as sacred ceremonies and parts of divine worship, yet in such a City as this which borders upon Enemies and is the Metropolis of a Kingdom lying in the midst of *Barbarians* and so alwayes at Warr, and where nothing else should be minded but Arms and Fleets, seem according to worldly Policy unprofitable and too frequent, as also so great a number

---

[1] This is the name given to those who voluntarily inflict corporal punishment on themselves by way of mortification, similarly to the well-known sect of fanatics called *Flagellantes*, who arose in Italy in the 13th century. A graphic description of a modern self-flagellation, similar to that here referred to by our traveller, will be found in the notes to *Childe Harold* (Canto IV), by Mr. Hobhouse.

[2] See *ante*, p. 156, note 7.

[3] See *ante*, p. 161, note 1.

of Religious and Ecclesiastical persons is burdensome to the State and prejudicial to the Militia.[1]

In the Evening of every *Fryday* of Lent there is a Sermon upon the Passion in the Church of *Giesù*[2]; and so likewise in other Churches, but upon other dayes and hours. At the end of these Sermons certain Tabernacles are open'd, and divers figures, representing some passages of the Passion (according to the subject of the Sermon), are with lighted Tapers shewn to the People; as one day that of the "*Ecce Homo*"; another day Our Lord with the Cross upon his shoulders; and the last day the Crucifix; and so every day one thing suitable to the purpose. Oftentimes they make these figures move and turn, as they made the Robe fall off from the *Ecce Homo* and discover the wounded Body; at which sight the devout People utter prodigious Cryes, and the Women force themselves to shriek out; and the *Signore*, or Gentlewomen, are so zealous that they not onely cry out themselves, but make their Maids do so too and beat them even in the Church if they do not and that very loudly, whether they have a will to it, or no. Strange devotion indeed!

III.—On *March* the third ten Ships of Warr were at length sent from *Goa* to the barr, or mouth, of the River, in order to depart (as they did) within two or three dayes towards *Ormùz* to *Ruy Freira*[3]; the Chief Captain of which was Sig: *Sancho de Toar*, Brother to the *Veador*[4] *da Façenda*, who was Treasurer and Captain of one of the Ships. Our Friend, Sig: *Michel Pereira Boralho*, who was sometime Captain of the Galeons, went also; his Brother, *Giovan Boralho*, was kill'd under *Ruy Freira*, in the battle with the English at *Giàsk*[5] last year, being Admiral of that Fleet,

---

[1] See *ante*, p. xv.

[2] See *ante*, p. 164, note 2.

[3] See *ante*, p. 279.

[4] Or Comptroller.

[5] See *ante*, pp. xxvii, and 8, 9 and 10, and p. 4, note 2.

which next to the General[1] is the prime charge, having been many times before Chief Captain, as they speak, or General, in the Streight of *Ormùz*. I make particular mention of him upon account of his relationship to Sig. *Michele Pereira* our Friend. But such a succour for *Ormùz* after so long a time is indeed a very inconsiderable matter. Yet, they say, other Ships are preparing to be sent after these.

On *March* the one and twentieth I took the Altitude of the Sun at *Goa* with my Astrolabe and found him to decline at noon from the Zenith towards the South fourteen degrees and forty minutes. He was this day in the thirtieth degree of *Pisces* and, consequently, in the Æquinoctial without any Declination; so that without making any Subtraction from, or Addition to, this number, *Goa*, that is the City, will lye just so many degrees (14° 40′) from the Æquinoctial towards the North, and also have the Northern Pole elevated as much.

On *March* the eight and twentieth news was brought to *Goa* how the great *Mogòl*[2] had caus'd all the English that were at his Court to be slain,[3] and imprisoned all the rest that were at *Súrat*.[4] As for those that were slain, some say it was by the *Mogòl's* Order in way of punishment, and that they were hang'd and otherwise executed; others say, it was by chance, as they endeavour'd to defend themselves by Arms, when he sent onely to arrest them prisoners, as he did those of *Súrat;* and this seems most likely. Be it as it will, this Accident may easily disturb their Commerce something in that Country. The occasion is reported thus. A few dayes, or moneths, ago, the English in *Súrat* ap-

---

[1] So in original.

[2] See *ante*, p. 30, note 1.

[3] This alleged massacre is not mentioned in the historical annals of he time referred to by the editor.

[4] See *ante*, p. 18, note 2. The imprisonment of the English residents at Sùrat, here referred to, is not mentioned in the ordinary works of reference.

prehending themselves aggriev'd to a considerable sum by the *Mogðl's* Ministers, (whether by exaction of Customs, or in Accounts, I know not) in order to repair the loss by force, since they could not do so in any other way, made reprisal on some of the *Mogðl's* ships, which were come abroad full laden; and being[1] the *Mogðl's* people were not able to deal with the English at Sea they were constrain'd, for recovering their surpris'd Vessels, to grant the English everything demanded, and satisfie them so far as they pretended to be aggrieved. Which thing coming afterwards to the King's knowledge, he caus'd all of that Nation to be apprehended wherever found in his Dominions, and hereupon happened the slaughter above-mention'd.

For my part, I think the English have not manag d their business discreetly in this case; for it is not possible for a few strangers and immigrants to contest with and get the better of a great King in his own Country. And upon the rising of the like differences I should account it the best course to settle them with good words, and amicably with the said King, by complaining of his Ministers, and procuring him to provide in such cases as well as may be; and this course may succeed happily; otherwise, if redress cannot be obtain'd, then, before a manifest feud, 'twere best to get out of his power and warr upon him securely, not in his own Country were there are so many people, and the King, undoubtedly, hath more power than any other. I believe the English made this attempt, upon supposition that the *Mogðl* hath great need of the Sea, and that, to the end his Ships might have free passage therein, without being molested by the English, he would suffer what they pleas'd. But herein, in my opinion, they are grossly mistaken; because the *Mogðl* is a very great and wealthy King, whose Revenews arise from his own Lands and not

---

[1] For "since"; see p. 28, *note*.

from the Sea; and one to whom that little which is to be had from the Sea (how great soever it may be) is nothing, and nothing he accounts it; because it accrues rather to some small Captain of his, as the Governour of *Suràt*, and the like, than to the King himself. So what is he concern'd for it? But indeed he will be concern'd for such an injury done to him in his own jurisdiction, as the English have done by making reprisal on Ships, which Princes much inferior to the *Mogòl* would not have suffer'd from any admitted as Friends into their Countries. Besides, the grievances alledg'd by the English were but pretences, and the *Mogòl's* Ministers had their Reasons for them; wherefore the case ought to have been heard before falling to violence; and, let the matter be how it will, 'twas just for him to be Judge in his own Country, and that this respect should be shewn him, if the English would have taken this course; if not, or if he would not do them Justice, they were alwayes at liberty to go out of his power, and so make Warr against him by Sea upon better terms. Concerning the Affairs of the *Mogòl* with his Son, they said that *Sultan Chorrom*,[1] having been twice routed,[2] had at last retreated with some few followers into the Dominions of *Cutab-Sciàh*[3]; and that his Father had given over pursuing him and, being retir'd to his own Court, left him there in quiet; that *Cutab-Sciàh* did not assist him out of awe of his Father,[4] nor yet drive him out of his Territories out of respect to himself, but let him enjoy the possession of a certain small circuit in his Country to which he had retir'd.

IV.—Concerning Persian affairs we heard a while since,

---

[1] Or *Kharram;* see *ante*, p. 59.

[2] At *Mewát*, and near *Allahabad;* see Elphinstone's *India*, pp. 497 and 498.

[3] Or *Kutb-Shah;* see *ante*, p. 147, note 4, and p. 148, note 5.

[4] *I.e.*, the Emperor Jahángir; see *ante*, p. 52.

and it was verifi'd, that not only the English Ships were gone thither, according to their custom, for the Trade of Silk, but also those of the *Hollanders* which come to *Suràt*; perhaps because the *Hollanders* are minded to set up a Traffick thither too, as I understood from a good hand last year at *Suràt*. In the mean time other Ships and Galeons are preparing at *Goa* to be sent to *Ormùz*.[1]

On *April* the tenth three Galeons freighted with Victuals departed from *Goa* to *Ruy Freira* for the war of *Ormùz*,[2] as two other Ships had done a few days before, besides the above-mentioned ten; and order was given for three other Galeons to go from *Mozambique*[3] with people sufficient to arm all the six; because the former three of *Goa* carried no Soldiers, but only Sea-men. They carried also from *Goa* a Petard,[4] wherewith they said they intended to attempt the little false Gate of *Ormùz* which stands towards the Sea, and several other preparations of War.

On the twenty-ninth of the same month, being the day of S. *Pietro Martire*,[5] who, they say, was the Founder[6] of

---

[1] See *ante*, p. 2, note 1.

[2] See *ante*, p. 279.

[3] On the east coast of Africa, where the Portuguese established a factory in 1508. This place and *Sofala* are the only places of importance on the coast of Africa still held by the Portuguese.

[4] Petards are said to have been invented by the French Huguenots in 1579, and to have been first used at the siege of *Cahors* in that year.

[5] Peter de Castelnau, one of the monks of *Citeaux* and of the monastery of *Fortfroide*, in Narbonnese Gaul, who was commissioned by Pope Innocent III to preach against the heresies of the Waldenses in 1203, and who was in this way the instrument for founding the Inquisition. He was assassinated in the dominions of the Count of Toulouse, and beatified in 1208.

[6] The Inquisition was founded by Pope Innocent III early in the 13th century, when he appointed a commission for the persecution of the Waldenses. It was established in the Portuguese dominions by King John III in 1536.

the *Inquisition*[1] against Hereticks, the Inquisitors of *Goa* made a Festival before their House of the Inquisition[2] which is in the *Piazza* of the Cathedral and was sometimes the Palace of *Sabaio*,[3] Prince of *Goa*, when the *Portugals* took it, whence it is still call'd *la Piazza di Sabaio*. After solemn Mass had been sung in the Church of *San Dominico*,[4] as Vespers had been the day before, in presence of the Inquisitors, who, coming to fetch the Fryers in Procession, repair'd thereunto *in Pontificalibus*; in the evening, many carreers[5] were run on horse-back by the *Portugal* Gentry, invited purposely by the Inquisitors; and a day or two after (for this Evening was not sufficient for so many things) there was in the same *Piazza* a Hunting, or Baiting, of Bulls after the Spanish fashion; but the Beasts, being tame and spiritless, afforded little sport; so that I had not the curiosity to be present at it. This is a new Festival lately instituted by the present Inquisitors, who, I believe, will continue it yearly hereafter.[6]

---

1 See *ante*, p. 156, note 2. The Inquisition at Goa was abolished by Royal letter in 1774, re-established under Doña Maria I in 1779, and finally abolished in 1812 (see Eastwick's *Handbook of Bombay*, p. 225), or in 1814, according to Mr. Sandberg (*Murray's Magazine*, Nov. 1890). See also Fonseca's *Hist. Sketch of Goa*, p. 219, and Capt. Marryat's tale of *The Phantom Ship*.

2 Marked No. 11 in the Plan of Goa, *ante*, p. 154. It was destroyed in 1829, and is now merely a "hill of bricks and stones and many mounds". It formerly covered a space of two acres, and contained three large halls and 200 prisoners' cells. (See "A Recent Visit to Goa" in *Murray's Magazine*, Nov. 1890; and Pinkerton's *Travels* vol. ix, p. 234; and Fonseca's *Sketch of Goa*, and De Kloguen's *Historical Sketch of Goa*.)

3 Sabaio is evidently identical with Sabaym Delcani (? Dekkani), mentioned by Barbosa in *East Coast of Africa and Malabar* (p. 75 of Hakluyt edition). See *ante*, p. 143, note 5.

4 Marked No. 32 in the Plan of Goa, *ante*, p. 154. It was completed in 1564, and demolished in 1841.

5 See *ante*, p. 412.

6 In Captain Marryat's tale of *The Phantom Ship* will be found a

On *May* the tenth a Packet-boat from *Mascàt*[1] arrived at *Goa* with Letters dated *April* the twenty-fourth, confirming what had some dayes before been rumor'd, that the King of *Persia* had taken *Baghdàd*,[2] and the *Persians* were about to go against *Bassorà*[3] by Sea, but were diverted from their designs by the *Portugal* Fleet, which they heard was preparing to succour that City, and by some Ships of theirs which they continually keep there in favour of the *Turks* against the *Persians* to guard the Mouth of the River, which is *Euphrates*[4] and *Tigris*[5] joyn'd together. The same Boat brought news also that twelve Ships were already departed from *Mascàt* under the conduct of my friend Sig. *Michele Pereira* to begin a new Siege of *Ormùz;* and that *Ruy Freira*[6] waited for the Galeons that he might go thither too with the greater Fleet.

---

graphic description of Goa in the zenith of its pride, with its festivals and processions.

[1] See *ante*, p. 158, note 7.

[2] *Baghdad* remained in the hands of the Persians until 1638, when it was taken by the Turks under Sultan Amurath IV, and has remained in their possession ever since that time. It is finely seated on the E. bank of the river Tigris, in Lat. 33° 20′ N., and Long. 44° 46′ E. It was formerly (before the discovery of the route to India by the Cape) the centre of a very extensive commerce, and still continues to be a place of considerable importance, having manufactories of silk, cotton, wool and leather, besides an iron foundry.

[3] Sometimes written *Basra.* The town is in Lat. 30° 30′ N., and Long. 47° 45′ E., on the W. bank of the Euphrates, about 65 miles from the mouth of the river. It is said to have been founded about the middle of the seventh century, and, previously to the discovery of the route to India round the Cape, was the most considerable trading town of Western Asia.

[4] This river rises near Erzeroum (Long. 41° 36′ E., Lat. 39° 57′ N.), and has a course of about 1,350 miles before its junction with the Tigris, 35 miles above Bassora.

[5] The Tigris rises near Diarbekir (37° 55′ N., and 39° 22′ E.), and joins the Euphrates near Bassora. It forms the boundary between Persia and the Turkish territory.

[6] See *ante*, p. 279.

If it be true that *Sciah Abbas*[1] has taken *Baghdàd* I am confident that in the long run *Bassorà* will fall into his hands too: if the *Portugals* may hinder him by sea, they cannot by land; and 'tis a clear case that if he hath *Baghdàd*, he intends also to have the port of *Bassorà*, which is of great importance. That he has taken *Baghdàd* may very well be true, during the present ill State of the Turkish Affairs, after the late Tumults in that Court, and the death of *Sultan Suleiman*,[2] who was lately murder'd and his formerly depos'd Uncle, *Sultan Mustafà*,[3] restor'd to the Empire, as I was lately assur'd here by an *Armenian* who told me that he was at *Constantinople* in the time of these Revolutions, and that *Sultan Mustafà* was very loth to re-assume the Government by reason of the ill deportment of the Ministers, and that he would have no more Women, or Concubines, but had married and dismissed all that were in the *Seraglio*[4]; that if any woman came into his presence he ran at her with his Ponyard, professing to lead a chaste and religious life, not meaning to have other Successors than his Brother's two Sons, the elder of which is *Sultan Mahomad*,[5] Son of *Sultana Kiosinè*, who, I alwayes believ'd, would by his Mother's Arts one day come to rule, and now without doubt, whether she be living or not, (if

---

[1] See *ante*, p. 402, note 1.

[2] This seems to be a mistake for *Osman* (the 2nd), who was assassinated in 1622.

[3] Sultan Mustafa I, who twice sat on the throne.

[4] The word *Seraglio* is here used in its usual sense of women's apartments. But its true meaning is that of a "large house" or "palace", and the Seraglio of the Sultan of Constantinople includes the residence of all the officers and dependents of the Court. The grand entrance on the western side is the *Baba-hoomajin*, or "Sublime Porte", which is, as is well known, the official title of the Turkish Court.

[5] He eventually succeeded to the throne, as Muhammad IV, in 1649.

the abovesaid relations be true) will at least reign after his Uncle *Mustafà*.

Now, forasmuch as in these violent mutations of Empires, the Government alwayes suffers deterioration, because without some evil disposition of the Government such violences in Royal Families cannot arise, therefore, I say, perhaps this ill posture of affairs hath afforded the *Sciàh* occasion of making himself Master of *Baghdàd*, especially if the Tyrant *Bechir Subascì*, who had in a manner usurp'd it to himself, have given it into his power, (which is an easie thing even in the good State of the *Turkish* Affairs) being, perhaps, afraid of *Sultan Mustafà*, who, they say, is very prudent and wholly intent on reforming the Disorders of the Empire without caring to attend to foreign enterprises; whence, perhaps having an eye too upon the Disorders of *Baghdàd*, he was about to raise a strong Army for removing the said Tyrant, who by this means became necessitated to yield it to the *Sciàh*. Nevertheless in these matters I have some doubt, because the same *Armenian* told me that *Sultan Mustafà* had made peace with the *Persian* for twenty years; and if the taking of *Baghdàd* be true it is a breaking of the peace; which amongst the Moors, and considering the Customs of *Sciàh Abbas*, is not impossible. At present I suspend my belief and desire to have more certain and particular informations of these matters, of which in *Goa* there is little supply.

By the same Vessel came a Letter from Sig. *Nicolao de Silva*, *Veador*[1] *da Façenda*, or Treasurer, at *Mascàt*,[2] to one of the Inquisitors,[3] wherein he signifi'd to him that he understood by the Letters of the *French* Consul at *Aleppo*,

---

[1] *I.e.*, Comptroller.

[2] See *ante*, p. 158, note 7.

[3] See *ante*, p. 421, note 2.

that at *Rome Gregory* XV[1] was dead, and a new Pope already chosen, Card. *Maffeo Barberini*,[2] about fifty-four years old, who had assumed the name of *Urban* VIII.[3] The same Letter further advertis'd that in *Spain* the Marriage between the Prince of *England* and the *Infanta* was celebrated[4] upon the day of our Ladie's Nativity in *September;* and that the *Infante Don Carlo*[5] was to accompany her into *England*, and from thence pass to his Government of *Flanders:* that in *England* the Catholicks had publick Churches open and enjoy'd Liberty of Conscience: that in *Italy* the business of the *Valtelin*[6] had been referr'd to his Holiness; but Pope *Gregory* died without determining it: that the King of *Spain*[7] kept a great Army ready in *Milan* about it; and that a League was made against him in *Italy* by other Princes; that some said *Don Carlo* of *Spain* was to marry the Heiress of *Lorraine*[8]; and otherlike news, which, being of things either uncertain, or future, I make small account of till I see the issue.

On *May* 11th the last vessels of the *Cafila* which went to China, and which had commenced to depart on the previous Wednesday, set sail, and my friends, Fathers *Morejon* and *Vincislao Pantaleone*, departed in it.

---

[1] Formerly Cardinal Alessandro Ludovisio. He had been Pope only since 1621. He it was who granted a dispensation, renewed by his successor, for the marriage of the Infanta with Prince Charles.

[2] The Barberinis were a celebrated Florentine family.

[3] It was Pope Urban VIII who in 1630 altered the title of the Cardinals from "*illustrissimi*" to "*eminentissimi*", of which change an illustration is seen in the Dedication of these Letters.

[4] This piece of intelligence must be included among the other false rumours which seem to have been prevalent. See *post*, p. 438.

[5] Brother of King Philip IV.

[6] The Valteline is the long valley in the north of Italy, traversed by the river Adda, to the east of Lake Como. The "business" here referred to was a dispute as to its possession.

[7] Philip IV, who came to the throne in 1621.

[8] Marie, daughter of the fourth Duke of Lorraine.

On *May* the seventeenth, by a Merchant's Ship from *Bassora*[1] which arrived at Goa the night beforè, we had more certain intelligence by *Luigi Medices*, through *Ramiro*, the *Venetian* Consul at *Aleppo*, that Pope *Gregory* XV died on the twenty-ninth of *July* 1623, having been sick only five days. The Report of the Conclave saith that the Pope died on the eight of *July*, the Cardinals[2] enter'd into the Conclave[3] on the nineteenth, and that on the sixth of *Augúst Urban* VIII was created Pope; that Card. *Montalto* died a little before the Pope, and Card. *Ludovisio*[4] was made Vice-Chancellor in his stead; and the Chamberlainship, being vacant by the death of *Aldobrandino*, was conferr'd upon the young Cardinal of the same name; that the new Pope *Urban* was sick for some dayes after his Election; but, afterwards recovering, was crown'd upon the day of S. *Michael* the Archangel; that, besides the Pope, almost all the Cardinals fell sick through the inconveniences of the Conclave in so hot a season; and many of them died, as *Pignatelli*, *Serra*, *Sauli*, *Gozzadino* and *Sacrati*; and the Card. *Gherardi* and *Aldobrandino* remained still grievously sick; and that of the Conclavists there died about sixty; which indeed was a great

---

[1] See *ante*, p. 422, note 3.

[2] The Cardinals were originally merely the principal priests of the parishes of Rome, and it was not until the eleventh century that they were established as a "College". Up to 1125 the College consisted of 52 or 53 Cardinals. The number was afterwards reduced to 20 or 25, but was subsequently raised by Pope Leo X to their present number of 70.

[3] The right of election of the Pope by the Cardinals was established by Pope Alexander III in 1179. Previously to that date the Popes were elected by the "tumultuary votes of the clergy and people". (See Gibbon's *Decline and Fall of the Roman Empire*, vol. vi, p. 353.) The word "conclave" is used for the apartment in which each Cardinal is confined during the progress of the election, as well as for the general assembly of Cardinals. As to the ceremonies attending the election of a Pope, see Gibbon, vol. vi, p. 354. The "Conclave" was instituted by Pope Gregory X in 1274.

[4] This Cardinal was nephew of Pope Gregory XV.

number for a Conclave that lasted so short a while. That *Telli*[1] (*Tilly*), the Emperor's General, had given a great rout to *Alberstat;* and the Emperor's Affairs in *Germany* pass'd very well. That 'twas true a confederacy was made against *Spain* about the business of the *Valtelin* between *France*, *Venice*, and *Savoy*, but that it will proceed no further, because *Spain* had deposited the *Valtelin* in the hands of the Pope. That the Prince of *Urbino*[2] was dead, and consequently that State would fall to the Church; which is a thing of much importance. That at *Venice* the *Doge Priuli* was dead, and a new *Doge* already elected, one *Contarini*, an eminent Person. That there was a great Plague, and that the King of *France* had subdu'd almost all the Garrisons of the Hereticks, except *Rochelle*,[3] which he also hop'd shortly to reduce to obedience. That the Espousals were pass'd between the *Infanta* of *Spain* and the King of *England's* Son, with hope that he is already a Catholick. That they have given her in dower the pretensions of Holland and Zealand, and money, on condition that Liberty of Conscience be granted in *England* and four Churches for Catholicks built in *London*, which was already executed, public Writings thereof going about in print; besides divers other Affairs of *Europe* of less consideration.

VI.—On *May* the nineteenth, one *Ventura da Costa*, a Native of *Canara*,[4] was married. He was a domestick servant to Sig. *Alvaro da Costa*, a Priest and our Friend, Lord of a Village near *Goa;* for whose Sake, who was willing to honour his servant's wedding in his own House,

---

[1] This celebrated General (originally a Jesuit) was born in 1559, and died in 1632 after a brilliant military career.

[2] The last representative of the Della Rovera family, Princes of Urbino, who had been invested with that Duchy by Pope Julius II.

[3] The well-known town of Rochelle, the capital of Lower Charente, was not taken for the Catholics until 1637 by Louis XIII of France.

[4] See *ante*, p. 168, note 1.

I and some other Friends went thither to accompany the Bride and the Bridegroom to the Church of *San Biagio,*[1] a little distant in another Village, which was in the Parish of the Bride, where the Ceremonies were perform'd in the Evening for coolness' sake. The Company was very numerous, consisting of many *Portugal* Gentlemen, such, perhaps, as few other *Canarini*[2] have had at their marriages. The Bride and Bridegroom came under Umbrellas of Silk, garnish'd with silver, and in other particulars the Ceremonies were according to the custom of the *Portugals;* onely I observ'd that, according to the use of the Country, in the Company before the Married Persons there march'd a party of fourteen, or sixteen, men oddly cloth'd after the Indian fashion, to wit naked from the girdle upward, and their Bodies painted in a pattern with white Sanders,[3] and adorn'd with bracelets and necklaces of Gold and Silver, and also with flowers and turbants[4] upon their heads, in several gallant fashions, and streamers of several colours hanging behind them. From the girdle downwards, over the hose which these *Canarini* use to wear short, like ours, they had variously colour'd clothes girt about them with streamers, flying about and hanging down a little below the knee; the rest of the leg was naked, saving that they had sandals on their feet. These danc'd all the way both going and returning, accompanying their dances with chaunting many Verses in their own Language, and beating the little sticks which they carry'd in their hands, after the fashion of the Country, formerly taken notice of at *Ikkerì.*[5] And indeed the dances of these *Canarini* are pleasant enough; so that in the Festivities made at *Goa* for the Canonization[6]

---

[1] This church does not appear in the Plan of Goa at p. 154.

[2] *I.e.*, natives of Kànara.

[3] See *ante*, p. 99, note 2.

[4] See *ante*, p. 248, note 4.

[5] See *ante*, p. 258.

[6] See *ante*, p. 170, note 2.

of the Saints *Ignatio*[1] and *Sciavier*,[2] though in other things they were most solemn and sumptuous, yet, in my opinion, there was nothing more worthy to be seen for delight than the many pretty and jovial dances which interven'd in this Tragedy.[3] The marry'd Couple being return'd from Church to the Bride's House, we were entertain'd with a handsome Collation[4] of Sweet-meats in the yard, which was wholly cover'd over with a Tent, and adorn'd with Trees and green boughs, the Company sitting round, and the marry'd Couple, on one side at the upper end, upon a great Carpet under a Canopy. After which we all return'd home, and the Husband stay'd that night to sleep in his Wife's House.

VII.—On *May* the twentieth a Galley of the Fleet expected from *Mozambique*[5] arriv'd at *Goa*. It brought Sig. *Don Nugno Alvares* (sometime General there, and Supreme Governour of all that Coast of *Cafuria*,[6] comprising under his Government the Rivers of *Coama*, *Mombace*,[7] and as much of *Africa* as the *Portugals* have from the Cape of Good Hope to the streight of *Meka*[8]) and with him a *Jesuit* that was a Bishop, one of those that were to go into *Æthiopia*.[9] The Patriarch[10] deputed thither, being also a *Jesuit*, remain'd behind in another Galeot, as likewise did the Ships of the last years *Portugal* Fleet, which came on by little and little; they brought news of the miserable

---

[1] See *ante*, p. 170, note 3.

[2] See *ante*, p. 170, note 4.

[3] This word is, of course, here used in its more strictly classical sense of any *dramatic* representation.

[4] See *ante*, p. 381, note 4.

[5] See *ante*, p. 214, and 420, note 3.

[6] For Kaffraria, or Kaffre-land, south of Mozambique.

[7] The *Coavo* and *Mombas* rivers of modern maps, in Lat. 8° 33′ S. and 4° 15′ S. respectively, on the east coast of Africa.

[8] See *ante*, p. 399, note 1.

[9] See *ante*, p. 131, note 1.

[10] Or chief Father.

wrack[1] of a Ship call'd *San Giovanni*, which two years before set forth from *Goa* for *Portugal*, very rich; and, meeting with the Dutch by the way, after a long fight being totally shatter'd, ran aground upon the Coast of *Cafuria*[2]; so that, saving the people remaining after the fight and the other disasters, and the Jewels, all was lost: which people, refusing both the offer of good entertainment made them by the Lord of the place, who was a Friend to the *Portugals*, till, upon advice sent to *Mozambique*, they might have passage thither, and also refusing his counsel to travel far within Land, where, he said, they would have less trouble in passing many Rivers, (which otherwise they would meet with) and would find an unarmed and more hospitable people, but unadvisedly, after the inconsiderate humor of the *Portugals*, resolving to go by land to *Mozambique* and to travel always far from the Sea amongst barbarous inhospitable people who eat human flesh, and withall not behaving themselves well with them in their passage, but out of a foolish temerity giving many occasions of displeasure, were assaulted in many places by the said *Cafiri*,[3] often spoyl'd and rob'd, and many of them kill'd; so that of the Women that were with them some were taken, others strip'd naked, till, after a thousand inconveniences and sufferings, and, as some say, about eight moneths' travelling on foot, during which they were fain to wade through abundance of Rivers, at last no more of the Company arriv'd at *Mozambique* than twenty-seven persons; all the rest being either slain by the way, or dead of hardships, excepting some few that were kept slaves by the *Cafiri*; amongst whom was a *Portugal* Gentlewoman of quality, whom they kept to present to their King, without hope, I

---

[1] This word, derived from the Danish *vrag*, is the old form of "wreck".

[2] See *ante*, p. 429, note 6.

[3] Or *Kaffres*.

believe, of ever being deliver'd; a misery indeed worthy of compassion! The Jewels sent from *Goa* to be sold in *Portugal* were almost all sav'd and deposited at *Mozambique* in the *Misericordia*[1]; some say to be restor'd to the owners, and others say at the instance of the King's Officer, who pretends the King's Right to them as shipwrackt goods; yet most conclude that the case will not be so judg'd, but that they will be restor'd to the owners upon payment of some small matter to those who sav'd them.

VIII.—On *May* the three and twentieth I visited the above-mention'd Bishop now arriv'd in *Goa*, at the Colledge of *San Paolo Novo*.[2] He was call'd *Dom Joanno da Rocha*, and is nominated, but not consecrated, Bishop of *Heliopoli*.

On the twenty-sixth I visited in the Convent of our Lady *della Gratia*, F. *Fra: Manoel della Madre di Dio*, formerly known to me in *Persia*, and now Prior of the Convent of *Spahan*,[3] who the day before arrived at *Goa* in a Shallop which had been long expected and judg'd lost, having been seven moneths in coming from *Mascat*.[4] He said that he came about Affairs of his Order and the Convents of *Persia* (for besides that which I left at *Spahan*, they have since made one at *Sciraz*,[5] and another at *Bassora*,[6] and they daily multiply) yet withall it was rumoured that he was sent by the King of *Persia* to treat with the Vice-Roy about the Matters of *Ormuz;* and I believe it, although he spoke nothing of it himself; otherwise, methinks, 'tis not likely they would have let him come out of *Persia* without the King's express Licence, or that the King would have granted it in time of War, unless he had come about some particular business of his. He informed me that all my friends in *Persia* were well, and so did

[1] See *ante*, p. 382, note 4.

[2] See *ante*, p. 185, note 3.

[3] Now generally written as *Ispahan*, the name meaning a "rendezvous", or place of meeting.

[4] See *ante*, p. 158, note 7.

[5] See *ante*, p. 9, note 1.

[6] See *ante*, p. 422, note 3.

a Letter of F. *Fra: Giovanni* to his Provincial at *Goa*, wherein mention was made of me, giving me intelligence of the well-fare of all my Friends, and how *Sitti Laali*, my connection by marriage, had brought forth a Son, whom she had nam'd *Avedik*, from *Chogia Avedik*, his Father's Uncle; which News was stale, for I knew it before my coming out of *Persia;* and, indeed, all the Letters F. *Manoel* brought were of a very old date; to me he brought none, because my Friends there conceiv'd that I was gone out of *India* into *Europe*.

On *May* the seven and twentieth a Ship of the *Portugal* Fleet that was coming from *Mozambique*[1] arrived in the Port of *Mormogon*[2]; it entered not into the River of *Goa*, because the mouth of the River, by reason of the lateness of the season, was insecure and began to be stopped; for every year all the mouths of the Rivers and Ports of this Coast are fill'd with sand during the time of Rain,[3] wherein the West wind blows very tempestuously, and are open'd again in *September* when the Rain ends. The Port of *Mormogon*, as I have elsewhere said,[4] is in the same Island of *Goa*, in the other mouth of the more Southern River, where sometimes old *Goa* stood, by which goods are convey'd by Boat from the Ships to the City, but by a longer way, going behind round the Island.

On *May* the twenty-eighth in the Evening, at the time of *Ave Maria*, the Bells of almost all the Churches of *Goa*, saving that of the *Jesuits*, were rung for the Beatification[5] of two Fryers of the Order of *San Domenico*,[6] whereof this Ship had brought News.

On *May* the twenty-ninth another *Portugal* Ship of the

---

[1] See *ante*, p. 420, note 3.

[2] See *ante*, p. 154, note 2, and p. 329, note 1.

[3] See *ante*, p. 32, note 2.

[4] See p. 392, *ante*.

[5] See *ante*, p. 170, note 2, and p. 411, note 5

[6] See *ante*, p. 189, note 5.

Fleet arrived, and, within two or three dayes after, all the other Ships expected from *Mozambique;* and in one of them the *Jesuit*, deputed as Patriarch into *Æthiopia*, whither he, with two Bishops, whereof one was dead by the way, and many other *Jesuits*, was sent at the instance of the King of the same Country, who, they say, is called *Sultan Saghed*,[1] and professes himself a Roman Catholick already, with great hopes of reducing all that Kingdom to the Church in a short time. As for the progress which the *Jesuits* affirm daily to be made in those Countries, being[2] I know nothing of them but by the information of others, I refer you to their Annual Letters; and it suffices me to have touched here on what I saw concerning the same, to wit the expedition of this Patriarch, Bishops and many Fathers who were sent thither by several wayes, attempting to open a passage into those Countries, lest such Commerce might be hindered by the *Turks*, who are Masters of some of those Passes. So that the F. Visitor of the *Jesuits* told me they had this year sent many people for *Æthiopia*, not onely by the Arabian Gulph,[3] and the Territories of the *Turks* bordering upon it, but also by *Cascem*,[4] a Country outside *Arabia* but govern'd by *Arabians*, by *Mozambique* and *Mombaza*,[5] Countries of the *Portugals*, on the Coast of *Africk*, by *Cafraria*,[6] *Angola*, and *Congo*[7]; that so by these several wayes they might send enough, being[2] the King demanded at least two hundred of their Fathers; and 'tis manifest that if the Conversion goes forward, as they presuppose, the Country is so large that there will be work

---

[1] See pp. 137 and 446. [2] For "since"; see *ante*, p. 28, note 1.

[3] Or Red Sea. See p. 11, note 1.

[4] Probably *Kishm*. See *ante*, p. 2, note 2.

[5] See *ante*, p. 420, note 3, and p. 429, note 7.

[6] See *ante*, pp. 429 and 430, note 2.

[7] This is one of the earliest references to the *Congo* route.

enough for a greater number of Fathers and Religious Catholicks.

IX.—On *June* the second we accompany'd, with a solemn Cavalcade, Sig: *Andrea de Quadro* from the House of Sig: *Gasparo di Melo*, Captain of the City, to the *Jesuits'* Colledge[1]; where, by the hands of the same Fathers, was given him the degree of Master of Arts, that is of Philosophy; the said Fathers having by Apostolical Authority jurisdiction in *India* to confer the said degree, and that of Doctor; for which reason I here have taken notice of this action.

On *June* the seventh I visited in the said Colledge of the *Jesuits* the Patriarch of *Æthiopia*, one of that Society, who is nam'd "*Don Alfonso Luigi de Santi*"; he told me much News from *Rome*, and of several of my Relations whom he knew, but it was stale News. The Patriarch and his Fathers had been inform'd of me, both by the Fathers of *Goa* and by a *Portugal* Souldier call'd *Pero Lopez*, whom I knew in *Persia*, and who went to *Rome* with my Letters, where he lodg'd many dayes in my House, from thence pass'd into *Spain*, and at length return'd into *India*, and came from *Mozambique* to *Goa* in the same Ship with the Patriarch. To gratifie whose desires of seeing me, upon their information I visited him; he not onely shew'd me many courtesies and offers of serving me, with like ceremonious words, but himself and all his Fathers enter'd into an intimate Friendship with me, and agreed to hold mutual correspondence of Letters from *Æthiopia* to *Rome*, and where ever else I should happen to be. We discours'd of many things, and he informed me concerning his Voyage, and how Fathers might pass at any time into *Æthiopia* from other parts, particularly from *Ægypt*. I

---

[1] See *ante*, pp. 142 and 185, note 2.

inform'd him of the *Æthiopick* Language, and some good Books for learning it, etc.

On *June* the sixteenth, if I mistake not in Computation, for which I refer myself to better diligence, (which I shall use with their *Ephemerides* of this year, in case I can procure the same) the Moors were to begin their *Rasandhan*[1] or Fast, of their 1633[2] year of the *Hegira*.

X.—On *June* the twenty-fourth, being in a house to see the careers[3] of the Cavaliers who ran in the Street before the Vice-Roy, according to the yearly Custom in *Goa* upon S. *John's* Day, I hapned to meet with Sig. *Luis de Mendoza*,[4] Chief Captain of the Fleet wherewith I went to *Calecut*,[5] and Sig: *Bento*, or *Benedetto*, or *Freites Mascarenhas*, in a Portugal Habit, who a few years before was taken by Pirates of *Argiers*,[6] and carried a slave to *Barbery;* whence being redeemed and return'd into his own Country, he was favourably look't upon by his King and sent again into *India* as Captain of a Galeon. This Cavalier, besides the relation of his own misadventures, told me how *Qara Sultan* (who in my time was sent Ambassador from the King of *Persia* into *Spain* in answer to the Embassy of *Don Garcia de Silva y Figueroa*,[7] and travelled in the same Ship, before it was taken by the Pirates), died by the Way, having first substituted another of his Company to perform his charge; which other Ambassador was taken with the said Ship and carried a slave into *Argiers;* whereof notice being given to the Persian Ambassador at *Constantinople*,

---

[1] Properly *Ramazan*. See *ante*, p. 179, note 1.

[2] A misprint for 1033.

[3] See *ante*, p. 412, note 7.

[4] See *ante*, p. 354.

[5] See *ante*, p. 344, note 1.

[6] For *Algiers*. The name is written as *Argier* in Shakespeare's *Tempest*, Act i, Sc. 2. The name does not occur here in the original Italian; in it the words are "taken by *Moreschi*".

[7] See *ante*, p. 188, note 4.

an order was expected from thence what to do with him; which not coming before this Gentleman was liberated, he could not tell what the issue was, but left him still a prisoner in *Argiers*.[1]

XI.—On *August* the fifth the *Indians* were to celebrate their solemn Festival of Washing and other Ceremonies accustomed to be performed at *Narva*,[2] and mentioned by me in the last year's relation as to be celebrated on the seventeenth of the same month. And because the Feast-day fell twelve dayes sooner in this year than in the last I perceived that the *Indian* year must be Lunar[3]; or if it be Solar, as I think I have heard, it cannot be just, or equal, but to be adjusted requires some great and extravagant intercalation. I went not to *Narva* to see the Feast, because the place lies beyond the River[4] in the Territory of the *Moors*, who at this time stood not upon good Terms with the *Portugals*. Neither did the *Gentiles* of *Goa* go thither for the same reason; and, if I was not mis-informed, they expected a safe conduct from *Idal-Sciah*,[5] from *Vidhiapor*,[6] to go thither another day.

On *August* the ninth, two hours and forty minutes before noon (if the Calculation and Observation of *Christofero Brano*, or *Boro*, be true) the Sun was in the Zenith of *Goa* and began to decline towards the South.

On *August* the twenty-fourth, on which day the Feast of St. *Bartholomew* uses to be celebrated, certain Officers, deputed for that purpose, with other Principal Persons entrusted with the superintendency of the Fields and Agriculture, offered to the Cathedral Church, and afterwards also to the Vice-roy, the first-fruits of the Fields,

---

[1] In the original *Algieri*. [2] See *ante*, p. 186, note 5.

[3] The lunar year was adopted in some parts of India, and the solar year in others. All festivals are regulated by the moon.

[4] The river *Mandavi*. [5] Or *Adil Shah*. See *ante*, p. 143, note 5.

[6] See *ante*, p. 117, note 2. More correctly *Bíjapúr*.

to wit of Rice newly eared, which is the most substantial of the fruits of the Territory of *Goa*.[1] I was told likewise that they made a Statue of an Elephant with Rice-straw, which I know not whether they carry'd about with them, or set up in some Piazza. This custom is practis'd annually upon the said day, because at that time precisely the said fruit begins to ripen.

On *August* the twenty-seventh one Galeon (of four that were coming from *Mascat*,[2] whither they had been sent last *April* with Provisions) arriv'd at *Goa;* they came, by the Vice-roy's Order, to be ready, if occasion requir'd, to afford new succours of large ships to be sent to *Ormùz*. This Ship related that the other three were possibly return'd back again to the streights of *Ormùz*, for fear of some *Dutch* Vessels which hover'd thereabouts; but this Galeon, being driven out to Sea, and having lost its company in the night, was forc'd to come directly forwards. It related further that *Ormùz* had been again besieg'd a good while by the Captains of *Ruy Freira*, to wit first by *Michel Pereira Boraglio* our friend, and afterwards by another, whom he sent thither by turns, because thereby the task would be easier to the besiegers: but that at the parting of these Galleys from *Mascat Ruy Freira* himself was upon the point to go to the said Siege with all the Men and Vessels with oars he had, which were about twenty, or twenty-five, Galeots, and many less *Morisco* Vessels called *Ternata's*.[3] A small preparation indeed to take *Ormùz* withall.

On *September* the second, a little before daylight, the safe arrival of the annual *Portugal* Fleet was saluted by

---

[1] See *ante*, p. 175, note 4. [2] See *ante*, p. 158, note 7.

[3] Should be *Terradas*. They were light rowing-boats employed generally in carrying supplies, but the term is also applied to small boats used in war. (See *Commentaries of Afonso Dalboquerque*, vol. i, p. 105, Hakluyt edition.)

all the Bells of *Goa*. It consisted of two Merchant Ships, lesser and lighter than the *Carracks*[1] which use to come in other years, one Galeon laden also with Merchandize, and order'd to return with the same Ships, in case it should not be required at *Goa* for the War, and five other Galeons equip'd for war, which were to remain at *Goa* with all the Soldiery, which was numerous and good, to be employ'd as occasion should require. The Chief Captain of this *Armada* was Sig: *Nugno Alvares Botelho;* the Admiral Sig: *Giovan Pereira Cortereal,* to whose diligence the happy and speedy arrival of this Fleet is attributed; the like not having come to pass in many years, and that through the fault and greediness both of the Pilots and Merchants: for before, without keeping order, or rule, in the voyage, or obedience to the Generals, everyone endeavour'd to have his Ship arrive first and alone. But this Sig. *Gio. Pereira Cortereal* having written and presented a printed Discourse about this matter to the King, his Majesty approv'd the same and gave strict charge that it should be observ'd with all exactness: and hence proceeded the good success of this Voyage.

This Fleet brought news that the Prince of *England* was departed from *Spain* without effecting the marriage between the two Crowns, because the Parliament of *England* would not consent to it[2]: which, considering all the pre-

---

[1] From a Portuguese word, *carraca*, a name given to large vessels built for voyages to India and South America, fitted for fighting as well as for trade. In the year 1592 one of these vessels was captured by Sir John Barrough, which is described as being of no less than 1,600 tons burthen, with thirty-two pieces of brass ordnance, having seven decks, and measuring 165 feet in length.

[2] This is, of course, a misapprehension. There is no doubt that the people of England disapproved of the match, but the consent of Parliament was never asked. There were several causes which led to the match being broken off. (See Hume's *Hist. of England*, vol. vi, p. 76.)

ceding transactions seems to me a strange case, and perhaps the like hath scarce happened between Princes; unless possibly there be some unknown mysterie in the business. That the Frosts, having obstructed the mouth of a River in *Holland*, had caus'd a great inundation, which broke the banks, or dikes, whereby they kept out the sea, and had done much damage to the Country. That twelve Ships which set forth from thence for *India*, being beset by the *Spanish* Fleet off *Dunkirk*, were partly sunk and partly shatter'd so that they could not come to *India*. That the Catholicks in *August* last, upon the precise day whereon *Urban* VIII was created Pope, had obtain'd a signal victory[1] in *Germany* against the Hereticks. That great Fleets were preparing in *England*, *Spain* and *France*, for unknown designs. That the King of *Spain* was at *Sevil*,[2] and the Queen had borne him a Daughter who was dead; but the Daughter of the *Conte di Vidigueira*,[3] present Vice-Roy here in *India*, had borne him a Son; at which the Queen was much displeas'd with the King. And that in *Portugal* it was expected that the Arch-Duke *Leopold* should go to govern that Kingdom.

XII.—On *September* the fifth the other three Galeons, which I said were to come from *Mascat*,[4] arriv'd at *Goa*. The cause of their delay was, as was rightly conjectur'd, that they had discover'd an *English* Ship upon those Coasts, and had spent some time in giving her chase, but in vain, through the fault, perhaps, of the *Portugal* Captain who was loth to fight her; for one of them made up to her and fought a while with her Artillery, but, perceiving her companions came not to do the like, gave over, and, having

---

[1] This was probably the victory gained by Count Tilly over Mansfeld at Stadt Loo on August 23rd, 1623.

[2] In the original written as *Siviglia*.

[3] See *ante*, p. 175.

[4] See *ante*, p. 158, note 7.

given and receiv'd many shots, let her go without doing her hurt and return'd to her company. The English Ship shew'd much bravery; for, seeing three Vessels coming against her, she waited to give them battle without flying.

The above-said Galeons brought Letters which signifi'd that *Mascat*[1] was molested with wars by the neighbouring *Arabians;* which, I conceive, may be upon some confederacy with the King of *Persia*, thereby to divert the *Portugals* from the Siege of *Ormùz*. That *Ormùz* was well provided with Men and Victuals; that, nevertheless, they hop'd it would be taken, if good succour were sent from *Goa*, particularly of Galeons to fight with the *Dutch* Ships which were expected to come to the Ports of *Persia* to assist *Ormùz* and recruit it with fresh soldiers. Of the *English* there is no mention, because, considering the late transactions in *Spain*, it is not known whether there will be War, or Peace, with them henceforward, though perhaps the Vice-Roy may know something privately.

On *September* the twenty-ninth a *Jesuit*, whose name I know not, was consecrated here in their Church of *Giesu*[2] Arch-Bishop[3] of *Angamale*,[4] and also, as they speak in the *Portugal* Language, "*da Serra*", that is, "of the Mountain", where live the Christians whom they call "*di San Tomè*",[5] of the *Chaldean* Sect,[6] and sometime subject to the Schismatical Patriarchs of *Babylonia*, but now of late years (by the diligence of the *Portugals*) Catholicks, and obedient to

---

[1] See *ante*, p. 158, note 7, and p. 187, note 3.

[2] See *ante*, p. 164, note 2.

[3] See *ante*, p. 199, note 2.

[4] A town in latitude 10° 20′ N., to the north-east of *Cranganur*.

[5] See *ante*, p. 199, note 1.

[6] Or Nestorians. They themselves do not accept this title, but style themselves *Nazaranies*.

Rome[1]; his residence is in *Cranganor*,[2] five leagues from *Cocin*[3] Northwards.

On *October* the one and twentieth proclamation was made by the Vice-Roy's Order for the Souldiers to come and receive Pay, in Order to their going to *Ormùz*.[4] The *Armado* wherein they were to go was very long in preparing through want of money; which the Vice-Roy was very diligent to raise, both from the Merchants and also from the *Gentiles*, who consented to pay a certain Annual

---

1 These Christians are still to be found existing as a religious sect. They were at one time an independent people, and elected a sovereign of their own. They were much persecuted by the Portuguese, in order to compel them to become Roman Catholics. When the Portuguese rule came to an end they regained their freedom, but remained divided in religion, and at present both the Syrian and Roman Catholic services are performed in the same church, and the Syrian division of the sect receives a superior from the Patriarch of *Antioch*, though before the Portuguese persecution they were governed by bishops deputed by the Nestorian Patriarch of *Mosul* (here called "of Babylonia"). (See Eastwick's *Handbook of Madras*, p. 317.) An interesting note on these Christians (said to number as many as 233,000 souls) will be found in Sir H. Yule's *Cathay and the Way Thither*, vol. i, p. 76.

2 More correctly *Kodangulùr*. In Lat. 10° 23′ N. Identified by Si H. Yule with the ancient *Cynkali*, or *Cyncilim*, or *Shinkala*, the seat of one of the old Malabar principalities, and celebrated as the place where St. Thomas first preached in India, and where Muhammadans, and Jews also, first settled in India. Called *Singugli* by Jordanus, and *Jangli* by *Rashid-udin*. (See Yule's *Cathay*, vol. i, p. 75.) Taken by the Dutch in 1662.

3 As this is one of the last references to *Cocin* in these letters, a few facts may be here mentioned in addition to those given *ante* at p. 199, note 1. The town is situated somewhat peculiarly on the extremity of a spit of land twelve miles long, to the east of which is an extensive backwater, which affords an advantageous means of communication, open at all seasons of the year. The town is well built, but it enjoys an unenviable reputation in regard to healthiness, owing to the prevalence of elephantiasis, otherwise called "Cochin leg". (See Eastwick's *Handbook of Madras*, p. 316.)

4 See *ante*, p. 2, note 1, and p. 395.

Sum (or else a greater sum once for all) that Licence might be granted them to celebrate Marriages in *Goa*, according to their own Rite, which ordinarily was not allowed them. But all these courses were not sufficient to dispatch the Fleet with that diligence which was desired; and in the mean time it was said that many *Dutch*, or *English*, Ships infested the Ports of *Ciaul*,[1] *Bassaim*,[2] and *Dabul*,[3] without controll; by all which it appears to me that matters in *India* go every day from bad to worse.

XIII.—On *October* the one and thirtieth news came to *Goa* that *Melik Ambar*,[4] who for a good while successfully warr'd against *Adil-Sciah*,[5] at length in a victory had taken one *Mulla Muhhamed*, General of *Adil-Sciah's* Army and much favor'd by him; who by his ill demeanor towards the said *Melik* (even so far as to endeavour to get him poyson'd) was the occasion of the present Warr, wherein *Melik's* chief intent was to revenge himself on the said *Mulla Muhhamed:* whom being thus taken, they say, he beheaded and caus'd him in that manner to be carry'd about his Camp with this Proclamation; that this Traytor *Mulla Muhhamed*, the cause of the Warr and present discords between *Adil-Sciah* and *Nizam-Sciah*,[6] (to whom this *Melik* is Governour) otherwise Friends and Allies, was thus in the Name of his Lord *Adil-Sciah*, as a Traytor and disturber of the publick Peace, put to death. By which act *Melik* meant to signifie that he had no evil intention against *Adil-Sciah*, but onely took up Arms for the mischiefs done him by *Mulla Muhhamed*, whom he desir'd to remove from the Government of *Adil-Sciah* and from the world. Yet it was not known how *Adil-Sciah* receiv'd this action, and what end the business would have.

---

1 See *ante*, p. 140, note 1.
2 See *ante*, p. 16, note 3.
3 See *ante*, p. 136, note 4.
4 See *ante*, p. 134, note 2.
5 See *ante*, p. 143, note 5.
6 See *ante*, p. 134, note 1.

In this Warr, they say, the *Mogol*[1] favor'd *Adil-Sciah* against *Melik* and supply'd him with 20,000 Horse: but, be that how it will, *Adil-Sciah* hath hitherto always gone by the worst and sometimes been in great danger; *Melik*, who is a brave Captain, having over-run all the State almost to the Gates of *Vidhiapor*,[2] which is the Royal City of *Adil-Sciah*, where he hath sometimes been forc'd to shut himself up as if it were besieg'd. A few moneths before *Adil-Sciah* put one of his principal Wives to death, for conspiracy which she was said to hold with *Melik*, and for having been a party in promoting this Warr, out of design to remove *Adil-Sciah* from the Government, as one become odious to his own people, either through his covetousness, or inability (being infirm), and to place his Son in his room, who therefore was in danger too of being put to death by his Father when the conspiracy was discover'd.

Further news came that *Adil-Sciah* had deposed from the government and imprison'd the Governour of the maritime Territories bordering upon *Goa*, who had lately given the *Portugals* so many disgusts; which seem'd to signifie that he was minded to give them some satisfaction: that he had given the place to *Chogia Riza* or *Regeb*, a *Persian*, lately Governour of *Dabul*,[3] who being in greater employments at Court will send a Deputy, and from whom, being prudent, and formerly a friend to the *Portugals*, they hope better dealings.

On *November* the first the Confraternity *della Misericordia*[4] made a solemn Procession in the evening, (as they use to do yearly upon this day) going with two Biers from their own Church to the Church of our Lady *de la Luz*,[5] to fetch the

---

[1] *I.e.*, the Emperor *Jahángir*. (See Elphinstone's *Hist. of India*, p. 498.)

[2] See p. 117, note 2, and p. 436, note 6.

[3] See *ante*, p. 136, note 4.

[4] See *ante*, p. 382, note 4.

[5] Marked as No. 23 in the Plan of Goa (*ante*, p. 154). It was built in 1540, and remained in use up to 1835, but is now removed.

bones of all such as had been executed this year and buried under the Gallows; which they carry in Procession, first to this latter, and then to their own, Church to bury, where also they make solemn Exequies for them.

On *November* the second, in the Evening, the *Dominicans*[1] made their solemn Procession *del Rosario* with much Solemnity, and so also the next morning, having deferr'd the same from the first Week of *October* till now, because the rain uses to disturb it in *October*.

This day news came to *Goa* that a Ship belonging to the *Mogol's* subjects, at her departing for *Gidda*[2] from the Port of *Diu*,[3] had there given security to return to the same Port to pay the usual Customs to the *Portugals*, which would have amounted to above five thousand *Scierifines*,[4] but the Ministers of *Diu* were contented with small security, which was no more than four thousand *Scierifines*: yet, when the said Ship came back very rich, she would not touch at *Diu*, little caring to discharge the small security, but put in at a place upon that Coast belonging to the *Mogul* between *Diu* and *Cambaia*.[5] The *Portugals*, understanding this, sent the *Armada* of *Diu*, consisting of small Vessels with Oars, to fetch her in to *Diu* by force; and, the Ship refusing to obey, they fell to fighting. In the fight those of the Ship kill'd, amongst others, the Chief Commander of the *Portugal Armada*; yet the *Armada* so beset the Ship that they first forced her to run on shore, and then burnt her. It was not true that the Chief Captain

---

[1] See *ante*, p. 156, note 2.

[2] For *Djidda*, or *Jedda*, on the west coast of Arabia, in lat. 21° 29′ N., a port formerly much frequented by vessels trading between India and Egypt.

[3] Or *Diul*. See *ante*, pp. 136, note 4, and 397, note 1.

[4] *Scierifines*, *Serafines*, or *Xerafini*, as they were called at Goa, were silver coins, equivalent to about 4*s*. 2*d*., and of about the same value as a *Pardao*. (See Yule's *Hobson-Jobson*.)

[5] See *ante*, p. 66, note 2.

was slain ; the Ship was taken indeed, but empty, the *Moors* having had time to save most of their wealth upon Land, but nevertheless they suffer'd much dammage. By this accident it may be doubted whether some disgust be not likely to ensue between the *Mogol* and the *Portugals;* and I know not whether it may not somewhat retard the *Portugal Armada* and *Cafila,*[1] which was ready to set sail for *Cambaia.*[2]

On *November* the fourth the *Armada* of *Colletta*[3] departed from *Goa* to fetch provisions ; it was to go to *Cocin,*[4] and therefore the newly consecrated Arch-Bishop of *Serra*[5] imbarqu'd in it to go to his residence ; so also did F. *Andrea Palmeiro,* Visitor of the *Jesuits,* my friend, to visit that his Province ; and F. *Laertio Alberti,* an Italian, with many other *Jesuits* who came out of *Europe* this year to go and reside there. The same day, an *Almadia,*[6] or small Boat, of *Ciaul*[7] came to *Goa* with news of a Vessel arriv'd there from *Mascat,*[8] and also a Ship from *Bassora*[9]; both which reported that *Ormùz*[10] was in much distress by the Siege, so that many *Moors,* soldiers, escap'd out of the Town to *Ruy Freira;* after whose arrival the Siege proceeded prosperously for us, with good order and much hope yet, if the succours were sent from *Goa,* which *Ruy Freira* very importunately desir'd. At *Bassora,* they said, all was quiet.

This will be the last that I shall write to you from *Goa,* being ready to depart out of *India* (if it please God) within a few dayes and desirous to return to my Country, where I may see and discourse with you ; the first object that I

---

[1] See *ante*, p. 121, note 3.
[2] See *ante*, p. 66, note 2.
[3] See *ante*, p. 354.
[4] See *ante*, p. 199, note 1.
[5] See *ante*, p. 440.
[6] See *ante*, p. 122, note 1.
[7] See *ante*, p. 140, note 1.
[8] See *ante*, p. 158, note 7, and p. 187, note 3.
[9] See *ante*, p. 442, note 3.
[10] See *ante*, p. 2, note 1.

propose to myself at my revisiting our dear *Italy*. However, I shall not omit in my way to acquaint you with my adventures, to the end that my Letters may forerun me and be the harbingers of my arrival. I reserve many things to tell the Sig. *Dottore*, and Signor *Colletta*, and those other Gentlemen my friends, who, I am confident, join in my prayers to God for my prosperous arrival; from whom wishing you all happiness, I rest, etc.

NOTE.—With reference to the mention made in this Letter of the mission to *Æthiopia* and of *Sultan Saghed*, king of that country (see p. 433), and to that of the Christians of *San Tomè* (see p. 440), it may be useful to remind readers that an account of the Nestorian sect, and of the Christians of "St. Thomas in India", as also of the Jesuit mission to *Abyssinia* (here called *Æthiopia*), will be found in chap. xlvii of Gibbon's *Decline and Fall of the Roman Empire*, in which account "*Sultan Saghed*" appears as the "Emperor Segued". On his death the Jesuits were expelled from the country by his son *Basilides*, and, in the words of the historian, "the gates of that solitary realm were for ever shut against the arts, the science, and the fanaticism of Europe".

INDEX.

ERRATA IN VOL. II.

P. 200, l. 3, *insert* IV.— at commencement of line.

P. 225, l. 5,	„	IV.—	„	„
P. 273, l. 15,	„	XXIII.—	„	„
P. 284, l. 26,	„	XXVII.—	„	„

P. 355, l. 16, "Mansel" should be "Manoel".

P. 424, l. 28, *insert* V.— at commencement of line.

THE

HAKLUYT SOCIETY

1892.

THE HAKLUYT SOCIETY, established for the purpose of printing rare or unpublished Voyages and Travels, aims at opening by this means an easier access to the sources of a branch ot knowledge, which yields to none in importance, and is superior to most in agreeable variety. The narratives of travellers and navigators make us acquainted with the earth, its inhabitants and productions ; they exhibit the growth of intercourse among mankind, with its effects on civilisation, and, while instructing, they at the same time awaken attention, by recounting the toils and adventures of those who first explored unknown and distant regions.

The advantage of an Association of this kind consists not merely in its system of literary co-operation, but also n its economy. The acquirements, taste, and discrimination of a number of individuals, who feel an interest in the same pursuit, are thus brought to act in voluntary combination, and the ordinary charges of publication are also avoided, so that the volumes produced are distributed among the Members at little more than the cost of printing and paper. The Society expends the whole of its funds in the preparation of works for the Members; and since the cost of each copy varies inversely as the whole number of copies printed, it is obvious that the members are gainers individually by the prosperity of the Society, and the consequent vigour of its operations.

Gentlemen desirous of becoming Members of the Hakluyt Society should intimate their intention to the Secretary, MR. E. DELMAR MORGAN, 15, *Roland Gardens, S.W.*, or to the Society's Agent for the delivery of its volumes, MR. CHARLES J. CLARK, 4, *Lincoln's Inn Fields;* when their names will be recorded, and on payment of their subscription of £1 : 1 to Mr. CLARK, they will receive the volumes issued for the year.

Members and the general public are informed that the Council has approved of the following scheme for the disposal of its surplus stock.

TO NEW MEMBERS.—*Complete sets of back publications*, omitting Nos. 1, 2, 3, 5, 6, 7 and 13, to be sold for . . . . £28.

TO MEMBERS ONLY.—*A limited number of sets up to* 1883 inclusive, omitting Nos. 1—13, 19, 36 and 37. 53 vols. in all, to be sold for £15 15s

TO THE PUBLIC GENERALLY.—*Also, a limited number of single copies* as follows:—

Nos. 17, 22, 23, 26, 29, 31, 34, 40, 47, 50, at . . . . . 8s. 6d.

Nos. 14 and 15, 18, 21, 24, 28, 30, 35, 46, 48, 51, 53, 55, 56, 58, 60 and 61, 62, 63, 64, 65, 69, at . . . . 10s.

Nos. 16, 20, 27, 32, 33, 38, 39, 41 to 45, 49, 52, 57, at . . . . 15s.

Nos. 54 and 59, at . . . . 20s.

*** Subject in case of Members to a discount of 15%.

Members are requested to bear in mind that the power of the Council to make advantageous arrangements will depend in a great measure on the prompt payment of the subscriptions, which are payable in advance on the 1st of January, and are received by MR. CHARLES J. CLARK, 4, *Lincoln's Inn Fields, W.C.* Post Office Orders should be made payable to MR. CHARLES J. CLARK, at the *West Central Office, High Holborn.*

WORKS ALREADY ISSUED.

1—The Observations of Sir Richard Hawkins, Knt.,

In his Voyage into the South Sea in 1593. Reprinted from the edition of 1622, and edited by Capt. C. R. DRINKWATER BETHUNE, R.N., C.B. *(First Edition out of print. See No. 57.) Iſſued for* 1848.

2—Select Letters of Columbus.

With Original Documents relating to the Diſcovery of the New World. Translated and Edited by R. H. MAJOR, Esq., of the Britiſh Muſeum. *(First Edition out of print. See No. 43.)* (1847.) *Iſſued for* 1849.

3—The Discoverie of the Empire of Guiana,

By Sir Walter Raleigh, Knt. Edited, with copious Explanatory Notes, and a Biographical Memoir, by SIR ROBERT H. SCHOMBURGK, Phil.D., etc. (1848.) *(Out of print.) Iſſued for* 1850.

4—Sir Francis Drake his Voyage, 1595.

By Thomas Maynarde, together with the Spaniſh Account of Drake's attack on Puerto Rico. Edited from the Original MSS. by W. D. COOLEY, Esq. (1849.) *Iſſued for* 1850.

5—Narratives of Early Voyages

Undertaken for the Diſcovery of a Paſſage to Cathaia and India, by the Northwest, with Selections from the Records of the worſhipful Fellowſhip of the Merchants of London, trading into the Eaſt Indies; and from MSS. in the Library of the Britiſh Muſeum, now firſt publiſhed; by THOMAS RUNDALL, Esq. (1849.) *(Out of print.) Iſſued for* 1851.

6—The Historie of Travaile into Virginia Britannia,

Expreſſing the Coſmographie and Commodities of the Country, together with the manners and cuſtoms of the people, gathered and obſerved as well by thoſe who went firſt thither as collected by William Strachey, Gent., the firſt Secretary of the Colony; now firſt Edited from the original manuſcript in the Britiſh Muſeum, by R. H. MAJOR, Esq., of the Britiſh Muſeum. (1849.) *(Out of print.) Iſſued for* 1851.

7—Divers Voyages touching the Discovery of America

And the Iſlands adjacent, collected and publiſhed by Richard Hakluyt. Prebendary of Briſtol in the year 1582. Edited, with Notes and an introduction, by JOHN WINTER JONES, Esq., of the Britiſh Muſeum. (1850.) *(Out of print.) Iſſued for* 1852.

8—A Collection of Documents on Japan.

With a Commentary by THOMAS RUNDALL, ESQ. (1850.) *Iſſued for* 1852.

9—The Discovery and Conquest of Florida,

By Don Ferdinando de Soto. Tranſlated out of Portugueſe by Richard Hakluyt; and Edited, with notes and an introduction, by W. B. RYE, Esq., of the Britiſh Muſeum. (1851.) *Iſſued for* 1853.

10—Notes upon Russia,

Being a Tranſlation from the Earlieſt Account of that Country, entitled Rerum Muscoviticarum Commentarii, by the Baron Sigiſmund von Herberſtein, Ambaſſador from the Court of Germany to the Grand Prince Vaſiley Ivanovich, in the years 1517 and 1526. Two Volumes. Tranſlated and Edited, with Notes and an Introduction, by R. H. MAJOR, Esq., of the Britiſh Muſeum. Vol. I. (1851.) *Iſſued for* 1853.

11—The Geography of Hudson's Bay.

Being the Remarks of Captain W. Coats, in many Voyages to that locality, between the years 1727 and 1751. With an Appendix, containing Extracts from the Log of Captain Middleton on his Voyage for the Discovery of the North-west Passage, in H.M.S. "Furnace," in 1741-2. Edited by JOHN BARROW, Esq., F.R.S., F.S.A. (1852.)

Issued for 1854.

12—Notes upon Russia. Vol. 2. (1852.)

Issued for 1854.

13—Three Voyages by the North-east,

Towards Cathay and China, undertaken by the Dutch in the years 1594, 1595 and 1596, with their Discovery of Spitzbergen, their residence of ten months in Novaya Zemlya, and their safe return in two open boats. By Gerrit de Veer. Edited by C. T. BEKE, Esq., Ph.D., F.S.A. (1853.)

(*First Edition out of print. See No.* 54.) *Issued for* 1855.

14-15—The History of the Great and Mighty Kingdom of China and the Situation Thereof.

Compiled by the Padre Juan Gonzalez de Mendoza. And now Reprinted from the Early Translation of R. Parke. Edited by SIR GEORGE T. STAUNTON, Bart. With an Introduction by R. H. MAJOR, Esq. 2 vols. (1853-54.) *Issued for* 1855.

16—The World Encompassed by Sir Francis Drake.

Being his next Voyage to that to Nombre de Dios. Collated, with an unpublished Manuscript of Francis Fletcher, Chaplain to the Expedition. With Appendices illustrative of the same Voyage, and Introduction by W. S. W. VAUX, Esq., M.A. (1854.) *Issued for* 1856.

17—The History of the Tartar Conquerors who subdued China.

From the French of the Père D'Orleans, 1688. Translated and Edited by the EARL OF ELLESMERE. With an Introduction by R. H. MAJOR, Esq. (1854.)

Issued for 1856.

18—A Collection of Early Documents on Spitzbergen and Greenland,

Consisting of: a Translation from the German of F. Martin's important work on Spitzbergen, now very rare; a Translation from Isaac de la Peyrère's Relation de Greenland; and a rare piece entitled "God's Power and Providence showed in the miraculous preservation and deliverance of eight Englishmen left by mischance in Greenland, anno 1630, nine months and twelve days, faithfully reported by Edward Pelham." Edited, with Notes, by ADAM WHITE, Esq., of the British Museum. (1855.)

Issued for 1857.

19—The Voyage of Sir Henry Middleton to Bantam and the Maluco Islands.

From the rare Edition of 1606. Edited by BOLTON CORNEY, Esq. (1855.)

Issued for 1857.

20—Russia at the Close of the Sixteenth Century.

Comprising "The Russe Commonwealth" by Dr. Giles Fletcher, and Sir Jerome Horsey's Travels, now first printed entire from his manuscript in the British Museum. Edited by E. A. BOND, Esq., of the British Museum. (1856.) *Issued for* 1858.

21—The Travels of Girolamo Benzoni in America, in 1542-56.

Translated and Edited by ADMIRAL W. H. SMYTH, F.R.S., F.S.A. (1857.)

Issued for 1858.

22—India in the Fifteenth Century.

Being a Collection of Narratives of Voyages to India in the century preceding the Portuguese discovery of the Cape of Good Hope; from Latin, Persian, Russian, and Italian Sources, now first translated into English. Edited, with an Introduction by R. H. MAJOR, Esq., F.S.A. (1857.)
Issued for 1859.

23—Narrative of a Voyage to the West Indies and Mexico,

In the years 1599-1602, with Maps and Illustrations. By Samuel Champlain. Translated from the original and unpublished Manuscript, with a Biographical Notice and Notes by ALICE WILMERE. (1859.)
Issued for 1859.

24—Expeditions into the Valley of the Amazons

During the Sixteenth and Seventeenth Centuries: containing the Journey of Gonzalo Pizarro, from the Royal Commentaries of Garcilasso Inca de la Vega; the Voyage of Francisco de Orellana, from the General History of Herrera; and the Voyage of Cristoval de Acuna, from an exceedingly scarce narrative written by himself in 1641. Edited and Translated by CLEMENTS R. MARKHAM, Esq. (1859.) *Issued for* 1860.

25—Early Indications of Australia.

A Collection of Documents shewing the Early Discoveries of Australia to the time of Captain Cook. Edited by R. H. MAJOR, ESQ., of the British Museum, F.S.A. (1859.) *Issued for* 1860.

26—The Embassy of Ruy Gonzales de Clavijo to the Court of Timour, 1403-6.

Translated, for the first time, with Notes, a Preface, and an Introductory Life of Timour Beg. By CLEMENTS R. MARKHAM, Esq. (1859.)
Issued for 1861.

27—Henry Hudson the Navigator.

The Original Documents in which his career is recorded. Collected, partly Translated, and Annotated, with an Introduction by GEORGE ASHER, LL.D. (1860.) *Issued for* 1861.

28—The Expedition of Ursua and Aguirre,

In search of El Dorado and Omagua, A.D. 1560-61. Translated from the "Sexta Noticia Historiale" of Fray Pedro Simon, by W. BOLLAERT, Esq.; with an Introduction by CLEMENTS R. MARKHAM, Esq. (1861.)
Issued for 1862.

29—The Life and Acts of Don Alonzo Enriquez de Guzman.

Translated from a Manuscript in the National Library at Madrid, and edited, with Notes and an Introduction, by CLEMENTS R. MARKHAM, Esq. (1862.)
Issued for 1862.

30—Discoveries of the World by Galvano,

From their first original unto the year of our Lord 1555. Reprinted, with the original Portuguese text, and edited by VICE-ADMIRAL BETHUNE, C.B. (1862.) *Issued for* 1863.

31—Marvels described by Friar Jordanus,

Of the Order of Preachers, native of Severac, and Bishop of Columbum; from a parchment manuscript of the Fourteenth Century, in Latin, the text of which has recently been Translated and Edited by COLONEL H. YULE, C.B., F.R.G.S., late of H.M. Bengal Engineers. (1863.)
Issued for 1863.

32—The Travels of Ludovico di Varthema

In Syria, Arabia, Persia, India, etc., during the Sixteenth Century. Translated by J. WINTER JONES, Esq., F.S.A., and edited, with Notes and an Introduction, by the REV. GEORGE PERCY BADGER. (1863.)
Issued for 1864.

33—The Travels of Cieza de Leon in 1532-50

From the Gulf of Darien to the City of La Plata, contained in the firſt part of his Chronicle of Peru (Antwerp 1554). Tranſlated and edited, with Notes and an Introduction, by CLEMENTS R. MARKHAM, Esq. (1864.)
Iſſued for 1864.

34—The Narrative of Pascual de Andagoya.

Containing the earlieſt notice of Peru. Tranſlated and edited, with Notes and an Introduction, by CLEMENTS R. MARKHAM, Esq. (1865.)
Iſſued for 1865.

35—The Coasts of East Africa and Malabar

In the beginning of the Sixteenth Century, by Duarte Barboſa. Tranſlated from an early Spaniſh manuſcript by the HON. HENRY STANLEY. (1866.)
Iſſued for 1865.

36—Cathay and the Way Thither.

A Collection of all minor notices of China, previous to the Sixteenth Century. Tranſlated and edited by COLONEL H. YULE, C.B. Vol. 1. (1866.)
Iſſued for 1866.

37—Cathay and the Way Thither. Vol. 2. (1866.)
Iſſued for 1866.

38—The Three Voyages of Sir Martin Frobisher.

With a Selection from Letters now in the State Paper Office. Edited by REAR-ADMIRAL COLLINSON, C.B. (1867.)
Iſſued for 1867.

39—The Philippine Islands.

Moluccas, Siam, Cambodia, Japan, and China, at the close of the 16th Century. Antonia de Morga. Translated from the Spanish, with Notes, by LORD STANLEY of Alderley. (1868.) *Iſſued for* 1868.

40—The Fifth Letter of Hernan Cortes

To the Emperor Charles V, containing an Account of his Expedition to Hondurasin 1525-26. Translated from the Spanish by Don Pascual de Gayangos. (1868.)
Iſſued for 1868.

41—The Royal Commentaries of the Yncas.

By the Ynca Garcilasso de la Vega. Translated and Edited, with Notes and an Introduction, by CLEMENTS R. MARKHAM, Esq. Vol. 1. (1869.)
Iſſued for 1869.

42—The Three Voyages of Vasco da Gama,

And his Viceroyalty, from the Lendas da India of Caspar Correa; accompanied by original documents. Translated and Edited by the LORD STANLEY of Alderley. (1869.)
Iſſued for 1869.

43—Select Letters of Christopher Columbus,

With other Original Documents, relating to his Four Voyages to the New World. Tranſlated and Edited by R. H. MAJOR, F.S.A., etc. 2nd Edit. (1870.)
Iſſued for 1870.

44—History of the Imâms and Seyyids of 'Omân,

By Salîl-Ibn-Razîk, from A.D. 661-1856. Tranſlated from the original Arabic, and edited, with Notes, Appendices, and an Introduction, continuing the Hiſtory down to 1870, by GEORGE PERCY BADGER, F.R.G.S. (1871.)
Iſſued for 1870.

45—The Royal Commentaries of the Yncas. Vol. 2. (1871.) *Iſſued for* 1871.

46—The Canarian,

Or Book of the Conqueſt and Converſion of the Canarians in the year 1402, by Meſſire Jean de Bethencourt, Kt. Compoſed by Pierre Bontier and Jean le V rrier. Tranſlated and Edited, with Notes and an Introduction, by R. H. MAJOR, F.S.A. (1872.)
Iſſued for 1871.

47—Reports on the Discovery of Peru,

Tranflated and Edited, with Notes and an Introduction, by CLEMENTS R. MARKHAM, C.B. (1872.) *Iſſued for* 1872.

48—Narratives of the Rites and Laws of the Yncas;

Tranflated from the original Spanifh Manufcripts, and Edited, with Notes and an Introduction, by CLEMENTS R. MARKHAM, C.B., F.R.S. (1873.) *Iſſued for* 1872.

49—Travels to Tana and Persia,

By Jofafa Barbaro and Ambrogio Contarini; Edited by LORD STANLEY of Alderley; and Narratives of other Italian Travels in Perfia, Tranflated and Edited by CHARLES GREY, Esq. (1873.) *Iſſued for* 1873.

50—Voyages of the Zeni

To the Northern Seas in the Fourteenth Century. Tranflated and Edited by R. H. MAJOR, F.S.A. (1873.) *Iſſued for* 1873.

51—The Captivity of Hans Stade of Hesse in 1547-55

Among the Wild Tribes of Eaftern Brazil; tranflated by ALBERT TOOTAL, Esq., and annotated by RICHARD F. BURTON. (1874.) *Iſſued for* 1874.

52—The First Voyage Round the World by Magellan.

Tranflated from the Accounts of Pigafetta and other contemporary writers. With Notes and an Introduction by Lord STANLEY of Alderley. (1874.) *Iſſued for* 1874.

53—The Commentaries of the Great Afonso Dalboquerque,

Second Viceroy of India. Tranflated from the Portuguese Edition of 1774; with Notes and Introduction by WALTER DE GRAY BIRCH, Esq., F.R.S.L. Vol. I. (1875.) *Iſſued for* 1875.

54—Three Voyages to the North-East.

Second Edition of Gerrit de Veer's Three Voyages to the North-East by Barents. Edited, with an Introduction, by Lieut. KOOLEMANS BEYNEN, of the Royal Dutch Navy. (1876.) *Iſſued for* 1876.

55—The Commentaries of the Great Afonso Dalboquerque. Vol. 2. (1877.) *Iſſued for* 1875.

56—The Voyages of Sir James Lancaster.

With Abstracts of Journal of Voyages preserved in the India Office, and the Voyage of Captain John Knight to seek the N.W. Passage. Edited by CLEMENTS R. MARKHAM, C.B., F.R.S. (1877.) *Iſſued for* 1877.

57—Second Edition of the Observations of Sir Richard Hawkins, Kt.,

In his Voyage into the South Sea in 1593, with the Voyages of his grandfather William, his father Sir John, and his cousin William Hawkins. Edited by CLEMENTS R. MARKHAM, C.B., F.R.S. (1878.) *Iſſued for* 1877.

58—The Bondage and Travels of Johann Schiltberger,

From his capture at the battle of Nicopolis in 1396 to his escape and return to Europe in 1427: translated, from the Heidelberg MS. edited in 1859 by Professor Karl Freidrich Neumann, by Commander J. BUCHAN TELFER, R.N.; with Notes by Professor B. BRUUN, and a Preface, Introduction, and Notes by the Translator and Editor. (1879.) *Iſſued for* 1878.

59—The Voyages and Works of John Davis the Navigator.

Edited, with an Introduction and Notes, by Captain ALBERT H. MARKHAM, R.N., F.R.G.S. (1880.) *Iſſued for* 1878.

The Map of the World, A.D. 1600.

Called by Shakspere "The New Map, with the Augmentation of the Indies." To Illustrate the Voyages of John Davis. (1880.) *Issued for* 1878.

60—The Natural and Moral History of the Indies.

By Father Joseph de Acosta. Reprinted from the English Translated Edition of Edward Grimston, 1604; and Edited, with Notes and an Introduction, by CLEMENTS R. MARKHAM, C.B., F.R.S. Vol. I, The Natural History. (1880.) *Issued for* 1879.

61—The Natural and Moral History of the Indies.

Vol. II, The Moral History. (1880.) *Issued for* 1879.

Map of Peru.

To Illustrate Nos. 33, 41, 45, 60, and 61. (1880.) *Issued for* 1879.

62—The Commentaries of the Great Afonso Dalboquerque. Vol. 3. (1880.) *Issued for* 1880.

63—The Voyages of William Baffin, 1612-1622.

Edited, with Notes and an Introduction, by CLEMENTS R. MARKHAM, C.B., F.R.S. (1881.) *Issued for* 1880.

64—Narrative of the Portuguese Embassy to Abyssinia.

During the years 1520-1527. By Father Francisco Alvarez. Translated from the Portuguese, and Edited, with Notes and an Introduction, by Lord STANLEY of Alderley. (1881.) *Issued for* 1881.

65—The History of the Bermudas or Somer Islands.

Attributed to Captain John Smith. Edited from a MS. in the Sloane Collection, British Museum, by General Sir J. HENRY LEFROY, R.A., K.C.M.G., C.B., F.R.S., etc. (1882.) *Issued for* 1881.

66—Diary of Richard Cocks.

Cape-Merchant in the English Factory in Japan, 1615-1622, with Correspondence. Edited by EDWARD MAUNDE THOMPSON, Esq. Vol. 1. (1883.) *Issued for* 1882.

67—Diary of Richard Cocks. Vol. 2. (1883.) *Issued for* 1882.

68—The Second Part of the Chronicle of Peru.

By Pedro de Cieza de Leon. Translated and Edited, with Notes and an Introduction, by CLEMENTS R. MARKHAM, C.B., F.R.S. (1883.) *Issued for* 1883.

69—The Commentaries of the Great Afonso Dalboquerque. Vol. 4. (1884.) *Issued for* 1883.

70-71—The Voyage of John Huyghen van Linschoten to the East Indies.

From the Old English Translation of 1598. The First Book, containing his Description of the East. Edited, the First Volume by the late ARTHUR COKE BURNELL, Ph.D., C.I.E., of the Madras Civil Service; the Second Volume by Mr. P. A. TIELE, of Utrecht. (1885.) *Issued for* 1884.

72-73—Early Voyages and Travels to Russia and Persia.

By Anthony Jenkinson and other Englishmen, with some Account of the first Intercourse of the English with Russia and Central Asia by way of the Caspian Sea. Edited by E. DELMAR MORGAN, Esq., and C. H. COOTE, Esq. (1886.) *Issued for* 1885.

74—The Diary of William Hedges, Esq.,

Afterwards Sir William Hedges, during his Agency in Bengal; as well as on his Voyage out and Return Overland (1681-1687). Transcribed for the Press, with Introductory Notes, etc., by R. BARLOW, Esq., and Illustrated by copious Extracts from Unpublished Records, etc., by Col. Sir H. YULE, K.C.S.I., R.E., C.B., LL.D. Vol. 1, The Diary. (1887.) *Issued for* 1886.

75—The Diary of William Hedges, Esq. Vol. 2.

Sir H. Yule's Extracts from Unpublished Records, etc. (1888.) *Issued for* 1886.

76—The Voyage of François Pyrard to the East Indies,

The Maldives, the Moluccas and Brazil. Translated into English from the Third French Edition of 1619, and Edited, with Notes, by ALBERT GRAY, Esq., formerly of the Ceylon Civil Service, assisted by H. C. P. BELL, Esq., of the Ceylon Civil Service. Vol. 1. (1887.) *Issued for* 1887.

77—The Voyage of François Pyrard to the East Indies, etc.

Vol. 2, Part I. (1888.) *Issued* for 1887.

78—The Diary of William Hedges, Esq. Vol. 3.

Sir H. Yule's Extracts from Unpublished Records, etc. (1889.) *Issued for* 1888.

79—Tractatus de Globis, et eorum usu.

A Treatise descriptive of the Globes constructed by Emery Molyneux, and Published in 1592. By Robert Hues. Edited, with Annotated Indices and an Introduction, by CLEMENTS R. MARKHAM, C.B., F.R S. To which is appended,

Sailing Directions for the Circumnavigation of England,

And for a Voyage to the Straits of Gibraltar. From a Fifteenth Century MS. Edited by JAMES GAIRDNER, Esq. ; with a Glossary by E. DELMAR MORGAN, Esq. (1889.) *Issued for* 1888.

80—The Voyage of François Pyrard to the East Indies, etc.

Vol. 2, Part II. (1890.) *Issued for* 1889.

81.—The Conquest of La Plata, 1535-1555.

I.—Voyage of Ulrich Schmidt to the Rivers La Plata and Paraguai. II.—The Commentaries of Alvar Nunez Cabeza de Vaca. With Notes and Introduction by DON LUIS L. DOMINGUEZ. (1891.) *Issued for* 1889.

82-83.—The Voyage of François Leguat

To Rodriguez, Mauritius, Java, and the Cape of Good Hope. Transcribed from the first English Edition. Edited and Annotated by Captain PASFIELD OLIVER, late Royal Artillery. (1891.) *Issued for* 1890.

84-85.—The Travels of Pietro della Valle to India.

From the Old English Translation of 1664, by G. Havers. Edited, with a Life of the Author, an Introduction and Notes, by EDWARD GREY, late Bengal Civil Service. (1892.) *Issued for* 1891.

OTHER WORKS UNDERTAKEN BY EDITORS.

The Voyages of Foxe and James to Hudson's Bay. Edited by MILLER CHRISTY, Esq.

The True History of the Conquest of New Spain, by Bernal Diaz. Translated from the Spanish and edited by Rear-Admiral LINDESAY BRINE.

The Voyages of the Earl of Cumberland, from the Records prepared by order of the Countefs of Pembroke. Edited by W. DE GRAY BIRCH, Esq., F.S.A.

Rofmital's Embaffy to England, Spain, etc., in 1466. Edited by R. C. GRAVES, Esq.

A Reprint of 17th Century Books on Seamanship and Sea Matters in General, including Captain John Smith's "Seaman's Grammar", from the edition of 1692, and Sir H. Manwayring's "Seaman's Dictionary", 1644, with extracts from unpublished MSS. Edited, with Notes and an Introduction, by H. Halliday Sparling, Esq.

The Travels of Leo Africanus the Moor, from the English translation of John Pory (1600). Edited by Robert Brown, Esq., M.A., Ph.D., F.L.S., etc.

Histoire de la Grande Isle Madagascar, composée par le Sieur De Flacourt, 1661. Translated and edited, with Notes and an Introduction, by S. Pasfield Oliver, Captain late Royal Artillery, etc.

The Travels of Ibn Jobair. Edited by Professor W. Robertson Smith, Fellow of Christ's College, Cambridge.

Raleigh's Empire of Guiana. Second Edition (see No. 3). Edited, with Notes, etc., by Everard F. im Thurn, Esq.

The Voyages of Keymis and Berrie to Guiana. Edited by Mr. James Rodway.

Dampier's Voyages. Edited by Lieut. Cecil Dampier, R.N.

WORKS SUGGESTED TO THE COUNCIL FOR PUBLICATION.

Inedited Letters, etc., of Sir Thomas Roe during his Embaſſy to India.

The Topographia Chriſtiana of Coſmas Indicopleuſtes.

Bernhard de Breydenbach, 1483-84, A.D. Travels in the Holy Land.

Felix Fabri, 1483. Wanderings in the Holy Land, Egypt, etc.

Voyage made by Captain Jaques Cartier in 1535 and 1536 to the Iſles of Canada, Hochlega, and Saguenay.

Ca da Moſto. Voyages along the Weſtern Coaſt of Africa in 1454: tranſlated from the Italian text of 1507.

J. dos Santos. The Hiſtory of Eaſtern Ethiopia. 1607.

Icelandic Sagas narrating the Diſcovery of America.

La Argentina. An account of the Diſcovery of the Provinces of Rio de la Plata from 1512 to the time of Domingo Martinez de Irala; by Ruiz Diaz de Guzman.

The History of Ethiopia, by Manoel de Almeida.

Journal of the Jesuit Desideri in Tibet.

Travels of Friar Rubruquis.

Voyages of Willoughby and Chancellor.

Letters of Ortelius and Mercator.

The Travels of Ibn Batuta.

Tasman's Voyages.

The Travels of Teixeiro (from the Portuguese).

Voyage of Sarmiento.

Travels of the brothers Sherley in Persia.

The Voyage of Ralph Fitch.

LAWS OF THE HAKLUYT SOCIETY.

I. The object of this Society ſhall be to print, for diſtribution among its members, rare and valuable Voyages, Travels, Naval Expeditions, and other geographical records, from an early period to the beginning of the eighteenth century.

II. The Annual Subſcription ſhall be One Guinea, payable in advance on the 1st January.

III. Each member of the Society, having paid his Subſcription, ſhall be entitled to a copy of every work produced by the Society, and to vote at the general meetings within the period ſubſcribed for; and if he do not ſignify, before the cloſe of the year, his wiſh to reſign, he ſhall be conſidered as a member for the ſucceeding year.

IV. The management of the Society's affairs ſhall be veſted in a Council conſiſting of twenty-one members, viz., a Preſident, two Vice-Preſidents, a Secretary, and ſeventeen ordinary members, to be elected annually; but vacancies occurring between the general meetings ſhall be filled up by the Council.

V. A General Meeting of the Subſcribers ſhall be held annually. The Secretary's Report on the condition and proceedings of the Society ſhall be then read, and the Meeting ſhall proceed to elect the Council for the enſuing year.

VI. At each Annual Election, ſix of the old Council ſhall retire, of whom three ſhall be eligible for re-election.

VII. The Council ſhall meet when neceſſary, for the diſpatch of buſineſs, three forming a quorum, including the Secretary, and the Chairman having a caſting vote.

VIII. Gentlemen preparing and editing works for the Society, ſhall receive twenty-five copies of ſuch works reſpectively, and an additional twenty-five copies if the work is alſo tranſlated.

RULES FOR THE DELIVERY OF THE SOCIETY'S VOLUMES.

I. The Society's productions will be delivered without any charge, within three miles of the General Poſt Office.

II. They will be forwarded to any place beyond that limit, the Society paying the coſt of booking, but not of carriage; nor will it be anſwerable in this caſe for any loſs or damage.

III. They will be delivered by the Society's agent, MR. CHARLES J. CLARK, 4, Lincoln's Inn Fields, to perſons having written authority of ſubſcribers to receive them.

IV. They will be ſent to the Society's correſpondents or agents in the principal towns throughout the kingdom; and care ſhall be taken that the charge for carriage be as moderate as poſſible.

LIST OF MEMBERS

OF THE

Hakluyt Society.

JUNE 2, 1891.

Abercromby, Hon. John, 62, Palmerston-place, Edinburgh.
Aberdare, Right Hon. Lord, F.R.S., 1, Queen's-gate, S.W.; and Duffryn, Mountain Ash, Glamorganshire.
Admiralty, The (2 *copies*).
Advocates' Library, Edinburgh.
Allahabad Public Library, India (Lt.-Col. C. A. Dodd, Secretary).
All Souls College, Oxford.
American Geographical Society, 11, West 29th Street, New York City, U.S.A.
Amherst, W. Amhurst T., Esq., M.P., Didlington Hall, Brandon.
Antiquaries, the Society of, Burlington House, Piccadilly, W.
Army and Navy Club, 36, Pall-mall.
Astor Library, New York.
Athenæum Club, Pall Mall.

Baer, Joseph & Co., Messrs., Rossmarkt, 18, Frankfort-on-Maine.
Bain, James, Esq., 1, Haymarket.
Ball, Valentine, Esq., C.B., LL.D., F.R.S., Director of the Science and Art Museum, Dublin.
Bank of England Library and Literary Association.
Barlow, R. Fred., Esq., 15, Ambrose-place, Worthing, Sussex.
Barrow, J., Esq., F.R.S., F.S.A., 17, Hanover-terrace, Regent's Park.
Basano, Marquis de
Bell and Bradfute, Messrs., 12, Bank-street, Edinburgh.
Bellamy, C. H., Esq., 97, Bishop-street, Moss-side, Manchester.
Berlin Geographical Society.
Berlin, the Royal Library of.
Berlin University, Geographical Institute of (Baron von Richthofen), 6, Schinkelplatz, Berlin, W.
Bethell, William, Esq., Rise, Hull.
Birch, W. de G., Esq., British Museum.
Birmingham Library (The).
Birmingham Central Free Library.
Bodleian Library, Oxford *(copies presented)*.
Bombay Asiatic Society.
Boston Athenæum Library, U.S.A.
Boston Public Library.
Bouverie-Pusey, S. E. B., Esq., 21, Grosvenor-street, W.
Bowdoin College, Brunswick, Maine, U.S.A.
Brazil, Emperor of, H.M. Dom Pedro II. (*Deceased.*)
Bremen Museum.
Brine, Rear-Admiral Lindesay, 13, Pembroke-gardens, Kensington.
British Museum *(copies presented)*.
Brooke, Thos., Esq., Armitage Bridge, Huddersfield.
Brooklyn Library, Brooklyn, U.S.A.
Brooklyn Mercantile Library.
Brown, Arthur W. W., Esq., 6, Sussex-square, Hyde Park, W.
Brown, J. Allen, Esq., 7, Kent-gardens, Ealing.
Brown, J. Nicholas, Esq., Providence, R.I., U.S.A.
Brown, H. T., Esq., Roodeye House, Chester.
Brown, Robert, Esq., M.A., Ph.D., etc., Fersley, Rydal-road, Streatham, S.W.
Brown, General J. Marshall, 218, Middle-street, Portland, Maine, U.S.A.
Bunbury, Sir E. H., Bart., 35, St. James's-street, S.W.
Burne-Jones, E., Esq., The Grange, West Kensington, W.
Burns, J. W., Esq., Kilmahew, Dumbartonshire.

Cambridge University Library.
Canada, The Parliament Library.
Carlton Club, Pall-mall.
Carlisle, The Earl of, Naworth Castle, Bampton, Cumberland.
Cavendish, H. F. C., Esq., 37, Eaton-place, S.W.
Ceylon Branch, Royal Asiatic Society, Colombo.
Chapman, Walter, Esq., Elsenham, Westwood Park, Southampton.
Chetham's Library, Hunt's Bank, Manchester.
Chicago Public Library.
Christiania University Library.
Christy, Miller, Esq., Pryors, Broomfield, near Chelmsford.
Cincinnati Public Library.
Clark, J. W., Esq., Scroope House, Cambridge.
Cleary, P., Esq., 200, Clarendon-street, South Melbourne, Victoria, Australia.
Cohen, Herr Friedrich, Kaiserplatz, No. 18, Bonn, Germany.
Colonial Office (The), Downing-street, S.W.
Collingridge, George, Esq., Hornsby Junction, New South Wales, Australia.
Congress, Library of, Washington, United States.
Constable, Archibald, Esq., 14, Parliament-street, Westminster, S.W.
Cooper, Lieut.-Col. E. H., 42, Portman-square, W.
Copenhagen Royal Library.
Cornell University.
Corning, C. R., Esq., West Fort Ann, Washington County, N.Y., U.S.A.
Corning, H. K., Esq., Villa Monnet, Morillon, Geneva.
Cotton, R. W., Esq., Woodleigh, Forde Park, Newton Abbot.
Crowle, Percival H. S., Esq., 36, Phillimore-gardens, Kensington, W.
Crowninshield, Colonel Benjamin W., 22, Congress-street, Boston, U.S.A.

Dalton, Rev. Canon J. N., per Messrs. Williams & Norgate, Henrietta-street.
Danish Royal Naval Library.
Davis, N. Darnell, Esq., Georgetown, Demerara, British Guiana.
Derby, The Earl of, 25, St. James's-square, S.W.
Dismorr, James Stewart, Esq., Wrotham-road, Gravesend.
Donald, C. D., Esq., 172, St. Vincent-street, Glasgow.
Doughty, Rear-Admiral Proby, care of Messrs. Hallett & Co., 7, St. Martin's-place.
Dresden Geographical Society.
Drummond, E. A., Esq.
Ducie, The Earl, F.R.S., Tortworth Court, Falfield.
Dundas, Captain Colin M., R.N., Ochtertyre, Stirling.
Dunn, John, Esq., 78, Michigan-avenue, Chicago, U.S.A.

Eames, Wilberforce, Esq., Lenox Library, 890, Fifth-avenue, New York, U.S.A.
EDINBURGH, Rear-Admiral H.R.H. the Duke of, R.N., K.G.
Edwardes, T. Dyer, Esq., 5, Hyde Park-gate, Kensington Gore, S.W.

Faber, Reginald S., Esq., 10, Oppidans-road, Primrose-hill, N.W.
Fellows Athenæum, per Messrs. Kegan Paul, Trench, Trübner, & Co.
Foljambe, Cecil G. S., Esq., M.P., 2, Carlton House Terrace, S.W.
Foreign Office (The).
Foreign Office of Germany, Berlin.
Franks, Augustus W., Esq., F.R.S., F.S.A., 103, Victoria-street, S.W.

Gale, Henry, Esq., 45, Elvaston-place, Queen's-gate, S.W.
Galignani, Messrs., Paris.
Georg, H., Esq., Lyons (2 *copies*).
George, C. W., Esq., 51, Hampton-road, Clifton, Bristol.
Gladstone Library, National Liberal Club, Whitehall-place, S.W.
Glasgow University Library.
Godman, F. Ducane, Esq., F.R.S., 10, Chandos-street, Cavendish-square, W.
Goodison, Rev. John, U.S.A.
Gore-Booth, Sir H. W., Bart., Lissadell, Sligo.

Göttingen University Library.
Grant-Duff, Sir Mountstuart Elphinstone, G.C.S.I., York House, Twickenham.
Gray, Albert, Esq., Palace Chambers, Westminster, S.W.
Grosvenor Library, Buffalo, U.S.A.
Guildhall Library, E.C.
Guillemard, F. Henry H., Esq., 1, Mill-lane, Cambridge.

Hamburg Commerz-Bibliothek.
Harvard College, Cambridge, Massachusetts.
Heawood, Edward, Esq., B.A., F.R.G.S., Caius College, Cambridge.
Hervey, Dudley F. A., Esq., per Messrs. H. S. King & Co., 45, Pall-mall.
Hiersemann, Herr Karl W., 2. Königsstrasse, Leipzig.
Hippisley, A. E., Esq., care of J. D. Campbell, Esq., C.M.G., 8, Storey's-gate, St. James's-park, S.W.
Horner, J. F. Fortescue, Esq., Mells Park, Somersetshire.
Horrick, Mrs. Perry, Beau Manor Park, Loughborough.
Hoskins, Rear-Admiral Sir Anthony H., K.C.B., 17, Montagu-square, W.
Hoyt Public Library, per Messrs. Sotheran and Co., Strand.
Hull Subscription Library.

India Office (21 *copies*).

James, Capt. Walter H., 5, Lexham-gardens, Kensington, W.
Johnson, General Sir Allen B., 60, Lexham-gardens, Cromwell-road, S.W.

Keltie, J. Scott, Esq., 1, Savile-row, W.
Kensington, South, Science and Art Department.
King's Inns Library, Henrietta-street, Dublin.
Kimberley Public Library, per Messrs. Sotheran and Co., Strand.
Kleinseich, M., National Library, Paris (2 *copies*).
Koehler, Herr K. F., Universitatsstrasse 26, Leipzig.

Larkin, M., Esq., South Melbourne, per Messrs. E. A. Petherick & Co., 33, Paternoster-row, E.C.
Leeds Library.
Lehigh University, U.S.A.
Lisbon National Library.
Liverpool Free Public Library.
Loescher, Messrs. J., & Co., Via del Corso, 307, Rome.
Logan, Daniel, Esq., Solicitor-General, Penang, Straits Settlements.
Logan, William, Esq. (Madras Civil Service), The Links, St. Andrews, Fife.
London Institution, Finsbury-circus.
London Library, 12. St. James's-square.
Low, Malcolm, Esq., 22, Roland-gardens, South Kensington, S.W.
Lucas, C. P., Esq., Colonial Office, S.W.
Luyster, A. L., Esq., 10, Silver-street, W.C.

Mackern, George, Esq., Buenos Ayres.
Macmillan, A., Esq., 16, Bedford-street, Covent Garden, W.C.
Macmillan & Bowes, Messrs., Cambridge.
Maiden, J. H., Esq., Technological Museum, Sydney, New South Wales.
Malcolm, W. Elphinstone, Esq., Burnfoot, Langholm, Carlisle.
Manchester Public Free Libraries.
Manierre, George, Esq., per Mr. B. F. Stevens.
Manila Club, The, per Mr. J. Bain, 1, Haymarket, S.W.
Mantell, Walter, Esq., Wellington, New Zealand.
Markham, Admiral Albert H., R.N., F.R.G.S.
Markham, Clements R., Esq., C.B., F.R.S., 21, Eccleston-square, S.W.
Massachusetts Historical Society, 30, Fremont-street, Boston, Mass., U.S.A.
Massie, Admiral T. L., R.N., Chester.
Maudslay, A. P., Esq., 11, Park-lane, W.
Maund, E. A., Esq., care of Mr. Kolchmann, 2, Langham-place, W.

Mayne, Rear-Admiral, C.B., 101, Queen's-gate, S.W. (*Deceased.*)
McClymont, Jas. R., Esq., Hobart, Tasmania.
Melbourne, Public Library of.
Meyjes, A. C., Esq., Aumerle-lodge, Wembly, near Harrow.
Mitchell Library, Ingram-street East, Glasgow.
Mitchell, Wm., Esq., Union Bank of Scotland, Ltd., Aberdeen.
Morgan, E. Delmar, Esq., 15, Roland-gardens, South Kensington, S.W.
Munich Royal Library.
Murchison, Kenneth R., Esq., 116, Park-street, Park-lane, W.

Nathan, Captain, R.E., Royal Horse Guards.
Natural History Museum, Cromwell-road, per Messrs. Dulau & Co. Soho-sq.
Netherlands, Geographical Society of the, per Mr. Nijhoff, The Hague.
Newberry Library, The, Chicago, U.S.A.
Newcastle-upon-Tyne Literary and Scientific Institute.
Newcastle-upon-Tyne Public Library.
New York State Library.
Nicholl, John Cole, Esq., Merthyr Mawr, Bridgend, S. Wales.
Nicholson, Sir Charles, Bart., D.C.L., The Grange, Totteridge, Herts, N.
Northbrook, The Earl of, G.C.S.I., Stratton, Micheldever Station.
Noailles, Countess de, Montclair, Hyères, Var, France.
North, Hon. F. H., C 3, The Albany, W.
Northumberland, His Grace the Duke of, Grosvenor-place, S.W.
Nutt, Mr. D., 270, Strand, W.C.

Oliver, Capt. S. P., Moray House, Monckton-road, near Gosport.
Oliver, Commander T. W., R.N., Oak Hill, Barsledon, Southampton.
Ommanney, Admiral Sir Erasmus, C.B., F.R.S., 29, Connaught-square, Hyde Park, W.
Oriental Club, Hanover-square, W.

Parlane, James, Esq., Rusholme, Manchester.
Peabody Institute, Baltimore, U.S.
Peckover, Alexander, Esq., Bank House, Wisbech.
Petherick, E. A., Esq., 33, Paternoster-row, E.C.
Philadelphia, Library Company of, U.S.A.
Phillimore, Charles B., Esq., F.R.G.S., Hurley Manor House, Great Marlow.
Poor, Henry W., Esq., 45, Wall-street, New York.
Portico Library, Manchester.
Pringle, Arthur T., Esq., Madras, c.o. Messrs. G. W. Wheatley & Co., 10, Queen-street, Cheapside, E.C.

Raffles Library, Singapore.
Ravenstein, E. G., Esq., Albion House, 91, Upper Tulse-hill, S.W.
Rawlinson, Major-General Sir H., Bart., K.C.B., 21, Charles-st., Berkeley-sq.
Reed, Mrs., Hassness, Cockermouth.
Reform Club, Pall-mall.
Richards, Vice-Admiral Sir F. W., K.C.B., United Service Club, Pall-mall, S.W.
Riggs, E. F., Esq., Washington, U.S.
Robson, J. R., Esq., Aden, Cockington, Torquay.
Rockhill, W. W., Esq., care of Fidelity Trust Company, Chestnut-street, Philadelphia.
Royal Colonial Institute (J. S. O'Halleron, Esq., Sec.), Northumberland-avenue, W.C.
Royal Engineers' Institute, Chatham.
Royal Geographical Society, 1, Savile-row, W. (*copies presented*).
Royal Scottish Geographical Society, Edinburgh (John Gunn, Esq., Librarian).
Royal United Service Institution, Whitehall-yard, S.W.
Russell, Lord Arthur, 2, Audley-square, W. (*Deceased.*)

Satow, Ernest, Esq., 104, The Common, Upper Clapton, E.
Schlichter, H., Esq., 25, Alma-square, Abbey-road, N.W.
Seebohm, H., Esq., F.L.S., 22, Courtfield-gardens, S.W.

Seybold, Dr. C. F., Hôtel Bon-Séjour, Cannes, France.
Shaw-Stewart, Major-General, R.E., 61, Lancaster-gate, W.
Signet Library, Edinburgh (Thos. G. Law, Esq., Librarian).
Silver, S. W., Esq., 3, York-gate, Regent's Park, N.W.
Sinclair, W. F., Esq., Bombay C. S.
Société de Géographie, Paris.
South African Public Library.
South Australian Legislature Library.
Stanley, Lord, of Alderley, Alderley Park, Chelford, Cheshire.
St. Andrew's University.
St. Martin's-in-the-Fields Free Public Library, 115, St. Martin's-lane, W.C.
St. Petersburg University Library.
Stechert, Mr. G. E., 30, Wellington-street, Strand, W.C.
Stockholm, Royal Library of.
Strachey, Mrs. Richard, 69, Lancaster-gate, Hyde-park, W.
Stride, Mrs. Arthur L., Bush Hall, Hatfield, Herts.
Stubbs, Captain Edward, R.N., 13, Greenfield-road, Liverpool.
Surrey County School, Cranleigh, per Rev. Dr. Merriman.
Sydney Free Library.

Temple, Capt. R. C., Pioneer Press, Allahabad, India.
Thomson, Sir William, F.R.S., LL.D., The University, Glasgow.
Thurston, Sir John B., K.C.M.G., Colonial Secretary, Fiji.
Toronto Public Library.
Toronto University.
Travellers' Club, 106, Pall-mall, S.W.
Tredgold, Miss E. M., Craneswater, East Southsea, Portsmouth.
Trinder, H. W., Esq., 65, Cadogan-square, S.W.
Trinder, Oliver Jones, Esq., Mount Vernon, Caterham, Surrey.
Trinity College, Cambridge.
Trinity House, The Hon. Corporation of, Tower-hill, E.C.
Trotter, Coutts, Esq., Athenæum Club, S.W.
Trübner, Herr Karl.
Turnbull, Alex. H., Esq., 7, St. Helen's-place, Bishopsgate-street, E.C.
Tylor, Professor E. B., D.C.L., The Museum House, Oxford.

Union Society, Oxford.
United States Naval Academy.
United States Navy Department, Library of, Washington, D.C., U.S.A.
University of London, Burlington-gardens, W.
Upsala University Library.

Vienna Imperial Library.

Washington, Department of State.
Washington, Library of Navy Department.
Watkinson Library, Hartford, Connecticut, U.S.A.
Watt, A. P., Esq., 2, Paternoster-square, E.C.
Webb, Captain Sir J. Sydney, The Trinity House, E.C.
Webb, William Frederick, Esq., Newstead Abbey, Nottingham.
Wharton, Capt. W. J. L., R.N., Florys, Princes-road, Wimbledon Park, S.W.
Whiteway, R. S., Esq., Bengal Civil Service, Meerut, N.W.P., India.
Wigram, R., Esq., Longcroft, Banstead, Epsom.
Wilson, Edward S., Esq., Melton, Brough, East Yorkshire.
Worcester, Massachusetts, Free Library.

Yale College, U.S.A.
Young, Sir Allen, C.B., 18, Grafton-street, W.

Zürich, Bibliothèque de la Ville.